DUKE UNIVERSITY PUBLICATIONS

RELIGIOUS ASPECTS OF THE
CONQUEST OF MEXICO

LONDON:

CAMBRIDGE UNIVERSITY PRESS

———

NEW YORK:

G. E. STECHERT & CO.

TOKYO:

MARUZEN AND COMPANY, LTD.

SHANGHAI:

EDWARD EVANS & SONS, LTD.

BUENOS AIRES:

J. LAJOUNE & CO.

RELIGIOUS ASPECTS OF THE CONQUEST OF MEXICO

By CHARLES S. BRADEN
Northwestern University

DURHAM · NORTH · CAROLINA
DUKE UNIVERSITY PRESS
1930

COPYRIGHT 1930
DUKE UNIVERSITY PRESS

PRINTED IN THE UNITED STATES OF AMERICA BY
THE SEEMAN PRESS, DURHAM, NORTH CAROLINA

TO

MY WIFE

FOREWORD

Conquest has its spiritual no less than its material aspects. With the latter, in so far as they affect Mexico, Prescott and his successors have made us reasonably familiar; but no corresponding narrative presents in detail the ecclesiastical penetration of Mexico, or attempts to measure the process in spiritual and social gain. Professor Braden bridges this gap for the sixteenth century in an account that is at once illuminating and convincing. Cortés to him becomes more than a mere conqueror; he is the forceful agent of a new faith, seeking outward signs of conversion as well as of submission and insisting upon religious conformity both in his own ranks and among the masses of new converts. The doughty warrior with due humility welcomes the humble Franciscans and other religious, who soon arrive to second his efforts, and furthers their stupendous task with the same zeal that he displayed in material accomplishments. Under Mr. Braden's treatment the leading *conquistador* becomes more than a daring ruffian wholly intent upon extorting from hapless captives the secret of hidden treasure or an undue share of personal service; he is the devout promoter of Mexico's evangelization.

In dealing with the early missionaries and the hindrances that beset or the factors that favored their work and in endeavoring to measure its consequences, the author undertakes a difficult task and one that calls for sympathetic and discriminating treatment. Not all, of course, will agree with his conclusions. Too much controversy was engendered among the early workers, regular and secular—not to mention their modern rivals—to expect agreement upon such mooted points as the extent and thoroughness of conversion, the survival of native practices, and the adequacy of mission or of parish in the spiritual training of an alien people. In

Mr. Braden's narrative the reader will detect the note of appreciation felt by a fellow worker—for the author's labors in Bolivia and in Chile entitle him in a very real sense to that designation—together with the scholar's critical judgment as developed by long training and teaching experience. It is this rare combination of fellow feeling, spiritual insight, and sound scholarship that will commend this pioneer study to a widening circle of appreciative readers.

ISAAC JOSLIN COX.

Northwestern University.

PREFACE

It is rather strange that, so far as we have been able to discover, no one has written specifically regarding the religious aspects of the conquest of Mexico. Of course, incidental references to it are frequent in works such as *The Ancient History of Mexico* by Clavigero, an Italian writer; in the great modern Mexican history, *México á través de los Siglos;* in Bancroft's *History of Mexico;* and in Prescott's classic *History of the Conquest of Mexico;* but the accounts are fragmentary and leave much to be desired. A modern Mexican Jesuit, Padre Mariano de Cuevas, has quite recently published *La Historia de la Iglesia en México*, in four volumes, which covers that period and comes nearer being an adequate treatment of it than any other. But the author, limiting himself too closely to the institutional history of the church, has altogether too little to say regarding the great contributing social and political factors which properly belong with a discussion of so vast and complicated a phenomenon as the conversion of a people. It is not too much to say also that it is written from the Jesuit Catholic standpoint and that on many occasions the historian becomes the apologist. Unfortunately, it is not available in English.

Quite the most comprehensive attempt to tell the story of the conversion is that of Mendieta, a writer of the sixteenth century, himself an active participant in the task. His book, *Historia Eclesiástica Indiana,* is one of the most valuable sources, but he stood too closely related to the process to evaluate properly all the elements that conditioned it.

One protestant missionary writer, Mr. H. V. Brown, in his book, *Latin America,* did attempt in a few brief chapters to discuss the subject, covering not only Mexico but the whole of Latin America. But his account is too brief to do justice to such an epoch.

It seemed worth while, therefore, to undertake an investigation of what really happened with reference to religion during the period of conquest and settlement. What happened to the native religions? What happened to Christianity? By what methods was the conversion of the Indians effected? To what extent was compulsion used? What were the results of conversion? What kinds of institutions resulted? To what extent do the resultant institutions display characteristics common to both the original forms of religion?

In the main, the most ancient and well authenticated source materials were employed in the study and these have been quoted extensively throughout the book. Indeed, certain sections of the study are somewhat of the character of a source book. Thus a great deal of very valuable material has been made available in English for the first time. In the case of one source very amply quoted, there does exist an English translation, two of them, indeed, but they have both long been out of print and are found only in the better libraries. In the appendix will be found a critical evaluation of the sources used.

Many friends and colleagues have aided me greatly in this investigation. I desire especially to acknowledge the encouragement and help received from my friend Professor A. G. Baker of the University of Chicago who read and criticized the entire manuscript and made many valuable suggestions. I am also indebted to my colleague Professor Isaac J. Cox, of the History department in Northwestern University, a recognized authority in the Latin American field, who graciously supplies a brief introduction to the book.

Grateful acknowledgment is made to the following publishers and owners of copyrights for permission to quote from their publications: G. P. Putnam and Sons, New York; The Macmillan Company, New York; University of California Press, Berkeley, California; Frederick A. Stokes Company, New York; The Smithsonian Institute, Washington, D. C.; The Viking Press, New York; The Missionary Education Movement, New York; the B. C. Forbes Company, Chicago, and Dr. Frederick Starr. Most of the works quoted are from the very nature of the study either very old or not copyrighted in the United States. The writer is no less grateful to their publishers, although formal recognition be not required. Especially is he indebted to the publishers of P. Mariano de Cuevas' *Historia de la Iglesia en México,* the Revista Católica, El Paso, Texas.

CHARLES S. BRADEN.

Northwestern University
Evanston, Illinois
March 15, 1930

TABLE OF CONTENTS

CHAPTER IX

THE PERMANENT INFLUENCES OF THE NATIVE RELIGIONS
OF MEXICO UPON ROMAN CATHOLIC CHRISTIANITY . 278

APPENDIX

RELIGIOUS ASPECTS OF THE
CONQUEST OF MEXICO

Chapter I

INTRODUCTION

History records no more interesting or romantic story than that of the sixteenth century conquest and conversion of the natives in the lands now known as Latin America. When, if ever before, was conquest on such a vast scale attempted? When, if ever, were such unnumbered hosts of people induced within so brief a period to abandon their age old religious beliefs and practices and embrace a strange cult brought from a distant land?

While it is true that accurate statistics relating to anything involved in that remote period are wholly lacking, there are estimates which, while undoubtedly exaggerated, serve, nevertheless, to indicate unmistakably the very rapid progress made by Christianity during the early years of the occupation of Mexico. Zumárraga, the first archbishop of Mexico, writing in 1531, only seven years after the coming of the first missionaries, and but ten years after the siege and capture of the capital, declared that his Franciscan monks alone had baptized more than a million and a half Indians. The fact is that within less than a century the entire region south of the Rio Grande was considered nominally Christian. It is true that the Indians still continued their ancient pagan practices in the more remote places, but most of the villages and cities had Christian churches which were recognized as the centers of the religious life of the people.

It is easy to say when confronted with these statements that, of course, the Indians became Christian because they were forced to do so, and that in a real sense they were not converted at all. Such a declaration has frequently been made. Indeed, it is the opinion rather generally held by Protestants; while not a few Catholics, viewing the state of Christianity in parts of Latin America, are inclined to agree.

But what are the facts? This is not a question to be decided on any sectarian basis. Something certainly happened during that first hundred years. What was it? Are there sources which may be trusted to reveal what really occurred? Some things are definitely known. There was a vast, complicated religious system in operation there when the Europeans first arived. Today it is no longer found. What became of it? Why did the natives abandon it and accept Christianity? Were they indeed forced to do so?

Every student of culture contacts knows well that one culture never wholly displaces another. Interaction is a universally recognized principle. There is always some degree of interpenetration. The resultant type of culture is never quite identical with either of the original cultures. The question very naturally arises, therefore, as to the effect of contact with the pagan faith upon Christianity. To what extent was Christianity modified? Here again generalizations are easy. But what really happened?

Obviously the first requisite for understanding what took place is a knowledge of the character of the two religions which met. What was Catholicism like in Spain at the time of the conquest? The facts here are easily accessible. Assuming, though possibly without warrant, a greater familiarity on the part of the reader with this subject than with the native religions, the author treats the religion of Spain very briefly. But the religion of Mexico, almost wholly unknown save to a very few, could not be dealt with so summarily. Here facts are not so easily available. Extended search in the extant source materials became necessary.[1]

It is a generally recognized principle that similarity of cultural elements facilitates fusion. Then any similarities between the two religions would be an aid in the process of conversion. These would help explain the rapidity with

[1] These are discussed and evaluated in Appendix I, p. 309.

which the Indians came over into Christianity, although Cuevas, a modern Jesuit writer, declares that so far from hastening the process, these similarities were a hindrance,[2] and the older writers, impressed by the likenesses between Christianity and the native faith, very frequently attributed the pagan form to malevolent spirits who copied the true religion in order to deceive the Indians. Certainly, however, no study of these religions would be complete which failed to note their various points of agreement, whatever their effect on conversion. If they were indeed a hindrance, it would be of the utmost importance to note them, for they would render just so much more difficult the explanation of the rapid shift of religious allegiance. Also, since the intimate connection of religion with the social and political life of a people is well recognized, one would naturally, in studying a period of such marked change, pay particular attention to those beliefs and practices which had a political or social bearing upon that change, such, for example, as the prophecies concerning the return of Quetzalcoatl.

Those familiar with the field may raise one objection with reference to the study of the native religion. No attempt has been made to distinguish between the religions of the various tribes of Mexico, the country being treated rather as a religious unit and the Aztec religion as *the* religion, except in a few cases where the Maya cult has been differentiated. As a matter of fact there is not a little difference between these religions at some points, sufficient indeed to render sweeping generalizations sometimes incorrect; but after all the similarities were very great. In view of this essential similarity, it seemed that an attempt to detail the differences would result in a loss of clarity hardly compensated for by the greater accuracy of detail.

With a background of understanding of the two reli-

---

[2] Mariano de Cuevas, *Historia de la Iglesia en México*, I, 231.

gions it is exceedingly interesting to watch them as they meet. First comes the military conqueror, Cortés, Apostle of the Faith, with his crusader's passion, and his zeal for religious as well as political conquest. After him came the missionaries. What sort of men were they? How did they go about their task? Did they make use of compulsion? What success had they? What were the factors that favored or hindered their work? What kinds of institutions resulted? What share had the Indians in them? What degree of accommodation to native practices and beliefs was necessary? These are questions that naturally arise, and it is to these and many others that this study attempts to find an answer in the source materials from that period.

The writer's interest in the subject grows out of several years' residence in South America, and it was his first intention to cover the whole of Latin-America in the study. Only a brief investigation, however, made it very evident that not only a geographical but also a time limit must be set. Accordingly, the field was narrowed to Mexico, largely because of the greater availibility of original materials, and to the sixteenth century, save for one chapter which, skipping over the intervening centuries, attempts to discover the permanent influences of the old pagan cult on Catholicism. However, such general reading as the writer has done over the whole Latin-American field leads to the conclusion that essentially the same process was carried on everywhere, with only such differences as would naturally arise out of the peculiar situation in each country. On the basis of one particular section, one may, therefore, with reasonable assurance, assume that he understands the general conversion process over the whole of Latin-America. It is to be hoped, however, that like studies will be made covering other parts, and that further work will be done on the subsequent development of religion in the various sections of the new world down to the present time.

CHAPTER II

RELIGION IN SPAIN AT THE TIME OF
THE CONQUEST

The period of the conquest and conversion of the Indians of New Spain was that of the Spanish Inquisition. Out of an atmosphere of religious fanaticism such as few epochs in the history of the Christian church have equalled and none surpassed, came the conquerors, and after them the priests who were to undertake the enormous task of converting a new continent to the Christian faith. Some knowledge of the institution which was so great a force in shaping the religious thought and expression of the time seems quite necessary as a basis for understanding what took place in Mexico.

The Inquisition was not born in the 15th century but had functioned more or less effectively throughout the middle ages in preventing defection from the church. It had stifled the Albigensian movement; it had sought to destroy the Waldensian reform. The Holy Office was one of the most powerful arms of the pope in holding in check any efforts at revolt against the Holy Faith and the Curia. It had not been very active in Spain for a long period. It had never existed in Castile until about the middle of the 15th century, when an application was made by John II for a delegation of inquisitorial power for the purpose of punishing Judaizing Christians.

There had been repeated attempts throughout the centuries at the conversion of the Jews who were numerous in the Peninsula. There had been not only peaceful attempts to induce voluntary acceptance of the Faith, but pressure and violence had been resorted to from time to time. About the middle of the thirteenth century the crown ordered that free access to the Jewish and Moorish communities be granted the friars. The people were required to assemble and to listen to sermons for their conversion. This ultimately led to trouble. An increasing tendency to persecution developed in which both state and church joined. By the end of the fourteenth century popular fanaticism had been so inflamed that massacres of Jews took place all over Spain. As many as fifty thousand were slain, according to some estimates. Only those who agreed to baptism were spared. The government made little or no attempt to punish the guilty.[1]

The enforced conversion of great numbers of Jews brought in its train many problems. Naturally such conversions were frequently not sincere. So, although some loudly denounced their former faith, the majority were content with a nominal profession of the new faith, and while attending mass and other Christian services, continued secretly to observe their own ancient practices. This laxity which increased during the reign of the weaker kings caused the church great anxiety. Added to this was the jealousy of the "old Christians" toward the "new Christians," as the proselytes were called, for these changed in no wise their economic habits and, by reason of the increased confidence and prestige which they gained on becoming Christians, profited enormously. In 1477 the king and queen were petitioned to punish the "detestable sin" of new converts, because if they left it unchecked, it would grow so rapidly that great harm would befall the Catholic Faith. Nothing would avail to end it but the Inquisition.

In 1474, Pope Sixtus IV had attempted to give his legate in Spain inquisitorial power, but Ferdinand and Isabella were unwilling to allow it under foreign control. Finally, in 1478, the pope authorized the monarchs to appoint inquisitors and to remove them at pleasure, and the Inquisition became peculiarly a Spanish institution. It was not, however, until 1480 that its work was really begun, and not until

[1] Henry C. Lea, *A History of the Inquisition in Spain,* I, 105-7. Quotations are reprinted by permission.

the appointment of Tomás de Torquemada as Inquisitor General in 1483 that it became well organized and systematized. Of Torquemada, Lea writes:

His selection justified the wisdom of the sovereigns. Full of pitiless zeal, he developed the nascent institution with unwearied assiduity. Rigid and unbending, he would listen to no compromise of what he deemed to be his duty, and in his sphere he personified the union of the spiritual and the temporal swords which was the ideal of all true churchmen. . . . If we cannot wholly attribute to him the spirit of ruthless fanaticism which animated the Inquisition, he at least, deserves the credit for stimulating it and rendering it efficient in its work by organizing it and directing it with dauntless courage against the suspect however high placed, until the shadow of the Office covered the land and no one was so hardy as not to tremble at its name.[2]

This is not the place to enter into a discussion of the Inquisition in any detail. Its activities covered a period of over three hundred years. Estimates as to the number of those who suffered through its powers vary widely. Frederick Meyrick, in *The Church in Spain,* states that, in all, thirty-two thousand were burned, seventeen thousand burned in effigy, and two hundred and ninety-six thousand degraded and imprisoned and their property confiscated.[3] Here it is only necessary to note that these years of fanatical persecution by means of the Inquisition, were the years of greatest activity in the conversion of pagan Mexico to Christianity.

In the religious background at the time of the discovery of America and the beginning of the Conquest belongs also quite properly the conquest of Granada in 1492 and the expulsion of the Moors who refused to become Christians. The presence of the Moors in the south of Spain had long been an offense to Catholic Spain. They were a constant menace to the peace and security of the Christian kingdoms

[2] Lea, *op. cit.,* I, 174-6.   [3] P. 401.

of the Peninsula. Yet every attempt to overcome them had failed prior to 1492, the year Columbus set sail for the discovery of the New World. That year, after a vigorous struggle, they were obliged to surrender to the superior strength of Christian arms. But so eager for their submission were the Christians that they granted them very liberal terms. In the treaty were numerous provisions for the security of the Moslem population. They were virtually promised that they would be in no way molested for their religious beliefs whether in Granada or in Castile. For a little while there was peace.

THE EXPULSION OF THE JEWS

About the same time, and as a result of the same general religious situation, came the expulsion of the Jews. Even the activity of the Inquisition against the "new Christians" and the "Judaizing Christians" did not satisfy the leaders of the church. The presence of any appreciable number of followers of any other than the Catholic faith also constituted a menace to the ideal of centralized absolutism toward which the Catholic kings were working.[4] Only a few months after the conquest of Granada, on March 31, 1492, a royal decree was issued requiring all Jews whether in Aragon or in Castile to accept the Christian faith or leave the domain. They were granted a brief period of only four months to dispose of their properties, arrange their affairs, and depart.

The enormous injustice of this is, of course, evident. It meant financial ruin for many of them, since, obliged to sell within so short a time, they had of necessity to sell at a big sacrifice. They were further harassed by restrictions as to the exportation of gold or silver coin. As a result, a great many of them accepted Christianity nominally. Great numbers of them, however, true to their faith, accepted the sacri-

---

[4] Charles E. Chapman, *A History of Spain*, p. 213.

fice and migrated to other lands, only to find themselves in some cases in a worse plight than before, for in Portgual and in North Africa they were more harshly dealt with than in Spain. Some of them in desperation returned to Spain and were baptized.

Statistics as to the expulsion vary widely. Chapman quotes the estimate of a Jewish historian which he thinks is perhaps reliable. According to this authority, one hundred and sixty-five thousand migrated, fifty thousand were baptized, and some twenty thousand lost their lives in the course of the execution of the decree.[5] The converted Jews were called Marranos. Many of them became genuine Christians, but many remained at heart loyal to the faith of their fathers while they outwardly assented to Christian beliefs and practices.

THE EXPULSION OF THE MOORS

For eight years after the fall of Granada, the Moors were allowed to live in peace, being regarded, as one writer says, with contemptuous toleration rather than antipathy. The principal reason for so long a period of security was the policy of the Archbishop Fernando de Talavera, who had enough faith in the appeal of Christianity to believe that, if it were but understood, it would be accepted. Accordingly, he learned Arabic himself and encouraged his priests to do likewise. An Arabic grammar and dictionary were prepared and the catechism and liturgy as well as portions of the gospels were translated into Arabic. Though, at first, suspicious of the motives of the Spanish, the Moors began soon to respond to the just and kindly treatment shown them and many of them accepted Christianity. Those who refused to go that far, learned, nevertheless, to revere and trust Talavera. Ferdinand and Isabella visited Granada in 1499 and expressed themselves as being pleased with the good order

[5] Chapman, *op. cit.*, p. 214.

and peace which they found. They had even allowed Moslem subjects expelled from Portugal two years before, to settle in the country under their special protection.[6]

Unfortunately the Archbishop of Toledo, Ximenes de Cisneros, who had gone with the sovereigns and, when they returned, had remained to lend assistance in the conversion of the Moors, was not satisfied with the slow progress made by the peaceful method of his colleague. Seeing the friendliness of the Moors, he declared that all they needed to bring them to Christianity was a little pressure. He called the leaders together, spoke to them on the faith and made them liberal gifts of rich clothing and other valuables. Whether they were moved by fear, or whether they were influenced by the gifts or the arguments, most of them accepted Christianity and brought with them a large number of followers, so that on a single day "three thousand candidates were said to have presented themselves for baptism, a number so great that the ordinary individual ablution proved impossible and the kneeling crowd had to be sprinkled with holy water from a brush."[7]

The activity of Ximenes called forth a protest from the stricter Mohammedans, on the ground that it violated the terms of the treaty. His reply was to throw the leader of the opposition into prison, whence he emerged ere long to be baptized by his own request. The archbishop's faith in strong measures was thus seemingly confirmed. He threw to the winds the restraints of the slower voluntary method. In his determination to put an end to their heretical studies he ordered the destruction of thousands of rare manuscripts of great value, thus enraging the Moors beyond measure, and setting an example for the wanton destruction, a few years later, of the vast wealth of ancient writings in Mexico by the early missionaries to the New World.

[6] I. L. Plunket, *Isabel of Castile and the Making of the Spanish Nation*, p. 273.   [7] *Ibid.*, p. 274.

Among those accorded especial protection by the treaty were a large number who had at one time been Christians but had become Moslems. The hatred of the Christians toward this class had made it necessary to provide especial protection for them. Cisneros, however, took the position that the children of such as had once been Christian must be baptized and come under the jurisdiction of the Inquisition. Enraged by the attempt to arrest the daughter of a renegade Christian, a mob formed, an official who tried to make the arrest was killed, and the frenzied people rushed to the castle where the archbishop lodged, determined to kill him. He managed, however, to escape, and the crowd was finally quieted, but the fires of resentment still burned. That it was not, however, so much anti-Christian as against Ximenes, was shown by the fact that Talavera made his way into the midst of the angry mob unprotected and the people crowded around him and kissed his robe.

The monarchs were at first displeased with the archbishop's action, but in the atmosphere of intolerance and fanaticism surrounding the court, he was able to win their support by declaring that the Moors had broken the treaty and had thus forfeited any rights that might have been guaranteed them, quite ignoring the fact that it was he who had provoked the rebellion by his own failure to abide by the treaty. The appeal of the Moors to the Sultan of Egypt at this juncture made it easier for the kings to listen to the fiery archbishop. He returned in triumph from the capital and from fifty thousand to seventy thousand Moors in and about the city were baptized. Twenty-five years later Franciscan missionaries condemned for using like wholesale methods in inducting Mexican tribes into the faith, were to appeal to the precedent thus set by the eminent archbishop of Toledo.

Outwardly, all was peaceful, but it could not last. Again the Moors rebelled, and this time they were reduced by the overwhelming superiority of the Spanish forces. The king was convinced that only in conversion or exile could there be any peace. Accordingly, he issued an edict in 1502 requiring the baptism or exile of all males over fourteen and females over twelve years of age. The restrictions as to wealth, property, and point of destination of the exiles were so severe that, virtually, their acceptance of Christianity was the only choice. So the great majority of them became nominally Christian, though not a few preferred loss and exile to the abandonment of their faith. The same rigorous treatment was not applied in Aragon, where a measure of toleration of existing Mohammedanism was allowed, though the erection of new mosques was forbidden. There, preaching and other methods were to be used for their voluntary conversion to Christianity, but in Castile, the land of Isabella the Catholic, the Roman Catholic faith alone was acknowledged.

Theoretically, the Catholic monarchs did not desire to force conversion upon the Moors. They wrote them explicitly at one time:

It has been told us that some have informed you that it is our will that you be commanded to turn Christians. But since it has never been, nor is it now our will that any Moor be forced to become a Christian, we hereby promise, on our word and honor, that we will not consent to any such procedure.

Again Isabella wrote:

I assure you that I will not permit that any of you nor your wives, nor your children, nor your grandchildren be forced to become Christians, against your will.[8]

Yet despite these fair words, a little later came the order of conversion or exile. How reconcile their words with their deeds?

[8] Don Modesto La Fuente, *Historia General de España*, VIII, 27.

La Fuente, the Spanish historian, attributes it to the fact that, whether or not it was true that the Moors were the first to break the terms of the treaty, at least Ferdinand and Isabella were persuaded that they were, and fanaticism did the rest. Perhaps this is true. An apologist for the Spanish monarchy would find it easier to believe so than would others without that interest.

However, La Fuente maintains that such action is not to be wondered at in that period, for even at the end of the sixteenth century a Spanish bishop, commenting on the Maccabees, wrote that anyone might with impunity slay a heretic, an infidel, or a renegade, and that the kings of Spain were obligated either to exterminate the Moors or at least to expel them from their borders. He discussed the question whether or not a child might not slay his parents, if they were discovered to be idolaters, or heretics, and held it to be quite permissible and indeed a current practice to kill a brother or a sister, or even one's own children under such circumstances. "If a prelate can teach such extreme ideas at the end of the century, what might they not have taught and practiced at its beginning?"[9]

SPANISH CONCEPTION OF RELIGION

Chapman says that the ideal of Catholic unity was carried to an excess which transcended unity itself, through an extension of the institution of "limpieza de sangre" (purity of blood). Certificates of this, that is, sworn statements that the bearer had no Jewish, Moslem or heretical antecedents, began to be required for the holding of various church offices, or for entry into religious orders, and often also for admission into the guilds. As a matter of fact few families could have withstood a close examination of their ancestry: the upper classes would almost surely have been found to

[9] *Ibid.*

have Jewish blood and the masses, certainly in the East and South, would have had a Moslem mixture in their veins.

Chapman continues:

> But the attainment of religious unity and the extreme sus-
> picion in which non-Catholics were held did not succeed in
> making the Spaniards respond to the moral code of their faith.
> Not only such licentious practices as have been alluded to were
> in vogue, but also a surprising lack of reverence was displayed
> by the improper use of sacred places and sacred objects and
> the mixture of the human and divine in masquerades. Never-
> theless it is not too much to say that the principal preoccupation
> of the Spaniards of the 16th and 17th centuries was the sal-
> vation of their souls. The worst of men would want to con-
> fess and seek absolution before they died, and many of them,
> no doubt, believed themselves to be good Catholics, even tho
> their every day life would not have borne inspection.[10]

Religion to the Spaniard of that day meant the acceptance of what the church taught, and a certain minimum amount of observance of the church's forms and ceremonies. That it had any large moral influence does not appear.

MORAL CONDITION OF THE CLERGY

Only a few years before the opening of the period of discovery, the lack of discipline in the monasteries and the lax
morality of the clergy, both regular and secular, as well as
the nuns, became so notorious that Isabella forced a reform,
which was carried out with excellent results by Archbishop
Ximenes, he of the forced conversion of the Moors. By
appointing only men of learning and integrity to the places
of greatest influence, she did much to raise the general level
of the clergy, but, even so, contemporary writers recount
abuses among them which to the modern reader seem incredible. The specific regulations as to the kind of priests
who might be permitted to go to the Indies in the *Recopila-*

---

[10] Chapman, *op. cit.*, p. 315. Reprinted by permission.

ción de Leyes, indicates that while there had been improvement, there was still much left to be desired.   The reference of Cortés to the conditions in Spain, and his evident desire to guard against such a condition in Mexico makes it clear that conditions were far from satisfactory.   He asks for monks rather than bishops or prelates for "if bishops and prelates come there would be the same wasting of funds in pomp and vices or in legacies to their children or relatives. . . . If the power of the church and the service of God were in the hands of the canons or other worthies and the Indians should see them practicing the vices and profanations such as in our time they are accustomed to practice in Spain, it would bring discredit upon our Faith."[11]

Happily the character of the earlier priests who came to Mexico was relatively high, as is shown in a subsequent chapter, but it was impossible to avoid the infiltration of the baser element as time went on.   Remembering these things, it will be more easily possible to judge properly the Christianizing process that went on in the western world.

THE CRUSADING SPIRIT IN SPAIN

During the reign of Charles V, who was considered the head of the Holy Roman Empire, there was almost constant conflict with the infidels, either in the region of the Danube or in North Africa.   While by no means wholly a religious crusade, for there were temporal ends to be conserved in the destruction of the Mohammedan powers, something of the crusading spirit burned still, and the appeal to it in support of his wars was effective.   The prevailing spirit in Spain during the period could hardly fail to have its effect likewise upon the Spanish attitude toward the infidels of the New World.

[11] Francis A. MacNutt, *Letters of Hernando Cortés to Charles V,* II, 213-16.

MacNutt has well said:

Sixteenth century Spain produced a race of Christian warriors whose piety born of an intense realization of love for a militant Christ was of a martial complexion, beholding in the symbol of salvation, the cross, the standard of Christendom around which the faithful must rally, and for whose protection and exaltation, swords must be drawn and blood spilled if need be. They were the children of the generation which had expelled the last Moor from Spain and had brought centuries of religious and patriotic warfare to a triumphant close in which their country was finally united under the crown of Castile. From such forbears the generation of Cortés received their heritage of Christian chivalry. The discovery of a new world, peopled by barbarians, opened a new field to the Spanish missionary zeal, in which the kingdom of God was to be extended and countless souls rescued from the obscene idolatries and debasing cannibalism which enslaved them. This was the white man's burden which that century laid on the Spaniard's shoulders.[12]

It should be recalled too that just at the time when Cortés was opening up Mexico, the influence of the Lutheran Reformation was beginning to make itself felt throughout Europe and produce a powerful reaction in Catholic Spain itself. Here, partly, and perhaps chiefly, in response to the necessity for some strong arm for defeating the spread of Protestantism, the Jesuit order was organized by Ignatius Loyola. Within a very few years after its organization, we find it appearing likewise in Mexico.

This then is the religious background of Spain out of which came the conquerors and the missionaries who attempted the Christian conquest of Mexico and the Western World. It was the period of the Inquisition; it followed by only a few years the religious wars with the Moors, their final defeat and conversion by force, as well as the forced conversion of the Jews, who were obliged to abandon their

[12] MacNutt, *Letters of Cortés,* I, 38.

faith or their country; it was a period of crusading wars by successive kings; it was the era of violent reaction to the Protestant reformation; and finally it was the age which saw the Jesuit order emerge.   It will help to understand what took place in Mexico, if these facts be constantly borne in mind.

CHAPTER III

THE RELIGION OF THE MEXICAN INDIANS AT THE TIME OF THE CONQUEST

RELIGION A CONTROLLING FACTOR IN THE LIFE OF THE PEOPLE

From the moment they stepped ashore in the New World, the Spaniards found themselves among a very religious people. The impression made on one of the early arrivals is recorded by Motolinia:

The idols which the Indians worshipped were numerous and were found in many places, especially in the temples of their demons and in the courtyards; in prominent places like forests, large hills and ports, or in high mountains and in every convenient pleasant resting place. Those that passed by drew blood from their ears or tongue and sprinkled them, or threw a little incense which they have in that land called "copalli"; others threw roses that they gathered along the way, and when they did not have anything else, they threw a bit of green grass or straw upon them; there they rested, especially those with burdens, for the Indians are accustomed to carry heavy loads. Likewise they had idols near the water, chiefly near fountains where they built their altars with covered steps. In many of the principal fountains they had four of these idols arranged in the form of a cross. . . . In the water they put much "copalli" and paper and roses and some devotees of the water gods sacrificed themselves there. Near the large trees like the great cypresses or cedars they likewise had altars and sacrifices. . . . At cross-roads, in different sections of the towns . . . they had oratories in which there were idols of diverse forms and figures. . . . Some had the figure of bishops with mitres and croziers . . . others had figures of men. These had a mortar on the head instead of the mitre. On them they threw wine because they were gods of wine. Some had the figures of women, some of wild beasts, lions, tigers, dogs, deer, etc. Also they had idols in the form of serpents, long and intertwined, some with the face of a woman. In front of these they offered snakes and serpents, and before some of them they placed strings of snake tails, for there are large snakes in this land which when they move their tails make a rattling noise.

Then also there were idols of birds like eagles, of night birds, vultures, kites and of large handsome plumed birds. The chief was the sun, also the moon, and the stars, the large fish and lizards of the water, even frogs and toads. . . . They had for gods the fire, the water, and the earth and of these they painted images. . . . They had figures of many other things, even of butterflies, fleas and lobsters, large and well carved.[1]

When one reads a book such as that of Sahagún which describes the religious feasts for each of the eighteen months which composed the Mexican year, one can but be impressed that religion in some of its aspects was the major preoccupation of the people. Evidently, however, in a civilization developed to such a degree as that of Mexico, religion will be found expressing itself in widely diverse forms, according to the classes of the population. Care must therefore be exercised not to attribute to the masses the relatively exalted religious conceptions which are here and there to be found in the Mexican records. Some writers on Mexico have apparently been misled into supposing a much higher general development than can be substantiated by the sources; but that there were a few who had advanced toward a much higher conception of religion than that commonly held, seems to be quite clearly evident.

Clavigero, an eminent Italian writer, declares that the Mexicans had some idea, though a very imperfect one, of a supreme, absolute being to whom they acknowledged owing fear and adoration. They did not attempt to represent him in any objective way, because he was held to be invisible. He was named in their language Teotl, a word which, he says, resembles still more in its meaning the Greek word *theos* than in its pronunciation. They applied to him certain

---

[1] Toribio de Motolinia, *Historia de los Indios de la Nueva España*, Joaquín García Icazbalceta, *Documentos para la Historia de México*, I, 32.

epithets expressive of the power and greatness which they conceived him to possess. They addressed him as Ipalneomani, that is "He by whom we live," and Tloque Nahuaque, "He who has all in himself." However, their knowledge and worship of this being was obscured "in the mass of deities invented by their superstition."[2]

Lewis Spence, in his *Myths of Mexico and Peru* declares that at least the priesthood was advancing toward a monotheistic belief. He says:

A superficial examination of the Nahua religion might lead to the inference that within its scope and system, no definite theological views were embraced and no ethical principles propounded, and that the entire mythology presents only the fantastic attitude of the barbarian toward the eternal verities. Such a conclusion would be both erroneous and unjust to a type of human intelligence, by no means debased. As a matter of fact, the Nahuan displayed a theological advancement greatly superior to that of the Greeks or Romans and quite on a level with that expressed by the Egyptians and Assyrians. Toward the period of the Spanish occupation, the Mexican priesthood was undoubtedly advancing to the contemplation of the exaltation of one god whose worship was fast excluding that of similar deities, and if our data be too imperfect to allow us to speak very fully in regard to this phase of religious advancement, we know, at least, that much of the Nahua ritual and many of the prayers preserved by the labors of the Spanish Fathers were unquestionably genuine and display the attainment of a high religious level.[3]

There is some ground for believing that the king Nezahualcoyotl, the flower of the culture of the Mexicans who lived but a generation before the conquest, did come to a conception of one supreme being. It is true that Ixtlilxochitl who gives us the story was a Christian, and there is always the possibility of his having read more into the actual occur-

---

[2] F. X. Clavigero, *Ancient History of Mexico*, II, 2.
[3] Lewis Spence, *Myths of Mexico and Peru*, p. 54.

rence than the facts warranted. He tells how the king Nezahualcoyotl had married a wife whom he had, in a way that
reminds one very much of the story of David and Uriah,
unrighteously obtained by securing the death of her husband
in battle. He was not however blest with a son as he had so
ardently desired. Nor was he having the success at arms
which he had formerly enjoyed. Consulting the priests, he
was told that it was because he had not sufficiently honored
the gods. More sacrifices must be made. So, again the
altars smoked with human sacrifice, but all in vain. The
gods did not respond. Then angered by their silence he
cried: "These idols of wood and stone can neither hear nor
feel, much less could they make the heavens and the earth
and man the lord of it. Some all-powerful unknown god is
creator of the universe on whom alone I must rely for consolation and support." He retired then to his rural palace
and prayed and fasted forty days, offering no other sacrifice
than the sweet incense of the copal tree, and aromatic herbs.
At the end of the period came a messenger announcing victory over the Chalcos and the birth of a son.

Overjoyed at the news, he went into the garden, fell upon
his knees and gave thanks to the Almighty Lord and Maker
of all things, promising to recognize him as the Creator and
Lord and to build him a temple for his worship. He then
openly professed his faith and earnestly commanded his subjects to worship the god who had heard and answered his
prayer. He built a temple in the usual pyramidal form and
on the summit of it a tower nine stories high to represent the
nine heavens. A tenth was surmounted by a roof painted
black and profusely gilded with stars on the outside and in-
crusted with metals and precious stones. He dedicated this
to the Unknown God, the Cause of Causes. No image was
allowed in the edifice, as unsuitable to the Invisible God, and
the people were expressly prohibited from profaning the

altars with blood or any other sacrifice than that of the perfume of flowers and sweet scented gums.[4]

Ixtlilxochitl repeats the story twice in his writings.   In the first volume it is told with such detail and with speeches so generously supplied, that it raises some question as to whether it is to be accepted as exact.   We would have felt less reason to suspect a Christian interpretation read back into what may have been indeed a real advance toward a less material conception of God, if the historian had given only the briefer narrative in his second volume.

However, Brinton, a very keen student of Mexican mythology and religion, recognizes as genuine this apparent advance toward the idea of a supreme God, but he adds in commenting on this and a similar story regarding the Inca of Peru:

In neither case was there any attempt to substitute another and purer religion for the popular one.   The Inca continued to receive the homage of his subjects as a brother of the sun, and the regular services to that luminary were never interrupted.   Nor did Nezahualcoyotl afterwards neglect the honors due to his national gods, nor even refrain, himself, from plunging the knife into the breasts of captives on the altar of the god of war.   They were but the expressions of that monotheism which is ever present, not in contrast to polytheism but in living intuition in the religious sentiments.   If this subtle but true distinction be rightly understood, it will excite no surprise to find such epithets as "endless," "omnipotent," "invisible," "adorable," and such appellations as "the Maker of All," "the mother and father of life," "the one god complete in perfection and unity," "the Creator of all that is," "the Soul of the world," in use and of undoubted indigenous origin, not only among the civilized Aztecs, but even among the Haitians, the Araucanians, etc.   It will not seem contradictory to hear of them in a purely polytheistic worship.   We shall be far from regarding them as familiar to the popular mind, and we shall never be led so far away as to adduce them in evidence of a monotheism in either technical sense of that word.

[4] *Obras Históricas de Ixtlilxochitl,* I, 247-8, and II, 224-6.

These were not applied to any particular god even in the most enlightened nations but were terms of laudation and magniloquence used by the priests and devotees of every several god, to do him honor. They prove something in regard to the consciousness of divinity hedging us about, but nothing at all in favor of the recognition of one god. They exemplify how profound is the conviction of a highest and first principle, but they do not offer the least reason to surmise that this was a living reality in doctrine or in practice.[5]

We owe to Brinton also the translation of a number of ancient songs and poems which indicate a comparatively highly developed philosophy of life. Some of these may properly be given here. While there is a question as to how widely current these may have been, it is not unlikely that they were known at least among the nobility of the land. They may very well, therefore, be considered as no unimportant element in the social and literary soil into which the early preaching of Christianity fell. One feels himself in the atmosphere of certain Old Testament sections as he reads these really charming bits of Indian verse. Though direct evidence that the early preachers actually made use of these possible points of contact is not found in the comparatively meager available source materials, it would have been most natural to do so, especially since we do find them using other similarities between the religions.

Nezahualcoyotl, prince of Tezcuco, who represents the highest point reached by native thought and literature, had reflected deeply on life and its problems. "Following the inherent tendency of the enlightened intellect to seek unity in diversity, the One in the Many," says Brinton, "he reached the conclusion to which so many thinkers of all ages and all races have been driven, that underlying all phenomena is one primal and adequate cause, the essence of all existence." This he expressed as follows:

[5] Daniel G. Brinton, *Myths of the New World,* pp. 74-5.

In the ninth series is the cause of all of us and of all created things, the one and only God who created all things both visible and invisible.[6]

To Thee, Cause of all, to Thee I cried out in sadness, My sighs rise up before thy face. I am afflicted here on earth, I suffer, I am wretched, never has joy been my lot, never good fortune. My labor has been of no avail; certainly nothing here lessens one's suffering; truly only to be with thee, near thee. May it be thy will that my soul shall rise to thee; may I pour out my tears before thee, thou giver of life.[7]

In a singularly beautiful poem he reflects on the fleeting character of human life and seeks to probe the future.

The fleeting pomps of the world are like the green willow trees, which aspiring to permanence, are consumed by a fire, fall before the axe, are upturned by the wind or are scarred and saddened by age.

The grandeurs of life are like the flowers in color and fate, the beauty of these remain so long as their chaste buds gather and store the rich pearls of the dawn, and saving it drop it in liquid dew; but scarcely has the Cause of All directed upon them the full rays of the sun, when their beauty and glory fail, and the brilliant colors which decked forth their pride, wither and fade.

The delicious realms of flowers count their dynasties by short periods, those which in the morning revel proudly in beauty and strength, by evening weep for the sad destruction of their thrones, and for the mishaps which drive them to loss, to poverty, to death, and to the grave.

All things of earth have an end, and in the midst of the most joyous lives, the breath falters, they fall, they sink into the ground.

All the earth is a grave and naught escapes it. Nothing is so perfect that it does not fall and disappear. . . . That which was yesterday is not today, and let not that which is today trust to live tomorrow.

He asks, then, where are the kings of yesterday?

---

[6] Brinton, *Ancient Nahautl Poetry*, p. 73.
[7] *Ibid.*, p. 36.

The same that I reply—I know not, for first and last are confounded in the common clay. What was their fate shall be ours, and all who follow us.

Unconquered princes, warlike chieftains, let us seek, let us sigh for the heaven, for there all is eternal and nothing is corruptible. The darkening of the sepulcher is but the strengthening couch for the glorious sun, and the darkness of the night but serves to reveal the brilliancy of the stars. No one has power to alter these heavenly lights for they serve to display the greatness of their creator, and as our eyes see them now, so saw them our earliest ancestors, and so shall see them our latest posterity.[8]

Brinton, commenting on these and other songs in his admirable collection, in the translation of which, it ought to be said, he has shown rare literary skill, says:

It will be seen that the philosophy of these songs is mostly of the Epicurean and "carpe diem" order. The certainty of death, the mutability of fortune, observations which press themselves upon the mind of men everywhere, are their principal staples and cast over them a hue of melancholy, relieved by exhortation to enjoy to the utmost what the present moment offers of pleasure and sensual gratification. Here and there a gleam of the higher philosophy lights the somber reflection of the bard; his thoughts turn toward the infinite Creator of this universe, and he dimly apprehends that by making him the subject of his contemplations, there is boundless consolation even in this mortal life.[9]

But if here as in other lands, some of the greater minds had arrived at the thought of a supreme God, the masses were immersed in a religious system which had numerous gods, some greater, some lesser, whom they worshipped. Prescott after considering these apparent tendencies to an exaltation of one god above all others, and the epithets which we have already noted as applied to them, says that while these sublime attributes infer no inadequate conception of

[8] *Ibid.,* pp. 45-6.   [9] *Ibid.,* p. 47.

the true God, the idea of unity, of a being with whom voli-
tion is action, who has no need for inferior ministers to
execute his purposes, was too simple or too vast for their
understanding and that they sought relief as usual in a plu-
rality of deities who presided over the elements, the changes
of seasons, and the various occupations of man.[10]   Of these
there were thirteen principal gods, and more than two hundred inferior ones, to each of which special days or festivals
were dedicated.

THE PRINCIPAL GODS OF MEXICO

Obviously, it is impossible in this limited study to discuss
even the principal gods at length, much less those of inferior
rank.   It will suffice here merely to list those that were accorded the principal places in the pantheon, and to characterize briefly the three great gods who so clearly overshadow
the rest, namely Tezcatlipoca, Quetzalcoatl, and Huitzilopochtli.   The thirteen usually listed are as follows:

Tezcatlipoca, who corresponds to Jupiter
Ometeucli and Omecihuatl, who grant men their wishes and
    direct the stars
Cihuacoatl, who corresponds to Eve
Tonatiuh and Meztli, representing the sun and moon
Tlaloc, Lord of Paradise, the Aztec Poseidon
Quetzalcoatl
Xiutecuhtli, god of fire
Centeotl, goddess of the earth and corn
Mictlanteuctli and Mictlancihuatl, god and goddess of the
    under world
Huitzilopochtli, god of war

Tezcatlipoca is characterized by Sahagún as the Jupiter
of the Aztec pantheon.   He represents him as a true, invisi-

[10] Prescott, *The History of the Conquest of Mexico*, I, 58.
    Note: Spelling of the names of persons, gods, and places differs con-
siderably in the various sources. The attempt has been made to avoid
variations in the spelling of any given proper name except in verbatim
quotations from authorities.

ble god going about everywhere through the sky, the earth
and the underworld. When he walked on earth he stirred
up wars and enmities and discord. He was called sometimes
the sower of discord. However, it was he also who "alone
had to do with ruling the world, and he gave or denied riches
and prosperity at will." He knew the secrets of men's
hearts.[11]

The priests of this god surpassed in number and power
those of any other deity. They are credited with the invention of many of the usages of their civilization. Spence
declares that they had all but succeeded in making his worship universal. Other gods were to be worshipped on certain
occasions, he says, but the worship of Tezcatlipoca was regarded as compulsory and to some extent as a safeguard
against the destruction of the universe, a calamity the Na-
huas had been led to believe might occur through his agency.
When any national danger threatened, or famine or plague,
universal prayer was made to him. The leaders and people
flocked to his temple and prayed earnestly that the calamity
might be averted.[12]

No god in the whole list had more different names by
which he was addressed, indicating thus the great veneration
in which he was held. The name by which he was most
commonly addressed in prayer was Titlacaoan, "we are his
slaves." Clavigero says that he was the god of providence
and the soul of the world, the creator of heaven and earth,
and the master of all things. He was always represented as
young to indicate that time had no power to lessen his
strength.[13]

The name Tezcatlipoca is translated by Clavigero as
Shining Mirror, by Brinton as Smoking Mirror. Some have
thought that this arose from the fact that his images were

[11] Bernardino de Sahagún, *Historia General de las Cosas de la Nueva
España,* II, Cap. ii.
[12] Spence, *op. cit.,* p. 67.   [13] Clavigero, *op. cit.,* II, 6.

always made of a sort of black stone called "tezcapoctli," smoky mirror. Others that it refers to the round disc of the moon as a mirror in the night sky. Brinton thinks that the mirror referred to is the surface of the water and that the smoke is the mist which rises from its surface at night, for he considers Tezcatlipoca the personification of darkness. He says that as presiding over the darkness and night, dreams and phantoms of the gloom were supposed to be sent by him and that to him were sacred the animals that prowl at night, such as the skunk and the coyote. Thus he thinks that his attributes, his sacred animals and myths unite in identifying him as a primitive personification of darkness, whether that of the storm or of the night. His idea is strengthened by the beliefs that were current as to his occasional appearances which were always at night and in the gloom of the forest. The hunter would hear a sound like the falling of mighty trees but which was only the breathing of the giant form of the god in his nightly wanderings. Sometimes the hunter would die of fright. Sometimes, however, he would seize upon the god who then was helpless and would grant whatever he asked. "Ask what you please," the god would say, "and it is yours. Only release me before the sun rises, for I must leave before it appears."[14]

Quetzalcoatl was perhaps the most interesting figure in the pantheon, and, from the practical point of view, the one who most influenced the relationships between the Spanish and the Indians in the early period of the conquest. He was, therefore, one of the important influences in the conversion of the natives to Christianity. The myths relating to his origin and earthly sojourn in Tollan (spelled sometimes Tula, and Tulla), his departure for Tlapallan and his expected return are very numerous. We can only mention the principal ones in this discussion. All the myths agree that

[14] Brinton, *American Hero Myths,* pp. 71-2.

he lived in Tollan, most of them agree as to his departure and his promise to return. Those concerning his origin, what he was and what he did in the city of Tollan vary widely. Sahagún says of him quite simply:

Quetzalcoatl, although a man was held to be a god, and it is said that he swept the way for the goddess of water, for before rains commence there are strong winds and dust storms, and for this reason they said that Quetzalcoatl, the god of the winds swept the road before the rain goddess.[15]

In another place he calls him "another Hercules, a great necromantic."[16]

One myth represents him as the son of the all-father, Tonaca Tecutli, by a virgin of Tollan named Chimalman. There were three sisters together when the god appeared to them. The other two died of fright, but Chimalman, conceived a son. She died at his birth and was transferred to the heavens. A variant of this story has it that she conceived from having swallowed a precious green stone. There are still other variants most of which, however, contain the idea of the virgin birth. Therefore, to the Indian mind there was no occasion for stumbling, when it came in contact with the story of the virgin birth of Jesus.

Other legends make no claim of a miraculous birth for the god. Las Casas tells of his arrival from the East, from Yucatan possibly, with a few followers. Torquemada and Ixtlilxochitl give a similar account. Mendieta says that the god or idol of Cholula called Quetzalcoatl was the most celebrated and most highly esteemed among all the gods. According to this writer he came from the region of Yucatan to the city of Cholula.[17] Veytia, another early writer, however, describes him as arriving from the north, "a full grown man, tall of stature, white of skin, full bearded, barefooted

---

[15] Sahagún, *op. cit.,* I, Cap. v.   [16] *Ibid.,* III, Cap. iii.
[17] Mendieta, *Historia Eclesiástica Indiana,* II, Cap. x.

and bareheaded, clothed in a long white robe, strewn with red crosses and carrying a staff in his hand."[18]

Thus it appears that there were two rather distinct representations of Quetzalcoatl; first, as a legendary, heroic but earthly figure, the high priest of Tollan; and second, as a great god about whom clusters a great mass of myth and story. The latter we may distinguish as the Quetzalcoatl of mythology.

The Quetzalcoatl of mythology was one of four brothers, divine sons of the infinite and uncreated deity known variously as *Tonaca Tecutli,* "Lord of our Existence," in his male manifestation and as *Tonaca Cihuatl,* "Queen of our Existence" in female form. Two of the four sons, one black, one red, were named Tezcatlipoca. These usually merge in the myths. The other two were Huitzilopochtli and Quetzalcoatl. These four in conference, discussed the creation of the universe but it was left to Quetzalcoatl and Huitzilopochtli to carry out the plan. Accordingly they made fire, a half sun, the heavens, the waters, and a great fish from the flesh of which they formed the solid earth. Man and woman were then created and in order that their son might have a wife, one was made for him by the two gods out of hair of their divine mother's head.

Then began a long struggle between Quetzalcoatl and Tezcatlipoca which time after time destroyed the world and its peoples and even the heavenly bodies. Tezcatlipoca made himself into a sun. Quetzalcoatl with a great club knocked him from the sky into the water and himself became a sun. Tezcatlipoca transformed himself into a tiger. In the midst of a period of happiness on earth, the tiger with a blow of his paw hurled Quetzalcoatl from the skies. In revenge Quetzalcoatl swept the world with a tornado, destroying the

[18] *Historia del Origen de las Gentes que poblaron la América Setentrional,* Cap. xv, quoted by Brinton, *American Hero Myths,* p. 96.

inhabitants, save a few who were changed into monkeys. So the struggle went on until at last the very skies fell in and the sun and the stars themselves were quenched. Seeing the havoc they had wrought the two gods united in again raising the sky, making it to rest on two beautiful trees, where it has ever since remained.

It was necessary that they have a sun, so Quetzalcoatl built a great fire and threw himself into the flames from which he rose into the sky as the sun that gives light to the world. "When the light god kindles the flames of the dawn in the orient sky, shortly the sun emerges from below the horizon and ascends the heavens. Tlaloc, god of waters, followed and into the glowing ashes of the pyre, threw his son who rose as the moon."[19]

Tezcatlipoca then re-peopled the earth by striking a rock with a stick and from it issued four hundred barbarians, who were, however, slain by five goddesses. The goddesses likewise died before the appearance of the sun, but came into being again as did also the four hundred Chichimecas. Brinton says:

It is not hard to guess who are these four hundred youths . . . the veil of metaphor which thus conceals to our mind the picture of myriad stars quenched every morning by the growing light, but returning every evening to their appointed places.[20]

However, it was not Quetzalcoatl, the mysterious creator god who was destined to play so important a role in the conquest of Mexico, but Quetzalcoatl the hero, the fabled high priest of Tollan, who like his more exalted counterpart, was forever in conflict with his jealous rival, Tezcatlipoca, reduced now to a clever, powerful magician. The period which Quetzalcoatl spent in Tollan was its golden age. Sahagún

[19] Brinton, *American Hero Myths*, p. 76.
[20] *Ibid.*, p. 77.

tells us that in his time the corn grew so luxuriantly that a
single ear was a load for a man; gourds were as long as a
man; cotton grew in great abundance and of all colors, red,
yellow, purple, gray, brown, and orange.   There were untold
numbers of the most beautiful sweetly singing birds.   His
people were rich and lacked nothing.[21]

But he was not long permitted to enjoy these blessings.
His ancient enemy, Tezcatlipoca, assuming various disguises,
deceived and robbed his subjects, brought pestilence upon
them and by cunning strategies, inflicted death upon great
numbers of them.   Finally he succeeded in humiliating Quetzalcoatl by making him drunk with *pulque,* thus causing him
to forsake Tollan and go to Tlapallan.   Of this departure
there are many stories.   According to Sahagún, he burned
all the beautiful houses which he had built, buried in the
earth many of the precious metals and other articles which
he possessed, ordered many kinds of birds to go ahead of
him, and set off.   Here and there through Mexico are to be
found the marks of his passing.   In one place the prints of
his fingers are on a rock which he took in his hands.   A seat
remains marked in a great stone where he sat down to rest.
He went sadly, for he was greatly afflicted at having to
abandon his city.   In passing through the mountains his
companions died of cold and exposure.   Sahagún says that in
his time the Indians were still accustomed to point out where
the mountains were cleft at his passing.

When he arrived at the edge of the sea, he ordered a boat
to be made of serpents, and entering into it, as into a canoe,
he sailed away over the sea and it is not known how he
arrived.[22]

But before he sailed away, he promised to come back.
Although none knew just where he had gone, it was expected

that he would some day return and take up once more his
beneficent rule. Nor did they know exactly when this would
be, but he himself had predicted that it would be in the year
Ce Acatl, "one reed," one of the fifty-two years which made
up the cycle into which the Mexican calendar divided time.
On some recurrence of this year he would return, though in
what cycle none could foretell. By a rare coincidence the
year 1519 was the year *Ce Acatl.* In that year Hernando
Cortés landed on Mexican soil.

Naturally at the approach of the year *Ce Acatl* the old
superstitions were revived. All sorts of omens were observed, in the sky and earth and water. They were, of
course, reported to the emperor. The soothsayers and the
wise men of the realm were called into conference regarding
them, but as usual their counsel was vague and equivocal.
Not satisfied with their answers, the emperor is said to have
summoned his hunchbacks and dwarfs, which he kept in
imitation of Quetzalcoatl, and sent them to a famous cave,
supposed to be the entrance to the underworld, to find out
the meaning of the portents. Twice they were commanded
to return for more definite answers. Each time they came
back with but hazy oracles. At last, Montezuma declared
that he would go there and find out for himself, but he was
finally dissuaded from his purpose.

It was at this time that rumors began to arrive regarding
the coming of the Spaniards, and when Montezuma had seen
the pictures of the bearded Spaniards, he could no longer
doubt that Quetzalcoatl had returned but exclaimed, "Truly
this is the Quetzalcoatl we expected, he who lived with us of
old in Tollan. Undoubtedly it is he, Ce Acatl Inacuil, the
god of One Reed who is journeying."[23] When the Spanish
ships for the first time touched Mexican shores, we are told
that the natives hailed the bearded strangers from the East

[23] Tezozomoc, *Crónica Mexicana,* Cap. cviii.

as gods, sons and brothers of Quetzalcoatl who had come
back from their celestial home to claim their own on earth
and to bring again the golden days of the past. Mendieta
says:

> The Indians always hoped that the prophecies of Quetzal-
> coatl would be fulfilled, and when they saw the Christians come
> they called them gods . . . although after they knew better
> and felt the weight of their practices they no longer considered
> them heavenly beings.[24]

This prophecy which is found not only among the Aztecs,
but the Mayas as well, greatly influenced the emperor Montezuma in his reception of Cortés, as we shall see later. The
account of the Conqueror may be, and probably is somewhat
embellished, but in its main features it is corroborated by
Bernal Díaz del Castillo, an eye witness, who gives substantially the same story. What enormous practical effect
the prophecy had on the conquest is related at length in a
later chapter, where the entry of Cortés into Mexico is
described.[25]

There has been much speculation as to the origin and
meaning of these stories of Quetzalcoatl. Chavero has discussed the subject in great detail[26] and it will be worth while
to note briefly the possible solutions of the problem which
have been offered. They may be summarized as follows:

There are those who simply deny that Quetzalcoatl ever
existed in any form, or in other words that he is pure myth.
This is the easiest way out. Others see in him only the sym-
bolism of the formation of the earth, a simple, but equally
useless explanation. Father Durán supposes that one of the
apostles preached in Mexico; García, Becerra Tanco, and
particularly the eminent Mexican writer Siguenza y Góngora

---

[24] Mendieta, *op. cit.*, II, Cap. x.   [25] See *post,* 104 ff.
[26] Diego Durán, *Historia de las Indias de la Nueva España y Islas de
Tierra Firme,* II, Appendix, pp. 77 ff.

believe that it was the apostle St. Thomas who left the tradition of his coming and passing which have come to surround the figure of Quetzalcoatl. The last mentioned writer has a work of 517 pages in which he deals with the subject. Since this idea came to have such wide acceptance among early Mexican historians, and has been championed even within the nineteenth century, it will be of interest if not of real profit to examine the grounds on which the belief is based.

The first reason given is the presence of the cross in Mexico at the coming of the first Christian conquerors, which presupposes the preaching of some Christian messenger. We shall discuss the matter of the cross at some length later in the chapter. Some think that it was St. Thomas the apostle who first brought it, some think that it was a St. Thomas of Meliapor, while Orozco y Berra thinks that it was simply a Christian bishop who arrived with the first European expedition to America, probably that of the Norsemen.

The second reason for presupposing an earlier Christian influence is the likeness between the native religion and Christianity in many respects such as the memory of the flood; the likeness of Cihuacoatl to Eve; the presentation of new-born children in the temple; baptism by immersion; communion with the body of Huitzilopochtli; confession of their sins to the god, Tezcatlipoca; their solemn processions; beliefs in a hell; the limbo of children and the paradise Tlalocan; the fact that they had a devil Tlacatecolotl; celebration of the memory of the dead; their fasts; abstinence; the organization of their priestly hierarchy; the giving of first-fruits to the gods; and belief in the destruction of the world by evil spirits. Finally, they said that Quetzalcoatl was white, light-haired and bearded; that he used a robe embroidered with red and black crosses; and they pictured him wearing a kind of mitre and carrying a staff in his hand.

The third reason given is the existence of the prophecies

themselves that Quetzalcoatl would return with bearded white men from the East.

Chavero having stated the case as presented, sets himself to the task of disposing of it, and no modern writer will fail to appreciate the cogency of most of his arguments. It seems perfectly clear when he has finished that the storied Quetzalcoatl could not have been St. Thomas, nor a bishop of the tenth century, nor indeed any Christian; but he has, in the course of his argument, noted a variety of similarities between native and Christian ceremonies and beliefs, which are of very great importance to this study. Nor does it matter whether the native traditions and practices had their origin in Christianity or not. Indeed it does not greatly matter that the similarities seem, some of them, to be very far-fetched. To the early Christian missionaries in Mexico the likeness was exceedingly real, and they made great use of that fact in the indoctrination of the people into the Christian faith. These similarities are discussed at greater length a little later.[27] Chavero's own theory, into which we need not go here, is that Quetzalcoatl was only a Nahuan priest, reformer of the religion and founder of a numerous sect. He was a great priest and a great king.[28]

In interpreting the prophecies about Quetzalcoatl, Chavero resorts to the formula of the light myth which has been held to explain so many of the worlds myths. Brinton holds a like view. Indeed one feels sometimes that he has gone quite beyond the canons of scientific method to work out his light myth theory. In the main, however, he is probably correct. He says:

Such presentiments were found scattered throughout America. They had excited the suspicion of historians and puzzled antiquarians to explain them. The primitive myth of the sun which had sunk but would rise again had, in the lapse of time,

[27] *Post,* 61 ff.
[28] Durán, *Historia de las Indias,* II, Appendix, p. 87.

lost its peculiarly religious sense and had been, in part, taken to refer to past historical events. The light-god had become merged in the divine culture-hero. He it was who was believed to have gone away, not to die, for he was immortal, but to dwell in the distant east, whence in the fullness of time he would return.

This is why Montezuma and his subjects received the whites as expected guests and quoted to them promises of their coming. The Mayas of Yucatan, the Muyscas of Bogota, the Quichuas of Peru, all did the same and all on the same ground —the confident hope of the return of the light-god from the underworld.

This hope is an integral part of the great myth of light, in whatever part of the world we find it. Osiris, the murdered and his body cast into the unclean sea, will come again from the eastern shores. Balder, slain by the wiles of Loki, is not dead forever, but at the appointed time will appear in nobler majesty."[29]

Bishop Landa, the first prelate of Yucatan, a close observer and accurate recorder of what he saw and heard in the Maya territory, gives the following account of the Maya prophecies. He is regarded as a trustworthy source by all historical writers. The world is indebted to him for one of the best and quite the earliest written description of the Maya calendar which has so challenged the admiration of men. He says that just as the Mexican people had signs and prophecies of the coming of the Spaniards, and the end of their own power and religion, so also had the people of Yucatan. Some years before the conquest of their territories by Montejo, an Indian priest, Ahcambal, who had to do with giving the oracles of the demon, announced publicly that soon they would be dominated by a strange people who would preach to them of a god and the virtue of a post which in their language they call "vahom che" which signifies an upright stick with great powers against the spirits. One of

[29] Brinton, *American Hero Myths*, p. 141.

the chief Indians, well known to the bishop, showed him a book in which was painted a deer. He said his grandfather had told him that when the great deer came, for thus they spoke of cattle, the worship of their gods would cease, and thus it had come to pass for the Spaniards brought large cattle.[30]

The whole matter of the prophecies which were found not alone in Mexico, but in nearly every part of the new world raises some very interesting questions, and there has been no little debate as to their genuineness. Alfredo Chavero who takes high rank as an historian, categorically affirms that they did not exist at all, but were fabricated by the conquerors after the conquest. He says: "All these prophecies and songs and legends which appear to have been confirmed by the arrival of the Spaniards, whether of Mexico or Tezcuco, or the Mayas, are works subsequent to the conquest. The truth is that no authentic poem of Nezahualcoyotl is known. Despite the opinion of Mr. Brinton to the contrary, I continue to believe that those in existence are either modern or adulterated ancient legends and songs."[31]

Brinton's own statement may well be given, since Chavero has called his opinion in question.

None of the American nations seem to have been more given to prognostication and prophecies and of none other have we so large an amount of this kind of literature remaining. Some of it has been preserved by the Spanish missionaries, who used it with very good effect in their own work of proselyting, but that it was not manufactured by them for this purpose, as some later writers have thought, is proven by the existence of copies of their prophecies made by native writers themselves at the time of the conquest and at dates shortly subsequent.

[30] Diego de Landa, *Relación de las Cosas de Yucatán* (Vol. III, *Collection de documents dans les langues indigénes etc.,* par l'abbe Brasseur de Bourbourg, Paris, 1864), p. 64.

[31] Footnote in *Obras Históricas de Ixtlilxochitl, Historia Chichemeca,* p. 236.

These prophecies were as obscure and ambiguous as all successful prophets are accustomed to make their predictions, but the one point that is clear in them is that they distinctly referred to the arrival of white and bearded strangers from the East, who should control the land and alter the religions.[32]

It is a question that cannot be decided absolutely without a great deal more information than is at present available. It is not even necessary, from the point of view of this study, that they be proved to have existed before the conquest, for it is certain that they were widely believed very shortly afterward and they would thus operate powerfully in the practical work of converting the Indians. Enough that they were believed to have existed. It seems to the writer, however, that the evidence points to the actual existence of such prophecies before the coming of the Spaniards. Two good reasons appear to support this opinion.

First, we find clear reference to the prophecies in the earliest writings regarding the conquest. Cortés wrote his own letters to the emperor but a few months after the events which he narrates, giving a full account of his meeting with Montezuma and the latter's use of the prophecy in welcoming him. This is given in full in another chapter.[33] Bernal Díaz, though he wrote much later, was actually present when the interview took place, and he gives it substantially as Cortés does. It is true that he might have made use of Cortés's writings to refresh his own memory of the conversation, but he has shown himself throughout his whole work so definitely interested in correcting what he alleges to have been given incorrectly by other writers, and in challenging statements attributed to Cortés, that it seems likely he would have noted any such misstatement as this if it had been made. He recounts the legend without raising any question whatever about it. Motolinia, who, it is true, might be more

[32] Brinton, *American Hero Myths,* p. 167.
[33] *Post,* p. 107.

easily suspected of a religious bias that might prompt such a representation, tells of it so naively that it bears every mark of genuineness. Likewise, Sahagún,[34] whose critical method of using his sources makes him one of the most authoritative writers of the period and who certainly took his materials in part from non-Christian sources, raises no doubt as to the existence of the prophecies.

Second, on no other basis does it seem possible to account for the hesitancy displayed by Montezuma to attack Cortés and destroy his forces before they reached Mexico City and were allowed to fortify themselves in the palace; and to explain his subsequent lack of resistance to the aggressiveness of the Spaniards in seizing his person, destroying his idols, and despoiling him of his treasure.

It may be doubted, as Brinton says, whether the prophecies were as definite as the form they took after the coming of the Spaniards, but, that there existed in some form prophecies which would seem to the credulous Indian mind to be fulfilled by the coming of the white men, it does not seem reasonable to doubt.

But the god most venerated in Tenochtitlán or Mexico City, was the patron god Huitzilopochtli, god of war. His was the highest temple, and his were the bloodiest sacrifices. To him, Sahagún ascribes a human origin. He says that he was their chief god; that he was like Hercules, a destroyer of peoples. In war he was like a fire. His banner was a dragon's head spewing fire from its mouth. He had the power of changing his form and frequently changed into either bird or beast. "This man for his strength and skill in war the Mexicans esteemed very highly while alive. After death, they honored him as a god and offered him human sacrifices."[35] Ixtlilxochitl likewise says of him that he and other gods were certain valiant men who came to be thought of as gods.

[34] *See* Appendix I, pp. 312-13.   [35] Sahagún, *op. cit.,* I, Cap. i.

There were, however, mythical stories of his origin also. We have seen that he figures along with Tezcatlipoca and Quetzalcoatl as divine brothers, sons of the All-Father. According to Sahagún, one of the myths represents him as born of Coatlycue, who was the mother of certain Indians called Centzonvitznaoa. One day as she was sweeping, there descended upon her a ball of feathers. She seized it and thrust it into her bosom, but later when she had finished sweeping and went to draw it out, she could not find it. Later it was discovered that she had conceived a son. When her sons knew of it, they were exceedingly angry and their sister counselled them to slay her. When Coatlycue heard this, she was much afraid, but the child within her comforted her, saying "do not be afraid, for I know what to do." The brothers armed themselves and came to kill her. When they were very near, Huitzilopochtli sprang full born to life and armed with bow and arrows, set upon them and slew a great many of them.[36]

This god became the special protector of the Mexicans and conducted them in their many wanderings until they came at last to the present site of the city of Mexico. The *Codex Ramírez* gives a very graphic account of the manner in which he led them, permitting them to settle for a time in a certain place only to be led on after a brief stay toward the land they were to occupy permanently and to make the center of a great empire.

"Thus did the Mexicans set out just as the children of Israel had done, in search of the promised land, taking with them their idol, enclosed in an ark made of rushes, just as the others had taken with them their ark of the covenant. . . . Under no conditions did the Mexicans ever move an inch without the advice and command of their idol, and never did an idol exist who conversed with his people as

[36] Sahagún, *op. cit.*, III, Cap. iii.

much as this one did. Thus in all their customs and the
cruel sacrifices in which these unfortunate people indulged,
it is quite clear that they were guided by this same enemy of
mankind. . . .

"The first thing they did whenever they wished to stop
at a certain place was to erect a tabernacle or temple to their
false god for the length of time they expected to stay there,
and they always built the temple in the center of the site
where they had established themselves, the ark being placed
upon an altar such as is used in a church, for the idol wished
to imitate our religion in many ways, as we shall afterwards
show."[37]

It was during their wanderings, led by Huitzilopochtli,
that the cruel sacrifice of human lives was begun. The
Codex Ramírez has it thus:

The people in disobedience to the god Huitzilopochtli undertook to settle permanently in a certain place. Their idol waxed
angry seeing this and said to the priest, "Who are these who
thus wish to transgress and put obstacles in the way of my
orders and commands? Are they greater than I? Tell them
I will take vengeance upon them before tomorrow for it is not
for them to give advice about matters which are for me to determine. Let them know that all they have to do is to obey."
Having said this, those who saw assert that the idol looked
so ugly and frightful that they were all terrified. On that very
night, it is said, when everything was quiet, a loud noise was
heard in that part of the camp, and when the people rushed
there in the morning they found that all those who spoke in
favor of remaining in the place were dead, with their breasts
torn open and their hearts torn out. In this way they were
taught that most cruel of sacrifices, a custom they always practiced after that, which consisted in cutting open a man's breast
in order to tear out the heart and offer it to the idols, for they
claimed that their god ate only hearts.[38]

[37] "Codex Ramírez," in Paul Radin, *Sources and Authenticity of the
History of the Ancient Mexicans*, p. 71.
[38] *Ibid.*, pp. 73-4.

It is an exceedingly interesting story, though beyond the particular limits of this study, how the god finally made it clear that they had at last arrived at the chosen spot.

The first thing they did on settling in their permanent home was to erect a temporary and very humble temple to Huitzilopochtli. This later became the greatest of the temples of Mexico, and on the site where it stood is built the present massive Catholic Cathedral. It was here in his honor that the cruelest of human sacrifices were performed literally by the thousands, according to early Spanish writers. We shall let Bernal Díaz del Castillo, who saw through a soldier's eyes, tell of his visit to the temple of the war god.

The ascent to the temple was by 114 steps. . . . When we had ascended to the summit we observed on the platform as we passed, the large stones whereon were placed the victims who were to be sacrificed . . . the priests then led us into a tower where was a kind of salon. Here were two altars, highly adorned with richly wrought timbers on the roof and over the altars, gigantic figures resembling very fat men. The one on the right was Huitzilopochtli, the war-god, with a great face and terrible eyes. This figure was entirely covered with gold and jewels and his body was bound around with golden serpents; in his right hand he held a bow and in his left a bundle of arrows. . . . He had around his neck the figures of human heads and hearts made of pure gold and silver, ornamented with precious stones of a blue color. Before the altar was a pan of incense with three hearts of human victims which were burning, mixed with copal. The whole of that apartment was stained with human blood in such quantity as to give a very offensive smell. . . . With their horrible sounding trumpets, their great knives for sacrifice, their human victims and their blood besprinkled altars, I devoted them and their wickedness to God's vengeance, and thought that the time would never arrive that I should escape from this scene of human butchery, horrible smells and more detestable sights.[39]

[39] *Memoirs of the Conquistador*, I, 146-7. Translation of *La Verdadera Historia de la Conquista de México*, by John F. Lockhart. All

We can, here, only characterize briefly a very few of the gods of lesser importance, for a complete description of the Mexican religion is not called for in this study. It is only the general impression of it as forming the background for the drama of the conversion of the people that we are interested in presenting.

Paynal was a sort of under-captain of the great god Huitzilopochtli. His name means 'swift.' When in life his people were attacked suddenly, he went swiftly and called together an army in order to go against the enemy. After his death he came to be celebrated as a god. At the time of his annual festival a long procession was held in his honor. It was peculiar in that everyone taking part in it ran at full speed, as befitting the name of Paynal.[40]

Tlaloctlamacazqui was the god of rain. He gave moisture to wet the earth, so that the trees and the grass and fruits might grow. He sent hail and lightning, storms at sea and perils on river and sea. The name means that he lives in the earthly paradise and gives to men the things necessary to their bodily life.

Civecoatl, or Cihuacoatl was the first of the goddesses. They thought that she caused adverse fortune such as poverty, weakness, and difficulties. Her name means, "woman of the serpent." Sometimes she is called Tonantzin which means "our mother." In these two respects, thinks Sahagún, it seems that this goddess is our mother Eve who was deceived by the serpent and that they had knowledge of what had passed between Eve and the serpent.[41] Brinton, in his *Rig-Veda Americana,* gives a number of prayers addressed to her. One of them runs in part as follows:

subsequent references to the work of Bernal Díaz del Castillo are to this edition. The more common English title is the "True History of the Conquest of Mexico." From this arises the epithet, the "true historian," applied frequently to the author.

[40] Sahagún, *op. cit.,* I, Cap. ii.

[41] *Ibid.,* I, Cap. iv.

Hail to our mother who caused the yellow flowers to blossom, who scattered the seeds of the *maguey* as she came forth from Paradise.

Ho! she is our mother, goddess of the earth, she supplies food in the desert to the wild beasts and causes them to live.

Thus, thus you see her to be an ever fresh model of liberality toward all flesh, etc.[42]

Her general function seems to have been that of the genius of fertility, which extends both to the vegetable and animal world. She was thus the patron of mid-wives and of women in child-birth. Her chief temple at Tepeyacac was one of the most renowned in Mexico, and "it was a felicitous idea of the early missionaries to have our Lady of Guadalupe make her appearance on the identical site of this ancient fane, already celebrated as the place of worship of the older female deity."[43] This matter is treated at length in the last chapter of the book.

Tlaculteotl was the Mexican Venus. The name signifies goddess of lust or carnality. It was she who had power to provoke unlawful passions. Yet according to Sahagún, it was to her also that lascivious men and women confessed their sins and vices and she pardoned them. He gives in detail a description of the confessional ceremony which they practiced toward this goddess. The confession took place generally but once in a life time and that in old age.[44]

Among the numerous lesser gods we may note only in passing, were:

Mixcoatl, goddess of hunting
Opochtli, god of fishing
Huistcihuatl, goddess of salt
Tzapotlatenan, goddess of physic
Texcatzoncatl, god of wine. Four hundred priests were consecrated to him in the capital alone. Sahagún mentions twelve other gods of wine.

[42] Brinton, *Rig-Veda Americana*, pp. 28-9.
[43] *Ibid.*   [44] Sahagún, *op. cit.*, I, Cap. xii.

Coatlicue, goddess of flowers
Omamcatl, god of mirth.

On the whole, the character of the gods of the Mexican pantheon was comparatively high. Clavigero, after contrasting the indecencies of the Roman and Greek gods, and the superstitions of the Egyptian gods, says:

The Mexicans entertained very different ideas regarding their deities. We do not find in their mythology any traces of that excess of depravity which characterized the gods of other nations. The Mexicans honored the virtues, not the vices of their divinities, the bravery of Huitzilopochtli; the beneficence of Centeotl, Tzapotlatman and Opochtli and others; and the chastity, justice and prudence of Quetzalcoatl. Although they feigned deities of both sexes, they did not marry them, nor believe them capable of those obscene pleasures which were so common among the Greeks and Romans. The Mexicans imagined that the gods had a strong aversion to every species of vice; therefore their worship was calculated to appease the anger of their deties, provoked by the guilt of man, and to procure their protection by repentance and by religious aspect.[45]

RELIGIOUS INSTITUTIONS

Religion among the Mexicans was highly institutionalized. There was a very definitely organized priestly hierarchy embracing a great variety of priestly orders. Torquemada tells us that there was one high-priest who ranked above all the others, some of whom were as bishops and others as ordinary priests. In some provinces of New Spain there were six principal priests all under the High Priest whom they recognized as head and obeyed. These were very honest and chaste. When they saw a woman, they lowered their eyes to the ground. They, like the Nazarites, never drank wine or any intoxicating beverage. They displayed self control, gravity, dignity, and majesty in their features,

[45] Clavigero, *History of Mexico,* III, 402-3.

with the result that everybody thought that they were good
and perfect in their false beliefs and teachings. They were
held in the greatest esteem by the people and allowed great
authority. Indeed they really governed everything through
the replies of oracles which kings and lords consulted in every
important matter, such, for example, as going to war.[46]

There were numerous grades of officials for carrying on
the various parts of the worship and other temple functions,
comparable, says Torquemada, to the dignitaries about a
cathedral. There was a treasurer who had charge of all the
temple properties, and the lands which supported the cult.
He guarded the sacred vessels, and ornaments, provided the
altar supplies, etc., and, says Torquemada, "fulfilled his duty
with great diligence in the house of the Devil." Under him
was a major sacristan who had direct charge of temple ornaments; there was a precentor who had charge of the temple
music; there were choir-boys; and one of the very important
officials was the school-master who had charge of the temple
school, and trained the youth who were there dedicated to
the service of the gods. In the capital city, there was a sort
of archdeacon called by some "the eyes of the bishop," a
kind of vicar-general over all the schools and monasteries of
the city. Here also was a special functionary, Ometochtli,
who presided over the four hundred priests dedicated to the
temple of the god of wine or *pulque*.[47] The High Priesthood was conferred by election, though it is not known
whether the electors were of the priestly orders alone or
were the same as those who chose the political head of the
empire.[48]

Chavero, who in discussing the matter betrays no small
anti-clerical bias, thinks that the priesthood was even more
powerful than the political rulers. He finds in the very name
of the High Priest, Teotecuhtli, an evidence of his supremacy

---

[46] Torquemada, *Monarquia Indiana,* II, 177-8.
[47] *Ibid.,* pp. 177-9.   [48] Clavigero, *op. cit.,* II, 42.

over the kings "who were no more than lords of men, but servants of the gods," for "tecuhtli" or lord was a title used by kings, while Teotecuhtli means literally, "lord of gods." The second in authority whose title translated means "Lord of the gods of Mexico," had the power of designating who should enter the school Calmecac, and who should occupy the important places among the priests of the empire. "What was the power of a king in comparison with this priest who at his will had power over magistrates and other function- aries?"[49] asks Chavero who had apparently come into contact with the priesthood of his own day in Mexico in such a way as to leave him with no very kindly feeling for the clergy.

The following estimate by Clavigero as to the number of priests may safely be considered as exaggerated, but it does serve to emphasize the fact that they were very numer- ous, and to indicate something as to the importance of religion in the life of the people. "The number of priests among the Indians corresponded with the multitude of the gods and temples; nor was the homage which they paid to the deities themselves much greater than the veneration in which they held their ministers. We may form some con- jecture of the immense number of priests in the Mexican empire from the number within the area of the great temple, which some ancient historians tell us amounted to five thou- sand. Nor will the calculation appear surprising when we consider that, in that place, there were four hundred priests consecrated to the service of Tezcatlipoca alone. Every temple indeed had a considerable number, so that I should not think it rash to affirm that there could not be less than a million priests throughout the empire.

"Their number could not fail to be increased from the great respect paid to the priesthood, and the high opinion they conceived of the office of serving in the worship of the

[49] *Mexico á través de los Siglos*, I, 586.

gods. The great even vied with one another in consecrating their children for some time to the service of the temple, while the inferior nobility employed theirs in works without, such as carrying wood, feeding and keeping up the fire in the temple stoves, all considering the honor of serving in the worship of the gods as the greatest to which they could aspire."[50]

With so large a priestly class in the land it is of very great importance to know what, in general, was their character. Unfortunately our sources are practically all Christian and therefore might be open to the suspicion of bias. Yet most of the early writers agree that, on the whole, they were morally a relatively high type, and that their influence on the people was for good. They taught them the cardinal virtues, and some surprising bits of moral instruction have been preserved.

Clavigero dwells on the austerity and chastity of the priests. He says that incontinence among them was punished very severely. He recounts the story of a priest who having violated his chastity was given over to the people to be beaten to death with clubs. On the failure of a high priest in Ichcatlan to do his duty, he was torn in pieces and his bloody limbs presented as a warning to his successors. Torquemada is obliged to recognize their chastity but is quite unwilling to attribute it to other than Satanic devices. He says of them:

The Indian priests of New Spain were under the same law of chastity, because the Devil wanted them to be chaste . . . not because he is clean, but in order to imitate God in some way in his purity, he required that his priests live chastely.[51]

The office was not necessarily permanent. Some gave their whole lives to it; others seem to have served for only a limited period. Women, too, were employed in some of the

[50] Clavigero, *op. cit.*, II, 40-42.
[51] Torquemada, *op. cit.*, pp. 214-5.

services in the temple, such as tending the sacred fires, sweeping, offering incense to the idols, preparing the daily offerings, but could not perform the sacrifices and higher functions of the priesthood. Some of them were consecrated to the services in infancy, and from the age of four or five years lived in the temple schools and were instructed in the duties of the office. Others in fulfillment of special vows entered for a year or two years of service. All writers agree in crediting them with living chastely, under the very strictest oversight on the part of superiors. So far as we have discovered, there has been no charge of anything like the temple prostitution so common among other religions. "Nothing," say Clavigero, "was more jealously attended to than the chastity of these virgins." They were not bound to perpetual celibacy, but at the age of sixteen to eighteen were usually married.

There were various orders, both of men and women, who devoted themselves to the worship of some particular god. Those dedicated to the service of Quetzalcoatl were perhaps the most noteworthy. There was an order of young men dedicated to Tezcatlipoca, who however did not live in communities, but met daily at sunset to dance and sing praises to him. There was an order dedicated to Centeotl, composed of old men of sixty years or over who were widowers. Their number were fixed and only on the death of a member was another received.[52]

The temples dedicated to the worship of their many deities were naturally numerous, and constituted the most imposing of the architectural wonders which caused the Spanish conquerors so to marvel. Clavigero, who estimated the number of priests at a million, estimates the temples in proportion. He thinks that Torquemada's figure of forty thousand is far below the actual number, if the lesser ones

[52] *Ibid.,* p. 50.

be taken into account, since there was no inhabited place that did not have one temple, nor any place of any size that did not have a considerable number. They called the temples *teocalli,* that is, houses of god, and *teopan,* the place of god, "which names," says Clavigero, "they applied with greater propriety to the temples erected in honor of the true God, after they embraced Christianity."[53] There were beside, as indicated in the quotation from Motolinia on page 20, all sorts of wayside shrines and altars on hills, mountains, and elsewhere.

The shape of the temple was rectangular, usually, though that of Quetzalcoatl was round. The great temple in Mexico City was like a truncated pyramid, with five stories rising one above the other, each smaller by several feet, leaving room for a walk around its base. The dimensions were about 250 by 300 feet at the bottom. According to a drawing in a very early document of "El Conquistador Anonimo,"[54] the steps leading from one level to the next could only be reached by walking entirely around the temple on each level. On the great level space at the top, were erected twin towers some fifty-six feet high, dedicated, one to Huitzilopochtli, and one to Tezcatlipoca.

While the great temple proper in the capital was not the greatest in size, being exceeded in height by the temples at both Tezcuco and Cholula, the whole group of greater and lesser temples within the vast compound was not exceeded by any other. Let us see it again through the observing eyes of soldier Díaz del Castillo.

The temple was surrounded by a great court as large as the square of Salamanca inside of a double inclosure of lime and stone. At a little distance from it stood a tower, a true hell or habitation for demons, with a mouth resembling that of an enormous monster, wide open and ready, as it were, to devour those who entered. At the door stood frightful idols; by it was

---

[53] *Op. cit.,* II, 21.   [54] *See* Appendix, p. 317.

a place for sacrifice, and within, boilers and pots full of water
to dress the flesh of the victims which was eaten by the priests.
The idols were like serpents and devils and before them were
tables and knives for sacrifice; the place being covered with
blood which was spilled on those occasions.   The furniture
was like that of a butcher's stall, and I never gave the accursed
building any name but that of hell. . . . Crossing a court we
came to another temple wherein were the tombs of the Mexican
nobility. It was begrimed with soot and blood. Next to this
was another, full of skeletons and bones, each kept apart but
regularly arranged.   In each temple were idols and each had
also particular priests who wore long vestments of black, somewhat between the dress of the Dominicans and our canons;
their long hair was clotted together and their ears lacerated in
honor of the gods.

At a certain distance from these . . . were a great many
houses where resided the priests who had charge of the idols.
. . . Hard by was a large building where resided a number of
Mexican women who resided there as in a nunnery. They worshipped two female deities who presided over marriages, and
to them they offered sacrifices to obtain good husbands.[55]

Sahagún describes it in very much greater detail, adding
many items not noted by Díaz. He describes the stone on
which the human sacrifices were offered, noting that a gutter
ran from it to carry away the blood. All the towers faced
east, and the ascent to them was by narrow and very steep
stairways. He enumerates seventy-eight different buildings,
giving each its name and describing its purpose. Among
others was the temple school where the sons of the principal
families were placed under the priests for a certain length of
time.[56]

We have already mentioned the school for girls. There
seem to have been two schools for boys. One was for
younger boys, in which they were drilled in monastic discipline, and were charged with decorating the shrines of the

[55] Bernal Díaz del Castillo, *op. cit.,* pp. 148-149.
[56] Sahagún, *op. cit.,* II, Appendix, p. 197.

gods with flowers, tending the sacred fires, and participating in the religious festivals. They were taught to sing under the direction of the director of music. The other was a higher school, Calmecac, where particularly the sons of the nobles were initiated into the traditions of their fathers, and learned the art of hieroglyphic writing, the principles of government, and such knowledge of the stars and of natural history in general as was current in that period.

Torquemada mentions still another school, not usually found in the temple enclosure, but near by, where the boys of the middle classes were gathered and kept, as in the case of the other schools, until the time of marriage. They had to do less with the interior service of the temple, and more with external matters connected with it. They brought wood from the mountains, cared for the temple buildings and grounds, worked the farms which provided support for the temples, and, besides, were taught good manners and habits, were corrected in their faults, and taught, according to Torquemada, that which natural religion required.

Thus, all of the institutional education of the Mexicans was centered about the temple. This fact constituted one more point of contact between the native religion and Roman Christianity which displaced it. Education at the hands of priests was the accepted practice among the pagan Indians; it became, therefore, the natural, normal practice among them as they turned to Christianity, with the transition from one to the other thus made just so much easier.

Lack of space forbids describing in detail all their feast days, their fasts, and other ceremonies. It will suffice here to give a brief discussion of sacrifice, leaving until later the description of a few other practices which resembled the rites and ceremonies of Christianity. The performance of sacrifice was the chief function of the priests. The sacrifices were of all sorts. There were over two hundred gods for whom special days were named, besides the chief gods, and to every god some kind of sacrifice was offered. To the god of the hunt, for example, offerings of wild animals were made. Blossoms were offered in spring time to the goddess of flowers. To the god of fire, a libation was poured out always before drinking, and the first morsel of food was thrown into the fire in his honor.

That which most marked the sacrificial system of the Mexicans was their resort to human offerings. There exist many descriptions of the method used in this sacrifice, from both lay and ecclesiastical writers. While both these groups may be charged with some degree of exaggeration, particularly the latter, because of their natural reaction to the horror of it all, there is no question that the Aztecs were among the cruelest of any people in the world, in their practice of human sacrifice. Sahagún thus describes one of these ceremonies.

When the masters of the captives took them to the temple to be sacrificed, they took them by the hair, and when they went up the steps to the altar they dragged them by the hair. Sometimes the victims fainted, but their captors dragged them on up to the great stone of sacrifice. Across this, the victim was laid on his back. Two priests held his arms, two his legs and one his head. Then another priest with a sharp stone instrument, with a quick skillful thrust, opened the breast and with one hand tore out the still palpitating heart and offered it to the sun. . . . After this, the body was thrown headlong down the steps where it was taken by the owner, cut into pieces and distributed to be cooked and eaten. Before being cut up, the body was flayed and young men put on the skins and disported themselves in mock warfare.

Apparently these skins were kept on for some time, for Sahagún continues in writing of the feasts of the following month:

Also in this month, those who had on the skins sacrificed the month before, went and threw them into a cave in the tem-

A Sacrificial Stone of the Aztecs Upon Which Human Sacrifices Were Doubtless
Performed. It is Preserved in the National Museum in Mexico City.

ple. This they did in procession and with much ceremony, and they went smelling like dead dogs. After they had taken off the skins, they washed with much ceremony. Sometimes sick people vowed to be present at this procession to effect a cure of their ailments, and it is said that some were healed.[57]

One of the remarkable feasts calling for human sacrifice was that in the fifth month, Toxcatl. Again the description is from Sahagún. This was the chief feast of all. It was like our Easter and indeed came at about Easter-time. The young man prepared for it was chosen a year ahead of time. Indeed during the festivities of the occasion, the choice of the victim for the next year, from among many young men, was a special feature. For the whole year before his sacrifice he went about the city elegantly dressed, and with flowers in his hand. Every one knew that he was the image of Tezcatlipoca and prostrated themselves before him and worshipped him wherever they found him. Twenty days before his death, he was wedded to four beautiful virgins with whom he lived in the greatest luxury for the twenty days. Five days before the sacrifice they feasted and banqueted him in the finest and most elegant surroundings possible. When finally the day came on which he was to be offered up, he himself chose the hour of sacrifice, bade goodbye to his erstwhile wives, climbed the steps to the altar, breaking on each step a flute on which he had played during the year, and arriving at the altar was sacrificed in the same bloody fashion as the others.[58]

One of the forms of human sacrifice was the gladiatorial. Within the temple enclosure there was a large flat circular stone, several feet in diameter, resembling a mill stone. On top of this the victim was tied with a chain long enough to allow him to move about freely. He was given a weapon and allowed to defend himself against the attack of a Mex-

---

[57] Sahagún, *op. cit.*, II, Cap. ii.
[58] Sahagún, *op. cit.*, II, Cap. v.

ican warrior. If he succeeded in defeating, one after the other, seven opponents, he had redeemed his life. If he fell, he was carried dead or alive to the altar and the usual sacrifice made.

The victims were usually captives of war or slaves. A great many children were sacrificed, some by drowning, some by being shut up in a cave and left to perish of hunger and terror. Some women were sacrificed to the goddesses. But most frequently it was the war captive, or sometimes the criminal, who was the victim. Usually he was dressed to represent the god to whom he was being offered. Sometimes the victims were given a certain drink which intoxicated them so that they seemed to go to death gladly.

How many lives were annually sacrificed is a matter of conjecture. Probably the number has been greatly overestimated by the Spanish writers. Zumárraga, the first bishop of Mexico, says in a letter of June 12, 1531, that in the capital alone, twenty thousand human victims were offered up to the gods. Acosta affirms that there was a certain day of the year on which five thousand were sacrificed in different parts of the empire, and another day on which they offered as many as twenty thousand. Las Casas reports a very small number, perhaps not over fifty to one hundred a year. It is very probable that all these writers have erred in their estimates, Las Casas, who was the defender of the Indians, by understatement, the rest by exaggeration of the truth. Without being able to estimate the number with exactness we may be quite sure that it was large, especially during the years of rapid expansion of the empire, when captives in war must have been taken by the thousands.

It is interesting to get the viewpoint of Montezuma regarding such sacrifices, as revealed in his reported conversations with Cortés. He said:

We have the right to take away the life of our enemies. We could kill them in the heat of battle as you do your enemies. What injustice is there in making those who are condemned to death, die in honor of our gods?[59]

Clavigero, whom we have frequently quoted, in comparing them with many other peoples, finds that they compare not all unfavorably unless it be in the greater number of lives which they took. He shows that the Mexicans are by no means alone in sacrificing human life, citing the practice by the Ammonities, Israelites, Egyptians, Phoenicians, Cretans, Gauls, Germans, the Pelasgians in Italy who sacrificed a tithe of their children, and the Spaniards. Moreover, he says, "the frequency of such sacrifice was certainly not less in Egypt, Italy, Spain, and Gaul than in Mexico."[60]

Although there was a belief in a life after death, it is not so very prominently mentioned by any of the writers regarding Indian beliefs and practices. The idea seems not to have been so important here as it was among other peoples. There is in the *Códice Vaticanus,* to be sure, a sort of a Book of the Dead, representing the journey of the soul after death through the gloomy dangers of the underworld. However, Sahagún, who treated most of their conceptions at considerable length gives but little space to it. According to him the souls of the dead went to one of three places; one was the inferno where dwelt a devil called Mictlantecutli and his wife Mictecacioatl.[61] There went the souls of those who died of sickness, either lords or princes or humble people. A dog was always sacrificed at the burial of such persons, for the Indians believed that the soul crossed the river into the inferno on the dog's back and that the dog served as a guide. Another place was the earthly paradise, a place of much joy and peace without pain. There went those who were struck

---

[59] Clavigero, *op. cit.,* III, 411.
[60] *Ibid.*
[61] Same as Mictlanteuctli and Mictlancihuatl, *ante,* p. 28.

by lightning or drowned, or lepers, the gouty and the drop-sical. The other place was the region where dwells the sun. Those killed in battle went there, as did also captives who died in the power of their enemies, those killed by sword, and those burned alive. After four years these souls were said to be transformed into various kinds of bright-plumed birds, and so fly about sucking honey from the flowers.[62] The souls of brutes as well as of men seem to have been con-sidered as immortal, certainly that of the dog, which was supposed to lead his master through the underworld.

In a few of the ancient Nahuatl poems in Brinton's col-lections, allusions to the future life appear, but there appear also statements which seem to imply that there is nothing beyond this present life. One cannot be sure that the quota-tions here given were not influenced by Christian teaching.

All of us are but mortal, and our home is there in the here-after where there is life without end.[63]

As many as live on earth, truly they go to God when they descend to the place where are their homes. Alas, we miser-able ones, may it happen when we die that we may see our friends, that we may be with them in grandeur and strength.[64]

There is a legend of the resurrection of one who had been in the tomb four days. She was the sister of Monte-zuma, and her purpose in returning was to warn her brother of the coming of the 'Sons of the Sun' from the East. She was to be privileged to enjoy the benefits of the faith that these strangers brought with them. Lewis Spence says of the legend:

Papantzin's resurrection is one of the best authenticated events in Mexican history, and it is a curious fact that on the arrival of the Spanish Conquerors, one of the first persons to

---

[62] Sahagún, *op. cit.*, III, 1. *App.*, p. 260 (edition 1829).
[63] Brinton, *Ancient Nahuatl Poetry*, p. 63.
[64] *Ibid.*, p. 77.

embrace Christianity and receive baptism at their hands was the princess Papan.[65]

What he means by authentication is that formal affidavits are on file in Rome purporting to substantiate it. One writer, of the nineteenth century even, apparently credits it. It seems to be one of the most outstanding of the numerous legends which got themselves either fabricated entirely or at least adapted for early propaganda purposes. It is introduced here only as evidence of their belief in a life beyond the present.

SIMILARITIES BETWEEN THE MEXICAN RELIGION AND CHRISTIANITY

The reader will already have observed in the course of the preceding survey of the religion of the Mexicans, some interesting similarities between it and Christianity, for example, the wandering of the Mexicans, led by their patron god whose presence was symbolized by a sort of ark; the departure of Quetzalcoatl and his expected return; the organization of their priesthood on lines not very different from the Roman Catholic plan; their monasteries in which young men were trained for the priesthood; their convents where young women were admitted for special service to the gods; and the rest of the whole long list given by Chavero in refuting the theory that St. Thomas had preached the gospel in Mexico.[66] It will be worth while to enter here into a somewhat more detailed discussion of some of the more pronounced similarities which were, doubtless, of very great importance in the conversion of the natives to Christianity, namely, the cross, baptism, confession, communion, and their feast days.

Without doubt, the finding of the cross in Mexico greatly impressed the early missionaries. It seemed to them certain

[65] Spence, *Myths of Mexico and Peru*, p. 148.   [66] *See ante*, p. 37.

proof that Christianity had by some means been preached in Mexico, and there is no doubt that they made great use of this idea in their work of converting the Indians. The cross was found in many different places and forms. Alfred Chavero gives an exhaustive list of the places. The more notable are the cross at Cozumel, which the natives held as the god of rain and the cross sculptured in relief in stone at Palenque. The cross appears in many ancient paintings; for example, the robe of Quetzalcoatl is represented as adorned with red and black crosses. Chavero cites more than a score of figures of the cross in the various codices, Vaticanus, Borgian, Teferiano, and Dresden. In some cases it takes the form of a tree. In one case the tree seems to be bleeding. Among them all, however, this author asserts that there is not one in the form of the Latin cross. All have arms of equal length. On one of the crosses there seems to be a person impaled; before another, a figure resembling an infant is being lifted up as if in adoration.

According to Ixtlilxochitl, when the Tlascalans saw that the Christians worshipped the god which they called Tonaca-quahuitl, meaning "tree of our sustenance," they marvelled greatly. The same writer says that it was also called Quia-huiteotl and Chicahualizteotl, meaning respectively god of rains and god of health.[67] Chavero holds that the cross was the tree of the sun, the god of the rain, as in another place it is called Tonacatecuhtli. In the Palenque cross, the sun image appears. In contrast to the Christian notion of the cross as a symbol of redemption, he says, it is simply the deity of the rains, and symbol of great chronological periods.[68] Brinton explains it as the symbol of the cardinal points, as in other religions where it is likewise found.

No matter what its origin may have been, or just what its significance was to the Indians before the coming of the

[67] Obras Históricas de Ixtlilxochitl, II, 370.
[68] México á través de los Siglos, I, 377-9.

Spaniards, it was one of the points of contact between the two religions which served the early preachers very effectively. To them it seemed sure proof that the gospel had been preached there, but that in some fashion the worship . of the cross had been taken advantage of by the devils, as they almost uniformly called the native gods.[69]

Although the meaning of baptism was very different among the Mexicans from what it was among the Christians, the rite was commonly practiced among them. In order to show the similarities of the ceremonies, and at the same time the wide differences, it will be well to reproduce almost in full, both the Aztec and the Maya forms, as given respectively by Sahagún and Bishop Landa, first bishop of Yucatán. The former has been translated, in part, into English by Prescott, though not so fully as here, but the latter has nowhere so appeared, so far as the writer has been able to discover. The translation in both cases is free, but accurate.

When the child was to be baptized, elaborate preparations were made for the ceremony. They made him a little bow and four arrows, and a shield. Then they made a little shield of the dough made of crushed seed of the wild amaranth, and placed on it a little bow and arrows of the same material. A special dish of beans and toasted corn was prepared, and if it were a girl, they made ready jewels and the materials and instruments for sewing, spinning, and weaving.

When everything necessary had been made ready, all the relatives of the child were assembled, and the midwife who was to perform the ceremony was called. At early dawn they met together in the courtyard of the house. When the sun had risen, the midwife taking the child in her arms, called for a little earthen vessel of water, while those who were about her placed the ornaments that had been prepared for the baptism in the midst of the court. To perform the rite, she placed herself with her face toward the west, and immediately began to go through certain ceremonies and to cry, "O Eagle, O Tiger,

[69] Mendieta, *Historia Eclesiástica Indiana*, IV. Pp. 536-40 contain some very interesting legends of pre-conquest Christian traces in Mexico.

O valiant grandson of mine, thou hast come to this world, and thy father and thy mother have sent thee, the great lord and the great lady.   Thou wast conceived and born in their house which is the place of the supreme gods, who dwell above the nine heavens.   Our son Quetzalcoatl hath done thee favor. Join thyself now with thy mother, the goddess of the water who is called Chalchivitlycue."

Having said this, she moistened her finger in the water and gave it to the child to taste saying:

"Take this.   See it is with this that thou are to live and grow upon the earth.   It is from this that the things necessary for our lives come; whereforth, receive it."

Then she touched the child's breast with her moistened fingers saying:

"Behold the heavenly water, very pure water which washes and cleanses thy heart and takes away all uncleanness.   May it cleanse and purify thy heart."

After this she sprinkled water on the head of the infant saying:

"O my child, take and receive the water of the Lord of the world, which is our life, and is given for the increasing and renewing of our bodies.   It is to wash and to purify.   I pray that these heavenly drops may enter into your body and dwell there, that they may destroy and remove from you all the evil and sin which was given you before the beginning of the world, since all of us are under its power, being all children of Chalchivitlycue."

She then bathed the whole body of the child with water, and spoke thus:

"Whencesoever thou comest, thou who art hurtful to this child; leave him and depart from him, for he liveth anew and is born anew; now he is purified and cleansed afresh and our mother Chalchivitlycue again bringeth him into the world."

Having thus prayed, the midwife took the child in both hands, and lifting him toward heaven said:

"O Lord, thou seest here thy creature, whom thou hast sent into the world, this place of sorrow, suffering and penitence. Grant him, O Lord, thy gifts and thine inspiration, for thou art the great god, and with thee is the great goddess."

Four times did she thus lift up the child toward heaven, each time with a different prayer, the last to the sun, thus:

Lord, Sun, and Tlaltecutli, who are our mother and father, behold this creature which is like a rich plume, Quechotl. Thine he is, and I have determined to offer him to thee, Lord, who art called Totonametl, painted like a tiger, brown and black, and who art valiant in war. See, he is thy creature, born to serve thee, and to give thee food and drink. His is a family of soldiers and fighters who fight on the battlefield."

Then taking the bow and arrow and shield, she said:

"Behold, the tools of war with which thou art served and in which thou dost delight. Give unto him the gift thou dost give to thy soldiers, that he may go to the house of pleasures where rest the valiant soldiers who die in war and who are there praising thee. Shall this little one be one of them? O Merciful Lord, have mercy upon him."

Torches of pine were kept burning during the performance of these ceremonies. When they were ended, they gave the child the name of one of his ancestors in the hope that he might shed new lustre upon it. The name was given by the midwife or the priestess who baptized him.

Then she put into his little hand the bow and arrow and shield, saying:

"O brave one, take thy bow and arrow, for these are thy diversions and the joy of the sun."

Meanwhile boys of the section entered the house and stole the food that had been prepared, representing thus men of war.[70]

In case it was a girl who was to be baptized, the ceremony differed somewhat in detail, although essentially it was the same.

It is worth while noting that it is the midwife and not a priest who performs the ceremony, though at the end of his description he does say "midwife or priestess" twice. It is probable that these midwives were trained in the temple school for women, as described, so that in a sense, they would

---

[70] Sahagún, op. cit., VI, 37.

be priestesses.   Certainly it is a highly religious ceremony,
if Sahagún's description is to be accepted as genuine, and it
seems to us that it is.   Apparently, however, the priests have
nothing at all to do with the rite.   Note too that it is performed in infancy; Durán says at four days of age.[71]   Note
also, that it was the occasion for naming the child, as in the
Christian ceremony.   It was given water to drink, was
sprinkled with it and finally immersed.   On the score of
water and method alone, the ceremony ought to have been
quite satisfactory to the Christians.

Bishop Landa gives a very interesting account of the
ceremony as practiced in Yucatan, among the Mayas, to
whom he thought it was peculiar, not knowing of the custom
among the Aztecs, as given by Sahagún.   Among the Mayas
it was not a ceremony of infancy, though always of child-
hood.   Here, it was performed definitely by a priest, and
upon groups rather than upon single individuals alone, and
upon boys and girls together.   It was by sprinkling only.
On the whole, it seems to resemble the Christian ceremony
somewhat more closely than does the Aztec.

Baptism is found among the Indians in Yucatan, and is
even expressed by the word which means "be born again," for
in the language of Yucatan, "zihil" means "to be born again."
. . . We have not been able to learn of its origin, beyond the
fact that it is a rite which they have always practiced, and to
which they are so devoted that no one omits receiving it.   So
great reverence do they have for it, that if they are conscious
of having committed sins, they must make it known to the
priest, and such faith have they in its efficacy that they in no
wise care to repeat it.   What they thought to receive from it
was a disposition to be good in their habits; to escape harm in
temporal matters at the hands of the demons; and to come by
means of it and a good life to enjoy the glory which they hoped
for, in which they thought as do the Mohammedans that there
was to be eating and drinking. . . . The ceremony was always

---

[71] Durán, *Historia de las Indias,* II, Appendix, p. 21.

performed between three and twelve years of age, and they never married before baptism.

When one wished to have his child baptized, he informed the priest of his desire and the latter made public announcement of the day, which they were always careful to see was not ill-omened. Having done this, the interested party chose one of his fellow townsman, a chief, to help in it. After this it was the custom to choose four other old men to help the priest on the day of the ceremony. In this choice, all the parents of the children to be baptized had a voice. . . . Three days before the feast, the parents and officials fasted and observed continence.

On the appointed day, all assembled in the house where the feast was to be celebrated together with the children who were to be baptized. They took their places in the patio of the house, which was clean and decorated with fresh leaves, the girls and boys in separate groups. An old woman was appointed to serve as sort of god-mother to the girls, and a man was put in charge of the boys.

When this was done, the priest proceeded to the purification of the place and the casting out of the demons. To do this, he placed benches in the four corners of the patio, on which he stationed his four assistants, with a rope stretching from one to another, so that the children were inside the enclosure. Then stepping over the ropes, the children's parents, who had fasted entered also. There was a bench likewise in the center of the square where the priest sat by a brazier, holding a little ground corn and incense in his hand. The boys and girls passed by in order, each receiving in his hand a bit of the cornmeal and incense which he or she cast into the brazier in passing. When this was completed, they took the brazier and the rope, poured out a little wine in a cup and gave them all to an Indian who should carry them out of the village, warning him that he should not drink nor look behind him in returning; and with this they believed that the devil was cast out.

This done, they swept the *patio,* taking up the leaves of the *cihom* tree and scattering others of the *copo* tree and brought in some large panniers, while the priest robed himself. Presently he appeared, dressed in bright colored vestments covered with long plumes, carrying a hyssop with an elaborately worked handle. For bristles of the hyssop were used the tails of a certain snake which are like little bells (rattlesnake). The helpers then went to each child and placed on his head a white cloth which the mothers had brought. They asked the older of them if they had committed any sin or evil, and if they had, they confessed it and were separated from the others.

Following this, the priest ordered the people to be seated and keep silence, then began to bless the children with many prayers and to sprinkle them with the hyssop, all with much serenity. When the blessing was concluded, the priest sat down and the chief of the feast, who had been elected by the parents, arose and with a bone which the priest gave him, went to each of the boys and passed it nine times across the forehead. Then he wet it and anointed the forehead and the cheeks and between the toes and fingers of each one without saying a word. The water used was made of certain flowers and cocoa, dampened and dissolved in pure water which they brought from hollow trees or from the mountains. Having finished this anointing, the priest arose, removed the white cloths from their heads and others which hung on the back, on which each one had tied feathers from some beautiful bird and some cocoa beans. . . . Then the priest took a sharp stone and cut off the stone bead which they carried tied to the hair.

After this the other assistants took a handful of flowers and a perfume pipe which the Indians were accustomed to smoke, and passed each nine times over each child, then allowed them to smell the flowers and smoke the pipe. The gifts which the mothers had brought were then collected and given to each child, as well as something to eat, for the rest were now eating. They then took a cup of good wine and offered it to the gods with fervent prayers, beseeching them to receive the gift of those children and, calling another one of the helpers called the Cayom, they gave him a drink which he swallowed without stopping, for to hesitate, they said, was a sin.

When this was ended, the girls were allowed to depart first, the mothers having previously, however, removed the cord and the shell which they had worn as a mark of their purity, which act was, as it were, a license to marry whenever the parents wished it. Then, the boys were allowed to go also, while the fathers distributed the pile of *mantillas* which they had brought among the guests and officers.

The feast was concluded with eating and drinking for a long time. It was called Emku, which means, "come down from god." The ones who had given it, beside the three days of fasting and abstinence already observed, must remain continent nine days longer, and this they did invariably."[72]

It would be quite easy to suspect that some of the really beautiful prayers given in Sahagún's accounts were the invention, not of pre-conquest Indians, but of Christians. If we had not his explicit statement of the great care which he exercised in securing his information and checking it with other authorities, this would seem very much more likely. It is difficult, however, to see why he would be inclined to paint an unduly favorable picture of the paganism of the Mexicans, which the early priests appeared so to abominate, by putting worthy Christian prayers into the mouths of priests and priestesses. Whether or not the descriptions are to be relied on as exactly accurate in every respect, there can be no reasonable doubt that in some form the rite was commonly practiced.

It is quite clear, therefore, that in accepting baptism at the hands of the Christians, the Indians would feel no violent break with their religious heritage. It will be well to remember this when reading a little later[73] of the early eagerness of the natives to be baptized.

Mendieta says that the Indians had a form of oral confession "in their times of infidelity." Twice a year they confessed to their gods, going alone to some quiet place in the house or the temple or the mountains, or to a fountain and there showed their contrition, sometimes with tears and wringing of the hands as they confessed their sins. During the period of this exercise they never laughed or enjoyed any pleasure whatever, but showed only sadness and regret and bitterness. In this, apparently, the priests had no part, though, he says that medical men sometimes heard confessions. The theory was that sickness was the result of sin. Confession of the sin therefore seemed necessary if one were to be healed, so he confessed to the one engaged in seeking to cure him. Sahagún, however, described at considerable length the confessions made to the priests of the goddess, Tlaculteutl, goddess of lust, who seems to have had not only the power to awaken human passions, but to pardon and absolve those who having fallen into the evil, confessed to her priests.

One desiring to confess went to the priest who was also a diviner, and arranged to come to him on such a day as might be favorable according to the signs. Confession might be made in his own home or in that of a priest. First the priest prayed to the goddess, then exhorted the penitent to a full and complete confession, keeping nothing back by reason of shame, for said he, "the goddess has wide open arms and is waiting to embrace you." Then the penitent took oath to tell the truth, according to the native custom, that is, by touching the hand to the ground, licking off whatever might have adhered to it, and throwing "copalli" into the fire; and finally, seating himself, made his confession. The priest, after hearing it, exhorted him as to what he ought to do in the future, then imposed upon him certain kinds of penance, such as fasting four days or more, or passing thorns through the tongue, or sometimes through the male organ, or the ears. In some cases as many as four hundred thorns were to be passed through the tongue, before pardon was granted.

In case of less terrible sins the penance was, of course, much lighter. When the confession was finished and the penance performed, says Sahagún, the sinner went home and tried not to fall again into such sins, for they thought that if one fell a second time, there was no remedy. This idea, of course, led to the postponement of the confession of the graver sins such as adultery until old age, and then chiefly to escape the temporal punishment due them, since by confession, it appears that they did avoid criminal punishment. The priests kept absolutely secret whatever was heard in confessions, alleging that it was not they who heard, but the god. The government recognized this right of the priesthood.

Sahagún closes his description by saying that there is no little foundation for believing that the Indians of New Spain felt themselves obligated to confess at least once in their lives, and this only by natural law, never having had notice of things of the faith.[74]

That there existed also a ceremony somewhat similar to the Christian Communion, is quite clear. Acosta indignantly ends his description of it exclaiming, "Who will not marvel that the devil should have taken such care to get himself worshipped and partaken of by the same method which Jesus Christ our God ordained and taught, and which the holy church practices."[75] It was the patron-god Huitzilopochtli, who, according to Acosta, usurped for himself thus the honor and cult which belonged to God, though Motolinia describes a somewhat similar ceremony in honor of Tezcatlipoca, which he says explicitly resembled a kind of commun-

[74] Sahagún, *op. cit.*, I, Cap. xii.

Note: Sahagún gives at length the prayer of the priest on behalf of the penitent and the address after he has heard the latter's confession, before assigning the penance which is to be performed. Both rise so close to the Christian level, that even with the declaration of Sahagún regarding his method, one suspects that at least Christian terminology has crept into the pagan forms. One must either assume this or admit a relatively high development of the Mexican faith, at least in its theoretical expression. Of course this latter is not impossible. See VI, pp. 57-63 (Edición Bustamante, 1829).

[75] Acosta, *Historia Natural y Moral de las Indias*, II, 96.

ion. We have found no reference to the latter in any other source.

According to Motolinia's account it was performed during a feast which took place in November, after the harvest. Taking the seed of a plant called *cenizos,* they mixed it with corn meal, and made something resembling *tamales,* which they cooked in a pot of water. During the cooking, the children beat on a sort of a drum made out of a stick of wood without leather or skin, singing meantime and saying that the *tamales* had changed into the flesh of Tezcatlipoca, who was their principal god or demon. Only the children ate the *tamales* as a kind of communion or flesh of the demon. The adults ate of the flesh of the human sacrifices.[76]

Both Sahagún and Acosta give detailed descriptions of the ceremony in honor of the patron-god, which agrees in the main. It was held in the month of Panquetzaliztli, or May, which was sacred to Huitzilopochtli. The nuns in the temple school, took the seed of a plant, the wild amaranth, carefully cleaned it, ground it very fine, and made a kind of dough, mixed with honey, according to Acosta, though some writers say with human blood. This they gave the size and the form of the idol, and dressed it in costly apparel, adorned with gold and silver ornaments. The following day, a man called Quetzalcoatl, in the presence of the king and four chief priests, shot an arrow into the idol's heart, thus killing the body. It was then borne in procession through the streets, and afterward placed on the summit of the temple where a sort of ceremony of consecration was performed. Acosta says that out of the same dough of which the idol was made were made also huge pieces in the form of bones which were to represent the flesh and bones of the god. These were placed before the idol and consecrated by special songs and dances as the flesh and bones of Huitzilopochtli.

[76] Motolinia, *Historia de las Indias,* Cap. ii, pp. 23-24, in García Icazbalceta, *Documentos para la Historia de México,* I.

When the consecration was completed, the bloody human
sacrifices of the day were carried out, large numbers of victims being offered up. Then the garments of the idol were
removed, the body was broken up into bits, the heart was
given to the king, and the rest passed out to the people in
order, "like kisses of the god Huitzilopochtli" says Sahagún.
They believed that it was the body of the god which they
received and ate. According to Acosta, "the whole people,
small and great, men and women, all received it with such
reverence, fear and weeping, that one was obliged to marvel.
Those who were sick begged for it and it was taken to them
with great reverence. All who communed were obligated to
give a tithe of the kind of seed of which the idol was
made."[77]

One other point of similarity between the Aztec and the
Christian religions was their system of feast-days and fasting. Mendieta tells us that there was a calendar by which
the feasts were regulated. There were certain days of the
year for each one of the devils which, said he, "was celebrated
just as we have certain days dedicated to certain saints, for
in this the devil seems to have imitated among the idolatrous
and deluded Indians the plan which the Catholic church has
adopted for the worship of God and the reverence for the
saints."[78] Sahagún gives the most complete account of their
sacred festivals. The whole of his second book, comprising
about one hundred and forty pages, is dedicated to a description of them. Each of the eighteen months of their calendar
had its peculiar feast or feasts, as did also the five extra days
of the year. There were, besides these, certain movable
feasts. The author details at least eighteen such festivals.

In the matter of fasting, they apparently went even beyond the Christian practice. Mendieta tells us that it was
quite common among the people, though chiefly practiced

[77] Acosta, *op. cit.,* II. 96.
[78] Mendieta, *Historia Eclesiástica Indiana,* p. 97.

among the priests. In this, he says that they "conformed to
the custom of the Catholic church, and rightly, for it is only
just that those who are dedicated to divine service be more
diligent in these penitential acts than those who are not."
These ministers had their special fasting periods of twenty
days or forty, and one chief fast of eighty days. The fast-
periods were begun with the most horrible acts of self-tor-
ture. A hole was made in the tongue of each devotee and
four hundred sticks varying in size from smaller to larger
were passed through the hole by the older and more experienced. The less experienced passed only two or three hundred. All of them at the end of twenty days repeated the
operation. During the eighty days fast therefore this would
be done four times. The fast was apparently not a complete
abstinence from all food, for that would have been manifestly impossible, especially during the eighty-days fast.
Just how much they were permitted to eat is not clear.
Mendieta says in one place:

> During this time the chiefs and people as well fasted, both
> men and women. They refrained from eating "aji of Chile,"
> did not bathe as was their frequent custom, were continent, and
> passed sticks through the tongue each twenty days.[79]

There is no need here to go into further detail regarding
these similarities, however interesting it might be to follow
them through. Of what importance was it to the conversion
of the Indians, that these and other similarities existed between the two faiths? They seem to the modern mind sometimes far-fetched and almost fanciful, and taken in the light
of the present knowledge of the history of the world's religions they do not appear so striking. However, it is necessary to recall that there is a wide difference between the mind
of the twentieth century reader and that of the sixteenth
century Catholic monk, while, of course, the distance be-

---

[79] Mendieta, *op. cit.,* p. 102.

tween our modes of thought and those of the Indians is very much greater still.

To those early preachers and fanatical Catholic conquerors of Mexico, not the differences, but the resemblances became the center of attention. As Prescott says:

They were not aware that the cross was a symbol of worship of the highest antiquity in Egypt and Syria, and that rites resembling those of communion and baptism were practiced by pagan nations on whom the light of Christianity had never shone. In their amazement, they not only magnified what they saw, but were perpetually cheated by the illusions of their own heated imaginations. In this they were admirably assisted by their Mexican converts, proud to establish—and half believing it themselves—a correspondence between their own faith and that of the conquerors.[80]

Unfortunately there is little record extant in Spanish of the actual preaching and teaching of the earliest propagandists of Christianity, though there are some such works in the native dialects; but, from occasional references of such writers as Motolinia, Mendieta, Torquemada, Ixtlilxochitl and Acosta, it seems quite fair to assume that every advantage of the similarities was taken by the early fathers. In a later chapter will be found definite instances of accommodation to Mexican practices on the part of Catholicism, in the case of certain parallel beliefs and ceremonies.[81]

In view of these similarities, it was a great deal easier for the Indians to yield to the various forms of external pressure which accompanied the more spiritual efforts to convert them, than if the two faiths had been totally unlike. Indeed many instances have come to light, some of which will be cited later, which indicate quite clearly that under the modified Christian form, for example of the worship of the cross or the Virgin Mary, the Indians carried over an almost wholly pagan content. This fact caused the *padres* no little spiritual concern.

[80] Prescott, *op. cit.*, III, 386-7.   [81] *See post*, Chap. ix.

CHAPTER IV

CORTÉS AND THE CONVERSION OF THE INDIANS OF MEXICO

THE CHARACTER AND MISSION OF CORTÉS

Every school boy knows something of Cortés as a soldier and conqueror. The amazing feat of marching with a mere handful of men into the very heart of a vast Indian empire, after having destroyed his ships behind him in order to cut off any possibility of retreat; the capture of the very emperor himself and his imprisonment in his own palace; the complete subjection of the Aztec empire to the king of Spain, all within a few months, has assured Cortés forever a place among the great dramatic military figures of history. Not so much, however, is known of Cortés the Apostle of the Christian faith, the man who planted Christianity on the American continent. Yet, that he so considered himself and was so considered by early Christian leaders in Mexico, is abundantly evident.

Mendieta, the eminent church historian of the period, thinks of him as a divinely chosen instrument for effecting God's purpose of winning the Indians to Christianity. He writes:

It ought to be well pondered how, without any doubt God chose the valiant Cortés as his instrument for opening the door and preparing the way for the preachers of the gospel in the new world, where the Catholic church might be restored and recompensed by the conversion of many souls for the great loss and damages which the accursed Luther was to cause at the same time within established Christianity. . . . Thus it is not without mystery that in the same year in which Luther was born in Eisleben, in Saxony, Hernando Cortés saw the light in Medellín, a village in Spain; the former to upset the world and bring beneath the banner of Satan many of the faithful who had been for generations Catholics; the latter to bring into the fold of the church an infinite number of peoples who had for ages been under the dominion of Satan in idolatry, vice, and sin.[1]

He notes further that Luther and Cortés began work the same year; that in the same year Cortés was born, indeed on the very same day, the great pagan temple which he later found in Mexico City, was dedicated with a feast which called for the sacrifice of eighty thousand human lives.[2] "Would not the cry of so many souls suffice that God should say, 'I saw the affliction of this wretched people,' and should send in His name one who should remedy the evil, as another Moses in Egypt?"[3]

The courage of Cortés, he thinks, and the manner in which he was protected in the numerous battles and dangers through which he passed, can only be accounted for by the fact that he was divinely called for the task.

And really to know clearly that Cortés was mysteriously chosen for this purpose, it is sufficient that he constantly showed such zeal for the honor and service of God and the salvation of souls, holding this as his chief end . . . for he said on leaving Cuba, "Friends, let us follow the cross, for if we have faith in this sign we shall conquer." Everywhere he went he destroyed idols, forbade human sacrifices, and preached faith in the one true God and His only begotten Son, our Lord Jesus Christ, a thing not all leaders have been accustomed to take so seriously.[4]

Cortés himself, in his reported speeches and writings, frequently appears to think of the whole enterprise of conquest as a holy crusade and of himself as God's appointed agent to free the natives of Mexico from the power of the devil. Through the whole account of his conquests which he wrote to the king of Spain runs the idea of dependence on

---

[1] Mendieta, *Historia Eclesiástica Indiana,* III, 174-5.
[2] During the whole period of the feast, not on a single day.
[3] Mendieta, *ibid.*   [4] Mendieta, *ibid.*

God for protection, direction, and help. After a notable victory and when discontented followers urged a return to Cuba, Cortés said:

Neither must we forget, gentlemen, that up to this moment the Almighty has lent us his protection and we may confidently expect that he will not desert us in the future for, from our first arrival in this country, we have announced his holy religion to the different tribes according to the best of our ability and destroyed the idols.[5]

Coming to a formidable wall of defense at the entrance to Montezuma's territory, they halted and deliberated as to whether they should go on. Pressed for his opinion, Cortés said, "Let us follow our standard, gentlemen. It bears the figure of the holy cross, and in that sign we conquer." "To which we added," says the historian, Díaz del Castillo, "Forward; whatever may happen, for God is our only strength."[6]

MacNutt, who translated the letters of Cortés into English and is one of the eminent students of his life and work, says of him in his introduction to the letters:

He was a man of unfeigned piety, of the stuff that martyrs are made of, nor did his conviction that he was leading a holy crusade to win lost souls to salvation ever waver. . . . Whatever else may be doubted, the religious sincerity and martial courage of Cortés are above impeachment. He was a stranger to hypocrisy which is a smug vice of cowards, and if his reasons for acts of policy which cost many lives may be deplored by the humane, their honesty may be impugned by none. Had the influence of his faith on his morals been proportionate to its strength, he would have merited canonization.[7]

An estimate of his character by Motolinia, one of the first group of Franciscan monks who arrived in Mexico, one who knew the conqueror personally and could not but be

---

[5] Bernal Díaz del Castillo, *op. cit.*, I, 162.
[6] *Ibid.*, p. 145.   [7] MacNutt, *op. cit.*, I, 207.

conscious of his serious moral lapses as well as his virtues, agrees with that of later writers. In relating the attitude of Cortés toward the branding of slaves, he writes:

Although as a man he was a sinner, he displayed the faith and works of a good Christian and had a great desire to employ his life and means in increasing faith in Jesus Christ and to die for the conversion of the gentiles (Indians). He confessed with many tears, communed with great devotion, and put his means and his spirit in the hands of his confessors. . . . He made great restitution and gave much alms. God visited him with great affliction, trials, and illnesses to purge his sin and cleanse his soul. I believe that he is a son of salvation and that he will have a brighter crown than many of those who seek to discredit him.[8]

But perhaps nothing more clearly reveals the religious character of Cortés than his will. It shows his interest in religion not alone in its phraseology but in the provision made for the founding of a hospital, a monastery, and a college for students of theology in training for the priesthood and for instructing the natives in the holy faith, as well as the endowment of certain churches. Item V provides for masses to be said in all the churches and monasteries, as many as possible on the day of his burial, and in addition five thousand more on successive days in the following manner: "One thousand for the souls in purgatory, two thousand for the souls of those who lost their lives serving under me in the discovery and conquest of New Spain, and the remaining two thousand for the souls of all those toward whom I have obligations of which I am ignorant or forgetful. . . . My executors shall recompense the five thousand masses according to custom, and I beg of them in all that concerns my funeral to suppress all worldly pomp and devote it rather to the good of souls."[9]

[8] Motolinia, in a letter written in 1555. *Documentos para la Historia de Indias,* VII, 285.

[9] MacNutt, *The Letters of Cortés to Charles V,* I, 78.

The motives behind his benefactions to the church are stated in Item XI:

I declare that since the Almighty has vouchsafed to advance and favor me in the discovery and conquest of New Spain, and I have always received from his merciful hand very great favors and mercies, both in my victories over the enemies of the Holy Catholic Faith and in the pacification and settlement of those kingdoms, from which I hope great service may accrue to God our Lord, I order that the following works be undertaken in grateful recognition of said favors and mercies, and also to discharge and satisfy my conscience for whatsoever faults or burdens may lie thereon, but of which my memory no longer takes account to enable me to specify them.[10]

These impressions of the religious character of Cortés will be deepened as we follow him in his marches from the moment of his first contact with the Indians on the island of Cozumel until he reached Mexico City and in his subsequent colonizing trips; in the provisions which he made for the prosecution of the work of conversion; and in his championing of the religious needs of the natives before emperor and pope.   •

It would be a mistake to suppose that Cortés stands alone among the Spanish conquerors as propagandist of the faith, for we find something of the same in Columbus, Pizarro, and other restless spirits of the age.   They were all, so far as religion was concerned, simply products of their times. But none surpassed Cortés in the constancy or the depth of his zeal for the Holy Catholic Faith.

He bore no special commission from the king of Spain for the conversion of the Indians, since he sailed not under direct royal orders but under the direction of Don Diego de Velazquez, governor of the Spanish Island, as Cuba was then called.   He was without doubt, however, familiar with the royal concern for the conversion of the natives.   It is

[10] *Ibid.,* p. 80.

therefore not strange that at his very first contact with the natives, he should begin his role as "converter" as well as conqueror.

In tracing this phase of the subject we shall follow chiefly the narrative of Bernal Díaz del Castillo, author of *La Verdadera Historia de la Conquista*, who, as a soldier of Cortés, was an eye witness of most of the episodes described; and the *Letters of Cortés to Charles V* in which he relates the story of his adventures and conquests. We shall, however, note here and there some variations in the narrative by Gomara and Andrés de Tápia who was also one of the conquerors. Gomara writes at second hand, though he is said to have had contact with those who marched with Cortés, and his history appeared before that of Díaz del Castillo.[11]

FIRST CONTACTS WITH THE INDIANS

On the island of Cozumel, Cortés first saw the native religious rites and ceremonies, for it was a place of pilgrimage from the mainland of Yucatan. Learning through an interpreter that the teaching of their priests "tended to ungodliness," Cortés assembled the chiefs together and gave them to understand that if they wished to become brethren "they must give up sacrificing to idols which were no gods but evil beings by which they were led into error and their souls sent into hell."[12] He then presented them with an image of the Virgin Mary and a cross which he wished them to put up instead. These, he declared, would prove a blessing to them at all times, make their seed to grow and preserve their souls from eternal perdition. The chiefs answered that their forefathers before them had prayed to idols because they were gods and that they were determined to follow their example. Cortés, however, ordered their idols to be destroyed and an altar built on which he obliged them to place

---

[11] See Appendix, pp. 316-20, for a detailed discussion of these various sources.   [12] Bernal Díaz del Castillo, *op. cit.*, I, 61.

an image of the Virgin Mary.   Thus was the conversion of the Indians of the new world begun.

While at Cozumel, Cortés learned of two Spaniards who were captives of the Indians on the mainland.   He at once despatched a letter to them saying that he would remain there a certain number of days awaiting them.   The message was delivered and one of the men, overjoyed at the news, managed to escape and reach the Spanish ships.   The other preferred to remain with the Indians, since he had married among them, become the father of a family, and had adopted native ways.   The finding of Aguilar was most fortunate, for he had lived long enough among the Indians to acquire the language and so became invaluable to Cortés as an interpreter.   Through him and through Doña Marina, an Indian woman who, a little later, was given to the Spaniards, along with a number of other women, by the chiefs at Tabasco, and who also proved to be a skillful interpreter, Cortés was able to communicate freely with the Indians.   It was through these two that he delivered the homilies which he addressed to the inhabitants in almost every place he visited.

Sailing from Cozumel, they came to the mainland and put in at the Tabasco or Grijalva river.   The inhabitants proved very hostile and threatened to attack if they landed. Cortés, who, it should in fairness be said, sought always to avoid violence if possible, requested that they be allowed to come ashore only for fresh water.   The natives refused permission, but before attempting to force a landing, Cortés sent the royal secretary with interpreters to ask once more for permission to replenish their supply of fresh water. "They were also to give them some notion if possible of the Lord God and His Imperial Majesty Charles V, and explain to them that if they attacked us, and we in defending ourselves killed any of their men, the guilt would be upon their heads, not ours."[13]

[13] *Ibid.*, p. 70.

Having done all he could by peaceful means and having cleared his conscience of guilt by throwing the blame for battle upon the Indians who well enough knew that they were defending their homes, Cortés attacked them, and though he was bitterly resisted, he gained a foothold upon the shore of the river at the cost of severe injuries to his men.

The Indians, retreating into the interior and securing the coöperation of all the chiefs of the province, returned to the attack. They outnumbered the Spanish many times over and fell upon them with such fury with arrows, stones, and lances that seventy of the Europeans were wounded in a very short time. But they were no match for the crossbows, the muskets, and the cannon of Cortés, nor particularly for the mounted soldiers. They were frightened by what they supposed to be a new sort of god-man, for they thought that horse and rider were one strange new being, having never before seen horses. After an hour of desperate fighting which cost the Indians over eight hundred men, the Spaniards were victorious.

The religious spirit of the men appears in the Thanksgiving service which they held at the conclusion of the battle. According to Díaz del Castillo, they praised God and the Holy Virgin and thanked them with uplifted hands for the complete victory which had been granted.[14] Gomara asserts that the Holy Apostle James, the patron saint of Spain, appeared, mounted on a gray charger and fought with them, inspiring great fear among the Indians.[15] To which the "true historian" who frequently finds fault with Gomara's history, says.

I can only say that for the exertions of our arms and this victory we stand indebted to our Lord Jesus Christ. . . . Certain it is that God showed his mercy to us here, and it may indeed have been one of the two glorious apostles, St. James

[14] *Ibid.*, p. 76.
[15] Gomara, *Historia de las Conquistas de Cortés*, p. 35.

or St. Peter, who thus came to our assistance. Perhaps, on account of my sins, I was not considered worthy of the good fortune to behold them. . . . Yet, I never heard any of the four hundred soldiers nor even Cortés himself, nor any of the cavaliers mention this wonder or confirm its truth.[16]

This is but one of the many legends that very quickly grew up about the conquest. Although Díaz del Castillo does not find any basis for this one and takes it as good opportunity to discredit his rival, Gomara, he himself in other instances repeats no less remarkable stories as though they were the solemn truth. Mendieta, who in another part of the book is relied upon as one of the principal sources, fills whole chapters with stories of miraculous happenings. Indeed, there is little choice between writers on this score, for it was a credulous age in which they wrote, one wholly a stranger to the modern habit of submitting everything to rigorous tests before accepting it. This instance is introduced here only as an illustration of the general religious spirit of the soldiers, for any such legend must have arisen out of the stories which they told. Not alone to Cortés, the leader, but to the soldiers as well, this was a conquest for faith as well as empire, and God was their leader and protector. Had not St. James appeared on the battlefields of Spain in her wars with the Moors? What more natural than that he should appear once more when the hosts of God were again facing the forces of Satan?

After defeating the Indians of Tabasco, Cortés invited them to return with their families, and they did so. The chiefs had already sent a present of gold trinkets, which, however, says Díaz del Castillo, "was not to be compared with the twenty females with which they presented us." Among these women one, named Doña Marina, subsequently became a convert and one of Cortés' best interpreters.

[16] Bernal Díaz del Castillo, *op. cit.,* I, 77.

The Indians showed readiness to comply with the wishes
of Cortés that they do away with their idols and human sacrifices when he had given them "some idea of our Holy Faith
and how we adored God."[17] Also he showed them the image
of the Virgin and they were much pleased, asking that it
be left in their village. So he caused a "very pretty altar to
be built." Likewise, Spanish carpenters, constructed there a
very high cross. The next day the cross and altar were set
up and the figure of the Virgin mounted. All fell upon their
faces before it while the priest, Bartolomé de Olmedo, read
mass. All the chiefs and villagers were present. To the
twenty women who had been given to the Spaniards Father
Olmedo said "many excellent things concerning our religion,
that they should abandon their belief in idols and no longer
bring them sacrifices, for they were not gods but evil spirits.
They had, up to this moment lived in gross error and should
now adore Christ our Lord."[18]

After this address the women were baptized, among them
Doña Marina, already referred to. These were the first to
be baptized as Christians in New Spain, and they were at
once distributed among the chief officers. Doña Marina was
given to Puertocarrero, a cavalier, but when subsequently
he returned to Spain, Cortés himself took her and had a son
by her called Don Martín Cortés. Still later, Cortés perhaps
having tired of her, she was given in turn to Juan Jaramillo,
one of the under officers in the army of Cortés.

The utter naiveté with which the writers mention these,
to us strange associations between religion and lax ideas
regarding the relations of the sexes, is perhaps the best indication of the standards of the times. Many of the officers
and soldiers had wives at home; certainly Cortés did. It is
particularly remarked by Díaz del Castillo that the officer to
whom later the daughter of the great chief of Tlascala was

[17] *Ibid.*, p. 81.   [18] *Ibid.*, p. 82.

given was a bachelor. Yet, these presents of women were of frequent occurrence as they went forward with the conquest. Nor does any disapproval seem to have been expressed by the representatives of the church who accompanied the expedition.

There is some question as to who were the first converts baptized in New Spain. By some later writers it is asserted that the first were five chiefs of Tlascala. Díaz del Castillo, however, mentions still other groups of women who were converted before the army came to Tlascala. No other first-hand writer has made any statement concerning the matter, so far as we have discovered. It seems safe therefore, to follow our soldier author who was an eye-witness of the events which he narrates.[19]

Not because it is of importance to the general trend of the history, but because of the light which it throws upon the religious ideas and feelings of the period, it is worth while noting here the story of Doña Marina as given by the historian, Díaz del Castillo. She was born a ruler, her parents being chiefs over a section called Painala. Her father died when she was but a child and her mother soon married a young chief. To this union was born a son to whom they wished to leave their territories. But to do this they must get rid of the daughter. Accordingly they gave her away to an Indian family in Xicalango, spreading the report that she had died. The opportune death of a female slave just at that time made it easy to circulate the story of the daughter's death. The family at Xicalango did not long keep the girl, but gave her to the people of Tabasco who later gave her to Cortés, along with other women.

Still later, Cortés, accompanied by Doña Marina as always, visited the province of her birth and ordered all the chiefs to assemble before him. Among others came Doña

[19] See *Post,* pp. 102-103, for further discussion of this question.

Marina's mother and her husband.   Mother and daughter recognized each other instantly.   The mother was in great fear lest they had been called there to be put to death for the wrong done the daughter, but Doña Marina besought them that they dry their tears and comforted them saying that she was sure they were unconscious of what they were doing when they had sent her away to the people of Xicalango and that she freely forgave them the past.   By this means, she declared, God had certainly directed everything for the best, turned her away from the errors of heathenism, and converted her to Christianity.   She then gave them presents. "The whole affair," says the 'true historian,' "reminds one of the history of Joseph and his brethren in Egypt."   This is but one of many parallels with Holy Writ which the pious Spanish authors have taken the trouble to point out.[20]

Since the name of Father Olmedo appears in one of the above quotations, it will be well to note as another indication of the religious purposes of the Spanish that this expedition, like most others of that time, was accompanied by priests, in this case Bartolomé de Olmedo, a Franciscan monk, and Juan Díaz a secular priest.   One is struck, however, with the fact that while Cortés at times consulted them, especially Olmedo, regarding religious matters, and while occasionally they are referred to as addressing themselves to the natives, most of the religious discourses came from the lips of their commander, Cortés.   This is a further evidence of the essentially religious interest of the conqueror.   The religious duties of the priests seem to have been confined largely to the saying of mass, the confession of the soldiers, and such other service as could be rendered by them, chiefly to the Spaniards.   Rather an amusing, and possibly also a revealing account of the priestly function is related, not by those who accompanied Cortés, but of an earlier expedition which touched Yucatan:

[20] Bernal Díaz del Castillo, op. cit., I, 85.

While we were fighting with the Indians, the priest, Gonzalez, ordered the gold and small idols to be removed to our ships by two Indians we had brought with us from Cuba.[21]

Non-combatants in the battles which were waged, they still had important work to do. Again and again, as we shall see, the good sense of Father Olmedo led him to counsel his chief to greater moderation in his religious zeal.

We need not detail all the efforts at conversion in the different places at which the conqueror halted. But at San Juan de Ulloa, on Easter day, an altar was set up and the priests performed mass in the presence of the assembled Indians, after which, Cortés explained something of the faith. Here they were met by representatives of Montezuma who had sent to find out who they were and what were their purposes, offering to supply them whatever they needed. They brought rich presents from their master to Cortés and he in turn sent to the emperor a string of fine pearls, a beautiful chair, and a number of other things, among them, a brightly polished helmet which had interested the ambassador because it bore a resemblance to that which had belonged to their ancient forefathers and now adorned the head of their war-god, Huitzilopochtli. This, the ambassador said, his lord would be pleased to see, so Cortés included it with his gifts.

Montezuma, on receiving the gifts, and hearing the reports, was greatly astonished; but when he saw the helmet and compared it with that of Huitzilopochtli, he no longer doubted for an instant that the Spaniards belonged to that people whom his forefathers had prophesied would some day come and subdue the country.[22]

Thus did the ancient prophecy pave the way for the entrance of the Spaniards into Mexico. While doubtless the superior arms of the Europeans would eventually have won

[21] *Ibid.*, p. 5.   [22] *Ibid.*, p. 89.

over the most stubborn opposition of the Mexicans, there is no question but that the way to the conquest was made immeasurably easier by the conviction which the Indians had regarding the rulers who should come from the rising sun. Although the emperor tried by every means to dissuade Cortés from coming to the capital, so deeply under the influence of the belief in the prophecies regarding the bearded blondes who should come from the east, given at the time of Quetzalcoatl's departure, was he that he was not prepared to use violence to restrain them. It is impossible to understand the attitude of the Aztecs, when later the Spaniards entered their capital, apart from a consideration of this myth.

On one occasion when the ambassadors of Montezuma were present, about the hour of Ave María, a bell was rung calling the Spaniards to assemble around the cross which had been set up upon a sand hill near the encampment. While the Spaniards were on their knees before the cross repeating the Ave María, the ambassadors were very much interested. They desired to know why they thus humbled themselves so greatly before "that pole." Cortés, turning to Olmedo the priest said, "this is a good opportunity Father, to give these people some notion of our holy religion through our interpreters." This Father Olmedo proceeded to do in a manner which, observers Díaz, would have done honor to the greatest of theologians. This is one of the few occasions on which Cortés permitted the priest to do the talking.

When Olmedo had finished speaking, Cortés explained to them further that one of the principal reasons why his emperor had sent them to Mexico was in order that the Mexican people might be led to abandon forever the religion of their accursed idols, do away with human sacrifices, and leave off the practice of kidnapping. He must therefore request that they set up crosses like the one before them in their towns

and in their temples, and also figures of the Virgin and her
most holy son. Thus God would bring great blessings upon
them.[23]

Not long afterward, the attitude of the Indians seemed
all at once to change. They no longer brought provisions as
before, nor came to barter with the soldiers. Later it was
learned that this was done by order of Montezuma who had
forbidden all intercourse with the strangers, induced to do
so by his idols Tezcatlipoca and Huitzilopochtli, for these
advised him not to listen to Cortés and to take no notice of
what had been said regarding the cross and the Virgin.[24]

While he was still at San Juan de Ulloa, ambassadors to
Cortés came from a tribe of Indians who were enemies of
the Aztecs. From them he learned a great deal about the
conditions within the empire and the attitude of the various
tribes toward it. A little later he broke camp and went off
to a place which had been seen by an exploring band which
he had sent out. At the point of landing a village was established called Villa Rica de la Vera Cruz, known today simply
as Vera Cruz, "the true cross." Thence a march inland was
undertaken.

Sempoalla was the first village of any size which they
entered. Here the people were very friendly until there suddenly appeared among them five tax-gatherers of Montezuma who reproached them for receiving the Spaniards and
giving them supplies. The chiefs were terror-stricken, for
they feared Montezuma's anger and they likewise feared the
white men. The tax-gatherers demanded twenty young
people of both sexes to be sacrificed to the god of war that he
might grant them victory over the foreigners.

Cortés urged the chiefs to make the five tax-gatherers
prisoners, saying that his great emperor had commissioned
him to punish those who did evil and especially to forbid

[23] *Ibid.*, p. 94.   [24] *Ibid.*, p. 95.

kidnapping and human sacrifices. Though fearful, they did
so. Then Cortés ordered them no longer to obey the commands of Montezuma nor to pay him tribute. Further they
were to make this known to all with whom they were allied.
He would send and make prisoners of any other tax-
gatherers who might be found among them. When the
chiefs expressed great fear of Montezuma, Cortés promised
to protect them. Anyone who molested them would forfeit
his life. In view of these promises the chiefs agreed to unite
their whole forces with the Spaniards against the emperor.
So a formal declaration of allegiance to Charles V of Spain
was drawn up.

An incident related with great gusto by Díaz del Castillo
shows the feeling of the Indians toward Cortés and his followers and is therefore worth considering for its influence
upon the conversion of the Indians. Their readiness to listen
to the religious teaching of the newcomers was in very direct
proportion to the fear and wonder which these excited in
their minds. It is also an indication of the attitude of
Cortés toward the Indians and reveals his disposition to fit
into the part which myth and tradition had created for him.

Soon after the formal declaration of subjection had
been made, some of the chiefs came to Cortés complaining
that a large group of Aztec warriors had assembled in a certain village and were attacking their brothers, at a distance
of some thirty miles from the camp. Cortés manifested
great sympathy for them and asked them to retire while he
considered what to do. Then turning to his followers who
stood near, one of them being the "true historian" who gives
us the story, he smilingly said, "Methinks, gentlemen, we
already pass here for great heroes; indeed, after what has
happened with the tax-gatherers, these people must look upon
us as gods or as a species of beings like their idols. Now, I
am of the opinion that we ought to strengthen them in this

notion, so in order that they may think that one single man of us is sufficient to dislodge the Aztecs from that fortress, we will send with them old Heredia of Biscay. The malignancy of his features, his huge beard, his half-mangled-countenance, his squinting eyes, and lame leg constitute him the most fitting person for this object, beside which, he is a musketeer."

Cortés then sent for the man and arranged that after he had proceeded a certain distance, he should fire off his musket. This would be the signal for some one to be sent after them to recall them. "All this is done," said Cortés, "in order that the Indians may suppose us to be deities, and as you have not the most pleasing of countenances, I trust that they will take you by preference to be some idol." Then calling in the native chiefs, Cortés said: "I send this my brother with you to drive the Mexicans out of the fortress and to bring those whom he does not kill as prisoners to me." When the chiefs heard this they were utterly amazed, not knowing whether Cortés were in earnest or not. But seeing that he did not change countenance, they were convinced that this was really his intention, and marched away with Heredia, sending notice to their allies that they were marching to their aid accompanied by a "teule" or god-man.

At the signal agreed upon, a messenger was sent to recall the party and Cortés explained that he had changed his mind and would himself and a group of soldiers go with them. "I have mentioned this laughable circumstance," says Díaz del Castillo, "that the reader may see what artifices Cortés employed to throw dust into the eyes of the Indians."[25] Cortés with his army marched to the fortress in question, Tzinpant-zinco, where the Indians sent ambassadors to beg for mercy. The Sempoallan forces which were following behind the Spaniards began to raid and plunder the country which had

[25] *Ibid.,* p. 115.

formerly been at enmity with them. Cortés issued peremptory orders that this cease and that the Sempoallans return home. This act of justice so impressed the people of Tzinpantzinco that they, seeing how friendly Cortés was, "were the more susceptible to the things he told them about our holy religion, respecting the abolishment of their human sacrifices and kidnapping, discontinuance of other abominations and obscenities, with other matters salutary to their well being."[26] They, like the other chiefs, also declared themselves vassals of the king of Spain. They complained bitterly of the oppression exercised by Montezuma upon them.

Later it developed that the Sempoallans had trumped up the story against the people of Tzinpantzinco to revenge themselves through Cortés and the Spaniards upon them. On learning this, Cortés was very angry and when they appeared before him at his summons, they were in great fear. As always, Cortés knew how to capitalize the situation both for the emperor and for the cross. He spoke to them harshly at first, then relented, effected a permanent reconciliation between them and the people of Tzinpantzinco, and left them so well disposed toward him that, in the words of Díaz del Castillo, "the only wish of the Sempoallans now was that we should never leave their country again, fearing that Montezuma would send an army about their ears."[27]

So anxious were they to effect a permanent alliance with the Spaniards that they proposed to Cortés and his followers that they choose wives from among the women of Sempoalla. As an indication of their sincerity they immediately made a present to the Spaniards of eight daughters of chiefs. The young women were dressed in all the Indian finery becoming to their station as daughters of chieftains. The leading chief in presenting them said: "Sir, these seven women are intended for your chief officers, and this my niece who herself holds dominion over a country and a people, I have destined for you." Cortés received them with expressions of pleasure, but declared that a permanent and brotherly union could exist between them only if they abandoned the monstrous heresy in which they lived. He could not endure to see or hear of such abominations, such cruel human sacrifices and unnatural offenses as they practiced. The women must be converted to Christianity before he could think of accepting them. All these atrocities must cease at once. Only thus could their union be secure.

To this the chiefs replied that it would be impossible to abolish their idols and their human sacrifices, for everything that was good they had received from the idols. It was they who made the seed to grow and supplied all their needs. However, with regard to unnatural crimes they would in the future strive to put an end to them.[28]

Las Casas, the most persistent defender of the Indians, denies that these unnatural offenses were so common as the other writers so constantly affirm. Whether he was not swayed to the opposite extreme in his desire to do justice to the Indians is an open question. Díaz del Castillo was an actual witness of much that he describes. He certainly lacks nothing in definiteness in writing of the matter, for he says in the same passage, "all unnatural crimes must be stopped and young men must cease to go about in female garb to make a livelihood by such cursed lewdness." It will be worth while to give in some detail what happened then, mostly in the words of the "true historian," for like scenes were to take place in a number of cities which the Spaniards later took. It is an excellent picture of Cortés, Apostle of the Faith, in action.

The reply of the chiefs made a disagreeable impression upon Cortés and his companions for, says Díaz del Castillo:

[28] *Ibid.*, pp. 119-120.

we could no longer bear to look upon their barbarities and the dissolute life they led. Cortés spoke a long time to us on the subject. He brought many holy and useful lessons to our minds and observed that we could do nothing more beneficial to the people nor more to the glory of God than to abolish this idolatry with its human sacrifice. It was certainly to be expected that the inhabitants would rise up in arms if we proceeded to destroy their idols; we should, however, make the attempt even if it cost us our lives.[29]

At this the Spaniards arrayed themselves for battle and Cortés informed the chiefs that he intended destroying the idols. The chief at once called out all his warriors to defend them. When Cortés and his soldiers started up the temple steps the chief became furious, and approaching Cortés menacingly cried: "Why would you destroy our gods? Such an insult will bring destruction upon us."

Thus hindered, Cortés lost all patience. He had already told them that they must not sacrifice any more to these monsters which were but liars and deceivers. There remained now no alternative but to lay violent hands upon the idols and hurl them from their bases. He must henceforth look upon the Sempoallans as enemies since they rejected his advice. He would withdraw his protection from them and their opposition would cost them their lives.

When these threats were interpreted by Doña Marina who had added on her own account the reminder of the wrath of Montezuma, the chiefs hesitated. Since the Spaniards were intent on destroying the idols, the destruction could not be prevented, but they, the chiefs, would never give their consent to it.

Hardly had they ceased speaking, when fifty of the Spaniards sprang up the steps of the temple, tore the idols from their bases and hurled them to the ground. Some of the idols were shaped like curious dragons and were about the

[29] *Ibid.,* p. 120.

size of young calves; others were half human in form; some like large dogs; all of them horrible to look at. "When the chiefs and the people saw their idols broken and lying on the ground,"writes Díaz del Castillo, "they set up a miserable howl, covered their faces and begged forgiveness of the idols, as they were unable to protect them against the 'teules' or god-men."[30]

The outraged warriors began to attack the Spaniards viciously, but at once Cortés seized the chiefs and declared that if the attack did not cease immediately their leaders would be killed. The chiefs gave orders to leave off fighting and peace was restored. Cortés then ordered the broken idols carried away and buried. This was done by six Indian priests. The description of these men by Díaz del Castillo is very interesting.

The dress of these priests consisted of a long black cloak, white cassock without sleeves which hung down to their feet, and a species of hood. Their dress was clogged together with blood with which they were besmeared from head to foot and impeded in their walk; they likewise smelled most offensively of sulphur and putrid flesh.[31]

When the idols had been disposed of, Cortés spoke to the Indians saying that he could now look upon them as true brothers and lend them assistance against Montezuma; instead of their idols he would give them the blessed Virgin, the mother of Jesus Christ in whom he and his followers believed and to whom they prayed, that she might intercede for them in heaven and protect them. The Indians listened with good nature, according to our chronicler. Masons were set to work to clean the walls of the temple and to plaster them, then an altar was erected and covered with a cotton cloth. The natives were ordered to bring fresh branches and flowers, and four priests were charged with keeping these renewed, their hair being cut off and their blood-soaked cloaks changed for white ones which they were ordered to keep clean thereafter. The Indians were taught to make candles and ordered to keep them burning always before the altar. A cross was also set up and next day Father Olmedo in the presence of the chiefs of the district said mass. This is the first notice of his having any part in the whole proceeding.

The eight women who had been given to the Spaniards were then baptized, "after an edifying discourse." The niece of the principal chief was presented to Cortés who received her "with every appearance of delight." "She was a very ugly woman," writes Díaz, not without a suggestion of humor. However, Cortés as usual gave her to one of his officers instead of keeping her for himself. The chiefs were highly delighted that their daughters had been accepted and the very best feeling existed between them and the Spaniards.[32]

THE MARCH TO MEXICO CITY

Though every circumstance might well have discouraged Cortés from carrying out his desire to see Tenochtitlán, as the capital was then called, and the emperor Montezuma, he continued, nevertheless, making his plans. The long difficult march through a hostile country; the opposition of Montezuma to his coming; the smallness of his force; the scarcity of his equipment; and the but half-concealed disloyalty of a considerable number of his little army would have been sufficient to prevent an ordinary leader from attempting it. But Cortés was no ordinary leader. He was himself utterly fearless and tireless; he was ambitious; he had unlimited confidence in his own powers, hesitating not at all to compare himself with some of the greatest military leaders of history in his addresses to his men; and beyond this he was

[32] *Ibid.*, p. 123.

fired with something of the crusader's zeal to win an empire
for Christ and the church.

He made every possible preparation, perhaps the most
important of all and certainly the most dramatic of all being
the destruction of his ships after all that was of value, such
as sails, anchors, and chains had been brought ashore, as a
precaution against possible desertion by the disaffected members of his party and their escape to Cuba. Before setting
out, Cortés spoke to his men at great length:

> They already knew of the contemplated campaign. It was
> of such a character that the aid of Jesus Christ our Lord only
> could bring us forth victorious from all the battles and engage-
> ments which awaited us. . . . Should we be worsted, which
> God forbid, considering our small numbers, we could expect no
> other assistance than that from above and our own arms, since
> we had no vessel in which to return to Cuba. He then ad-
> duced many beautiful comparisons from history and mentioned
> several heroic deeds of the Romans.[33]

They answered, according to the soldier author, that they
would follow his orders. The die had been cast. They, with
Caesar, had passed the Rubicon. They had no other choice
left but to follow on; besides, everything was for the glory
of God and the emperor.[34]

The march to the capital led first through the district of
Tlascala which was at enmity with the Aztecs and friendly
with the Sempoallans who supplied Cortés with two hundred
Indians as porters and a group of warriors. On leaving
Sempoalla, he gave strict orders that the church and the
cross should be cared for and reverenced. An old soldier
was left behind in charge of it. On their march they sought
to introduce Christianity wherever they stopped. At Xalapa,
says Díaz del Castillo:

> Doña Marina and Aguilar told the people a good deal about
> our Holy Religion and how we were subjects of the emperor

[33] *Ibid.*, p. 135.   [34] *Ibid.*, p. 135.

Don Carlos who had sent us to bring them back from kidnapping and from sacrificing human beings. . . . We erected a cross in every township and explained its significance to the inhabitants, and what reverence was due it.[35]

At Castilblanco, Cortés declared to Olintecle the chief that he came by command of his emperor to put an end to human sacrifices. As the Indians made no answer, Cortés said to his followers, "I think, gentlemen, that we can do nothing further here than to erect a cross." To which Father Olmedo replied, "I believe, sir, that even this would be doing too much at present, for these people as subjects of Montezuma are neither afraid of nor shy of us and would only destroy the cross. What we have disclosed to them concerning our religion is sufficient until the time when they shall be susceptible of understanding more of it."[36]

It is no part of our purpose to follow the fortunes of Cortés except in so far as they have a bearing on the conversion of the Indians. Tlascala proved very hostile and opposed the advance of the Spanish forces with an army of fifty thousand warriors. The night before the great battle, the "true historian" tells us that being human and being faced by death, they all confessed to Father Olmedo and the priest Juan Díaz. This occupied the whole night and they did not fail to offer up fervent prayers to the Almighty that he would grant them victory. Faced by such fearful odds and winning as they did, it is little wonder that they felt they had enjoyed God's special care during the gruelling battle, and that their first act after the fight was over was to offer up glad thanks to the Almighty.[37]

It was only after repeated battles that peace was finally negotiated and the Spaniards were allowed to enter their capital. In winning over the Tlascalans, Cortés paved the way for the final conquest of the Aztecs, for these people

[35] *Ibid.*, p. 139.   [36] *Ibid.*, p. 141.   [37] *Ibid.*, p. 152.

were the most feared enemies of Montezuma. They remained loyal to the Spaniards throughout the whole contest and it is doubtful if, without this aid, Mexico could ever have been taken.

The next morning after entering the city, Cortés ordered an altar to be set up, and mass was then said in the presence of several of the chiefs. Gifts were brought to the conquerors and to Cortés the principal chief Xicotencatl said: "In order that you may have clearer proof of our good feeling toward you . . . we are resolved to give you our daughters in marriage, that they may have children by you. . . . I myself have a daughter who is very beautiful and who has never been married, whom I have destined for you."

Cortés made a suitable response, then turned to Father Olmedo. "What is your opinion?" he said. "Would not this be the proper moment to request these people to abolish their idols and human sacrifices? From fear of the Mexicans they will undoubtedly do anything we require of them." "It will be time enough" answered the priest, "when they bring us their daughters. Then we shall have the best opportunity of telling them that we cannot accept their gift until they have promised to abstain from human sacrifices. If they comply, it is well. If they refuse, we know what our duty and our religion require of us."

The next day the chiefs brought five young women with them, each accompanied by a maid in waiting. Cortés received them with expressions of pleasure, but said that for the present they must remain with their own people. The chiefs desired to know why. To which Cortés replied: "I have no other reason than that I am bound first to fulfill my duty to the God whom we adore and the emperor our master, which is to require you to abolish your idols, the human sacrifices, and other abominations practiced among you, and exhort you to believe in Him whom we believe, who is the only true God."

At the same time he showed them an image of the Virgin holding her Son in her arms. "If you are indeed our brothers and are really inclined to conclude a lasting peace with us, and if we are to take your daughters as affectionate husbands should do, they must abandon their horrible idols and believe in the Lord God whom we adore." They would soon discover the beneficial effect of this, he continued, blessings would be showered upon them; the seasons would be fruitful and all their undertakings would prosper; after death their souls would be transplanted to heaven and partake of the eternal glory. On the other hand, by the human sacrifices made to their idols who were nothing but devils, they would be led to hell where eternal fire would torment their souls.

In answer to the address of Cortés they said: "Malinche (the name by which he was known to the natives), we have heard all this from you on former occasions and willingly believe that this god and this illustrious woman are right good beings. But you should reflect how very recently you have arrived in our country and that you have but entered our city. You should certainly give us time to learn more of your doings, your manner of behavior, and the nature of your gods. When we have satisfied ourselves respecting their qualities, we shall certainly make choice of those we consider best. How can you ask us to abandon our gods whom we have adored for so many years and prayed to and sacrificed to? If we should do so to please you, what would our priests, our young men, yes, even our boys say to it? Believe us, they would rise up in arms. The priests indeed have already spoken to our gods who have told them not to abandon human sacrifices nor any of our ancient practices; otherwise they would destroy our whole country by famine, pestilence, and war."

Father Olmedo found himself obliged to address Cortés

on the subject. "My opinion is, sir, that you should no longer urge the matter with this people. It is not acting right to force them to become Christians. I could likewise wish that we had not destroyed the idols at Sempoalla. This, I am convinced, ought not to be done until the people have gained some knowledge of our Holy Religion. What indeed do we gain by pulling down the idols from their temples? They have merely to repair to another temple. But, on the other hand, we should never cease to exhort them with pious lessons. In this way the time will certainly come when they will find that our intentions and our advice are good."

Cortés then contented himself with ordering the idols to be taken down from a temple which had been recently built in the neighborhood, the latter to be cleansed and freshly plastered and the image of the blessed Virgin to be placed in it. To this the chiefs readily consented, and when all was finished, mass was said and the daughters of the chiefs were baptized. Afterward, they were received by the chief officers for whom they were destined.[38]

Thus far, the converts to Christianity of whom we have knowledge number twenty-five, all of them women who were given immediately after baptism as mistresses to the Spanish officers and soldiers. We know little about any of them except Doña Marina who seems to have developed into a devout Christian woman. One cannot help wondering just how far superior to their former faith they found Christianity, given the conditions under which they embraced it and under which they lived. So far as the record goes the women themselves had nothing to say one way or another regarding their conversion or their being given to the Spaniards.

It is probable that they made no resistance to the arrangement, for in that early period, it will be recalled, the Spaniards were still considered as god-men. Marriage to such

---

[38] The entire account of the Tlascalan episode as given here is taken from Bernal Díaz del Castillo, *op. cit.*, I, 178-82.

BAPTISMAL FONT WHICH, ACCORDING TO TRADITION, WAS USED IN BAP-
TIZING THE FIRST CHRISTIANS (MALE) IN MEXICO. IT IS PRESERVED
IN THE FRANCISCAN CHURCH IN TLASCALA.

(Translation of the inscription: At this font the four senators of the ancient
republic of Tlascala received the Christian faith. The rite took place in the year
1520, Juan Díaz, chaplain of the army of conquest, being minister. Captain Hernando Cortés and his distinguished officers acted as sponsors, etc.)

beings would doubtless be looked upon as a distinct honor by the women, and, since polygamy and concubinage were both commonly practiced among the Indians, the fact that the Europeans might have wives at home would not enter into their thinking as at all important. Of course, in the Aztec civilization woman had not attained a place which entitled her to be consulted on such matters.

Ixtlilxochitl, in his *Historia Chichemeca,* asserts that at this time the four chiefs of Tlascala were baptized,[39] but he is quite certainly mistaken in this. It is true that the chiefs were baptized, but at a later time during the stay in Tlascala, while preparations were under way for the siege of Mexico City. Torquemada is authority for this. He says that a painting depicting the event hung in the convent of Tlascala, showing the four chiefs receiving the sacrament at the hands of Juan Díaz and not Bartolomé de Olmedo, as other writers affirm. The names of the chiefs were written in the painting, and the garb of the minister proved that he was not a monk but a secular priest.[40] Later, on the death of one of the chiefs, Maxixcatin, his son was baptized and made his successor. These were the five who are said to have been the first converts in Mexico, but of course this does not take into account the conversion of the twenty-five women who have been reported thus far as having been baptized.

The route chosen for the march from Tlascala to the capital lay through Cholula, one of the chief cities of the empire, the seat of a large garrison of Montezuma's warriors. It was religiously the most important city after the capital. Its principal temple was even larger than that in Mexico City. Díaz del Castillo says that over a hundred temple towers were to be seen from the top of the great

[39] *Obras Históricas de Ixtlilxochitl,* II, 370. Cf. *México á través de los Siglos,* I, 889.
[40] Torquemada, *Monarquía Indiana,* I, 523.

temple, which was only slightly lower than the one in the capital. It was said to have a hundred courts.

At first the Cholulans received the Spaniards with great cordiality but later sought by treachery to destroy them. Though greatly outnumbering the intrepid invaders, they were no match for them and were severely punished by Cortés for their attempted deceit. Afterwards he assembled the chiefs and priests and admonished them very much as at Tlascala. They promised to destroy their idols, but kept putting it off. Cortés became impatient, but Olmedo reassured him by declaring that it would mean little, even if the people abolished their idols, unless they had previously received some notion of the Holy Faith. For the moment, he thought that enough had been done in admonishing them to piety, and in erecting a cross.

An argument of no small weight which Cortés used with them and with other conquered cities was that their gods had promised them the victory, yet they had suffered defeat. This proved the falsity and the impotence of the idols. They ought, therefore, to pull down and destroy such deceitful and lying gods. Later, as we shall see, the success of the siege of Mexico City depended in no small degree on such an appeal.

Meanwhile, as Cortés advanced toward Tenochtitlan, Montezuma continued sending messengers with gifts, seeking to dissuade him from attempting to come to the capital. When it no longer seemed worth while trying to discourage him, Montezuma sent the most important ambassador of his court, his own nephew, Prince of Tezcuco, to bid him welcome, and he himself met the white men well out at the edge of the city and conducted them to his palace.

What strange influence was it that restrained this semi-savage emperor, ruler of a vast empire, with unnumbered eager, almost savage warriors at his command, with hundreds of smoking altars and hungry idols awaiting the offering of quivering human hearts of slain captives in sacrifice—what restrained him from crushing this pitiful handful of adventurers who, with their ships destroyed behind them, advanced steadily toward his capital, subjecting the tribes as they came to allegiance to a distant foreign king? There were less than five hundred of them all told, and but a small escort of Sempoallan and Tlascalan warriors. A mere word of command from Montezuma would have finished with them forever, especially after they had entered the city across the long cause-way which led from the mainland to the island on which the capital was built, and before they had been allowed to fortify themselves in the palace to which they were assigned.

There can be but one answer, his religion. Quetzalcoatl had departed promising that others should come out of the east, bearded white people who should rule Mexico. The gods had spoken. All the portents of the recent years had indicated that the time was near at hand when the prophecy should be fulfilled. Now they had come. With a grim fatalism, he bowed to the inevitable. So did his people at first. One is reminded as he reads the accounts of the march to the capital and the subsequent dealing of the Spaniards with Montezuma, of the traditional rabbit or bird being charmed by a rattler, looking on, knowing that destruction eventually awaits it, but powerless to do anything to save itself. This feeling on the part of the Mexicans must be held in mind not alone in the physical and political conquest, but in the religious conquest as well.

The feelings of the Spaniards as they entered the city can well be imagined. No wonder the "true historian" is moved to write:

And we who were gazing upon all this, passing through innumerable crowds of human beings, were a mere handful of

men, in all but four hundred and fifty; our minds still full of
the warnings which the inhabitants of Huexotzinco, Tlascala
and Tlalmanalco had uttered, and with the caution that they
had given us not to expose ourselves to the treachery of the
Mexicans. I may safely ask the kind reader to ponder a moment and say whether he thinks any men in the world ever
ventured so bold a stroke as this.[41]

CORTÉS AND MONTEZUMA

Just at the edge of the city a thousand of the principal
inhabitants came out in procession to meet Cortés and his
company, and a little within the city proper, they were met
by the emperor Montezuma himself, accompanied by his
brother and a numerous retinue of lords, "two hundred
chiefs, all barefooted and dressed in a kind of livery, very
rich, according to their custom,"[42] says Cortés in his letters.
Montezuma, who alone of the company was shod, came between two lords. As they approached, Cortés dismounted
from his horse and was about to embrace the monarch, but
was prevented by the two lords who together with their ruler,
performed the ceremony of kissing the ground. Rich gifts
were exchanged; then, Montezuma preceding them, they continued through the streets to the palace which he had
prepared for their lodgement.

As Montezuma moved away before them in the direction
of the palace and the Spaniards followed, Díaz de Castillo
who marched among the soldiers says:

The road before us now became less crowded, and yet, who
would have been able to count the vast numbers of men, women
and children who filled the streets, the balconies, and the canals,
merely to look upon us? Indeed at the moment I am writing
this, everything becomes as lively to my eyes as if it had happened yesterday; and I am daily more sensible of the great
mercy of our Lord Jesus Christ, that He lent us sufficient
strength and courage to enter this city.[43]

[41] Bernal Díaz del Castillo, *op. cit.*, I, 220.
[42] MacNutt, *Letters of Cortés to Charles V*, I, 233.
[43] Bernal Díaz del Castillo, *op. cit.*, I, 220.

When they had established themselves in the palace, Montezuma had other valuable gifts spread before them and, seating himself on a platform near where Cortés had been placed, addressed him as follows:

We have known for a long time from the chroniclers of our forefathers, that neither I nor those who inhabit this country are descendants from the aborigines of it, but from strangers who came to it from very distant parts; and we are also told that our race was brought here to these parts by a lord whose vassals they all were and who returned to his native country. After a long time he came back, but it was so long that those who remained here were married with the native women of the country and had many descendants, and had built towns where they were living; when, therefore, he wished to take them away, they would not go, nor still less receive him as their ruler, so he departed. And we have always held that those who descended from him would come again to subjugate this country and us, as his vassals. According to the direction from which you say you come, which is where the sun rises, and from what you tell us of your great lord or king who has sent you here, we believe and hold for certain that he is our rightful sovereign, especially since you tell us that since many days he has word of us. Hence you may be sure that we shall obey you and hold you as representative of this great lord when you speak, and that in this there will be no lack or deception; and throughout the country you may command at will (I speak of what I have in my own dominions), because you will be obeyed and recognized, and all we possess is at your disposal.[44]

Gomarra records that Montezuma spoke sadly; that tears fell from his eyes while he was speaking; and that his followers wept also, for it seemed that they foresaw the troubles which were to come upon them.[45] Cortés himself gives no indication as to his own reply beyond saying the suitable thing and confirming the Indian belief that it was the king of Spain that they were expecting. Díaz del Castillo, who

[44] MacNutt, *Letters of Cortés to Charles V*, I, 234-5.
[45] Gomarra, *op. cit.*, p. 129.

was himself present during the conversation, says that Cortés in this his first conference with Montezuma, made particular mention of his desire for the conversion of the people of Mexico to Christianity.   The emperor, Don Carlos, he declared, had expressly sent to beg him, Montezuma, and his subjects that they become converts to Christianity for the salvation of their souls, and that they adore only one true God as he had expressly explained to the various ambassadors who had been sent to meet him on his march to the capital.[46]

The very next day, Cortés made a visit of courtesy to the emperor's own palace where he was very cordially received and given an elevated seat at Montezuma's right hand. Although Bernal Díaz del Castillo alone is authority for the account that follows, and though he wrote it down only after a great many years of strenuous soldier life, and may, therefore, hardly be credited with strict verbal accuracy in his report, it seems fair to assume that at least it represents the spirit and method of Cortés in his attempt to win Montezuma to the faith.   It is worth while giving at considerable length if only as a sample of the sort of homilies which Cortés was accustomed to make to the Indians.

After formal greetings had been exchanged, Cortés, through his interpreters, addressed the emperor as follows:

He said that all his and our wishes were now fulfilled, since he had reached the end of his journey, and obeyed the commands of his emperor.   There only remained now to disclose to him the commandment of God.   We were Christians, believing in the one true God and Jesus Christ who suffered for our salvation.   We prayed to the cross as an emblem of that cross on which our Lord and Savior was crucified.   By his death the whole human race was saved.   He rose on the third day and was received in heaven.   By him heaven, earth, sea, and every living creature was formed, and nothing existed but by his divine will.   Those figures which he, Montezuma, considered

[46] Bernal Díaz del Castillo, op. cit., I, 224.

as gods, were no gods but devils which were evil spirits.   It
was very evident how powerless and what miserable things they
were since in all those places where we had planted the cross,
those gods no longer durst make their appearance. . . . Of this
his ambassadors were fully convinced and he himself would in
the course of time be convinced of this truth.   He begged that
he would also pay particular attention to something else which
he had to communicate.

Here Cortés very intelligently explained to him how the
world was created; how all the people were brothers and sons
of one father and mother, Adam and Eve; and how grieved
our emperor was to think that so many souls should be lost and
sent to hell by those false idols, where they would be tormented
by everlasting fire.   For this reason he has sent us hither to
put an end to so much misery and to exhort the inhabitants of
this country no longer to adore such gods nor sacrifice human
beings to them; and also to abstain from robbery and committing unnatural offenses.   In a very short time our emperor
would send to this country men of great piety and virtue, of
whom there were numbers in our country, who would explain
these things more fully to them.   Of all this we were merely
the first messengers and could only beg of them to support us
in our labors and assist us in their completion.

As Montezuma was about to reply, Cortés stopped short
and turning to us said, "Verily, I am determined that they shall
comply with this, and let this be the beginning of our work."

Montezuma in reply expressed himself as follows: "Malinche, what you have just been telling us about your gods has
indeed been mentioned before to me by my servants to whom
you made similar disclosures upon your arrival off our coast.
Neither am I ignorant of what you have stated concerning the
cross and everything else in the towns you have passed through.
We, however, maintained silence, as the gods we adore were
adored in bygone ages by our ancestors.   We have once for all
acknowledged them as good deities, in the same way as you
have yours; let us therefore talk no further on this subject."[47]

After four days of rather close confinement within the
palace and gardens, Cortés and his soldiers began to be rest-

[47] *Ibid.*, pp. 225-6.

less and desired to see more of the city. Permission was sought of Montezuma, but he, fearing that some outrage might be committed on the idols about the city, resolved to accompany them. Accordingly they set out, the Spaniards heavily armed, led by Montezuma and a large retinue. They visited the market and the courts, then came to the great temple. Arrived at the foot of it, the emperor who had already ascended while they were still in the market and was sacrificing to his gods on top of it, sent six priests to escort Cortés up the one hundred and fourteen steps that led to the great upper court. Here spread out before them were the altars and all the implements for human sacrifice to the gods, already described in an earlier chapter.[48] Cortés, after looking out over the vast city which lay at their feet, turning to Father Olmedo, said, "I have just been thinking that we should take this opportunity to apply to Montezuma for permission to build a church here."

In modern parlance, Cortés might have been described as a "fast worker." Father Olmedo apparently thought so, for he replied that while the site was wonderful, and it would be a splendid thing if the emperor would grant the request, it would be acting too hastily to make such a proposition just then, since to gain his consent at any time would be difficult. For the moment at least, Cortés desisted from his purpose.

Turning to the emperor, however, he begged of him that they might see his gods. After first consulting the priests, the Spaniards were led into one of the towers in which stood the image of the war god Huitzilopochtli, of horrible mien. In front of him were burning three hearts of human victims sacrificed but a short time before. The walls of the chapel were besmeared with blood and the stench was fearful, "worse than a Spanish slaughter house," says the soldier author.[49] After seeing this and other horrors, Cortés turned smilingly to the emperor and said:

[48] See *ante,* pp. 53-54.   [49] Bernal Díaz del Castillo, *op. cit.,* I, 239.

I cannot imagine that such a powerful and wise monarch as yourself should not have discovered by this time that these idols are not divinities but evil spirits called devils. In order that you may be convinced of this and that your priests may satisfy themselves of this truth, allow me to erect a cross on the summit of this temple where stand your Huitzilopochtli and Tezcatlipoca. Give us a small space that I may place there the image of the Holy Virgin. Then you will see what terror will seize these idols by which you have been so long deluded.[50]

One is continually amazed at the tactless daring of this Spanish adventurer. Commander of only a little handful of fellow adventurers, his ships burned behind him, completely surrounded by half-savage hordes, in the heart of the capital city of a great empire, on the summit of the most sacred temple in the land, he has the temerity to request the monarch to allow him to set up the cross and Virgin alongside the great gods of Mexico! At the moment, practically the whole of the Spanish company was on the temple top, cut off from their fortification, and with but a few rounds of ammunition each. The utter destruction of the whole band would have been comparatively easy had the emperor given the order.

Montezuma was angered at the suggestion. He answered indignantly;

Could I have conjectured, Malinche, that you would use such reviling language as you have just done, I would certainly not have shown you my gods. In our eyes they are good divinities; they preserve our lives; give us nourishment, water and good harvests, healthy and growing weather, and victory whenever we pray for it. Therefore, we offer up prayers to them and make them sacrifices. I earnestly beg of you not to say another word to insult the profound veneration in which we hold these gods.[51]

Cortés, seeing the excitement with which the words were pronounced, very wisely decided that it was time to go. Montezuma, however, declared that he himself must stay and

[50] *Ibid.*, p. 240.   [51] *Ibid.*, p. 240.

atone to the gods for the sin he had committed in permitting them to ascend the temple and insult his gods.

The Spaniards, immediately on occupying the palace assigned to them, had fortified themselves as best they could and set up tables as altars. However, this was not regarded as sufficient. They desired to erect a chapel in their quarters, and to this Montezuma readily assented. Indeed, he ordered masons to do the work. In three days it was finished and a cross planted in front of their quarters. Mass was celebrated every day so long as the wine held out, and after that even they went into the church and prayed on their knees in front of the altar, because, says Díaz, "it was our Christian duty, and in order that Montezuma and his grandees might notice it and become accustomed to these holy things by seeing us kneel before them, particularly when we repeated the Ave María."[52]

Accidentally, in looking for the best place to erect the altar, a door which had been plastered over was discovered leading into the emperor's treasure room. "I concluded on seeing it," says the "true historian," "that the whole of the remaining part of the world put together could not produce such a vast collection of riches."[53]

Neither the officers nor men could for a moment be unmindful of the risk they ran of being attacked and put to death. The palace they occupied lay near the center of the city. Numerous canals cut across the island, spanned by bridges which must be crossed before reaching the causeway that offered the only avenue of escape to the mainland. The causeway itself was, moreover, broken at intervals by gaps, bridged over for strategic purposes. How easily any one or all of these bridges could be destroyed and all chance of escape from the capital cut off! The only guarantee of safety they could see was the capture of the emperor's own

---

[52] *Ibid.*, p. 242.   [53] *Ibid.*, p. 245.

person, and this they suggested to Cortés. He at first demurred but was later convinced that in such a bold stroke lay their only security. They had already begun to note a change of demeanor toward them on the part of the house-steward who furnished their supplies. Might not this reflect a change in the attitude of Montezuma himself?

After much deliberation, it was decided to make the attempt next morning. "The whole night," writes the soldier historian, "was spent in prayer with Father Olmedo to ask the support of the Almighty in this holy cause."[54] How the capture was effected is no part of this account. It is enough to say here that Montezuma was obliged to abandon his own palace and go live in that of Cortés, and to inform his generals and attendants that he did it of his own free will and on the advice of Huitzilopochtli, their war god. He was accorded every courtesy and attention and, after a little while, was even permitted to go out of the palace on hunting excursions and to the temple, unguarded by soldiers. He was naturally much affected at first but became used to the condition and even seemed to enjoy the companionship of the Europeans. He carried on his governmental responsibilities as before, refusing to listen to his followers who wished to revenge his humiliation by attacking the Spaniards.

Cortés conferred frequently with him and from time to time talked of religion, urging the emperor to accept Christianity. When Montezuma asked to go to the temple and fulfill his religious duties, Cortés at first refused for fear that the people might seize him and fall upon his captors. However, Montezuma persuaded him that it would be a good opportunity to show the people that he really, of his own free will, remained in the custody of the foreigners. Cortés then consented to his going but forbade any human sacrifice, as

[54] *Ibid.*, p. 246.

that was a 'sin against God.' It would be much more profitable, he suggested, if his devotions were made before the altar and the image of the Virgin Mary within the palace. Father Olmedo also, now and then, spoke to him about the holy faith.

Meanwhile, trouble was brewing for the Spaniards. Plots were being laid for a revolt against them. The power of Montezuma was being lessened daily. Notwithstanding this, however, Cortés was able to persuade the emperor to call a council and declare allegiance to Charles V of Spain. The chiefs bitterly opposed such a step, but Montezuma declared it to be the will of the gods, according to the current tradition. Moreover, when the priest of Huitzilopochtli sought another oracle, none was given. It was, therefore, necessary to bow to the will of the gods for the present. Perhaps later the gods would respond. Finally all consented and with tears agreed to take the oath of allegiance. Again, it will be noted, religion played a major role in their submission. After this, Montezuma seemed nervous and depressed. He could not keep back the tears. The Spaniards sought by every means to cheer him. Cortés and Father Olmedo scarcely left him alone for a moment, says our soldier chronicler, "while we employed every means to cheer him, we never lost an opportunity to exhort him to abolish his false gods."

The emperor, about this time, offered one of his daughters in marriage to Cortés, who, however, suggested the propriety of her being previously initiated into the mysteries of the Christian religion, by being baptized. To this Montezuma readily consented. He himself, however, continued as much attached as ever to his worship and sacrifices. This fact placed Cortés and his captains in a dilemma. What should they do? As good Christians could they permit this to continue? On the other hand, situated as they were, did they dare attempt to oppose these pagan practices? Finally they resolved that it was most consistent with their duty as Christians to incur even the danger of insurrection by destroying the idols of the Mexicans in order to plant the true cross in their place. Or, if that were found impossible, they resolved to content themselves for the moment with making a chapel for Christian worship on the temple.

With this in mind, Cortés approached Montezuma and said to him:

Great monarch, I have already so many times begged of you to abolish those false idols by whom you are terribly deluded and no longer to sacrifice human beings to them; yet these abominations are continuing daily. I have, therefore, come to you now with these officers to beg permission of you to take away the idols from the temples and place in their stead the image of the Holy Virgin and the cross. The whole of my force feel determined to pull down your idols even should you feel averse to it, and you may well suppose that some of your priests will become victims.[55]

When the emperor heard this he cried:

Alas, Malinche, why is it that you wish to compel me to bring down destruction upon this city? Our gods are already angry with us, and who can tell what revenge they contemplate against you? I will, however, assemble the priests to know their opinion.

Cortés, thereupon, begged a private interview with him and when the officers had withdrawn, told him that there seemed no other way of saving the town from rebellion and the idols from being destroyed than to permit the building of an altar and a cross and the image of the Virgin on the summit of the great temple. If this were permitted, he would be able to silence the mutterings of his men, and the Mexicans would soon be convinced of the value to their souls

[55] *Ibid.*, p. 285.

from such a change, for blessings and a good harvest would result from it.

Montezuma called together the priests and discussed the matter with them, and it was agreed that the Spaniards be allowed to build an altar, the cross, and an image of the Virgin opposite the idol, Huitzilopochtli, on the summit of the temple. Greatly did the Spaniards rejoice at this and set to work to build as they had planned. An old soldier was put in charge of the shrines and the Indian priests were strictly enjoined not to obstruct the man in any way in the performance of his duties.

The account so far given is from Díaz del Castillo. There are, however, two other accounts, both by eye-witnesses, which tell a different story. Díaz says nothing about the actual destruction of the idols, while Cortés declares that he did overturn the principal ones. His report of the affair is found in his letters to Charles V. It is in part as follows:

The principal idols in which they have the most faith and belief, I have overturned from their seats and rolled down the stairs, and I had those chapels where they kept them cleansed, for they were full of blood from the sacrifices; and I set up images of our Lady and other saints in them, which grieved Montezuma and the natives not a little. At first they told me not to do it, for it if became known throughout the town, the people would rise against me, as they believed that these idols gave them all their temporal means and, in allowing them to be ill treated, they would be angry and would give nothing, and would take away all the fruits of the soil and cause the people to die of want. I made them understand by interpreters how deceived they were in putting their hope in idols made of unclean things by their own hands, and I told them they should know that there was but one God, the Universal Lord of All who had created the heavens and the earth and all things else and them and us, who was without beginning and immortal; that they should adore and believe in Him, and not in any other creature or thing. I told them all I knew of these matters so as to win them from their idolatries and bring them to the

knowledge of God our Lord; and all of them, especially Montezuma, answered that they had already told me that they were
not natives in this country and that it was a long time since
their fathers had come to it, therefore, they might err in some
points of their belief, as it was so long since they had left their
native land, whilst I, who had recently arrived, should know
better than they what they should believe and hold; and if I
would tell them and explain to them, they would do what I told
them as being for the best. Montezuma and many of the chiefs
remained with me until the idols were taken away and the
chapels cleansed and the images put up, and they all wore happy
faces. I forbade them to sacrifice human beings to the idols,
as they were accustomed to do, for beside its being hateful to
God, Your Majesty has also prohibited it by laws and commanded that those who killed should be put to death. Henceforth, they abolished it, and in all the time I remained in the
city, never again were they seen to sacrifice any human being.[56]

Still another account, while agreeing more nearly with
that of Cortés, is of interest for its more dramatic quality.
It is from the pen of Andrés de Tápia, one of Cortés officers
who distinctly asserts that he was present at the destruction
of the idols.

Walking in the court of the idols, the marquis said to me,
"Climb up that tower and see what there is in it." So I went
up with some of the native priests and came to a thickly-woven
veil on which were hung many small bells. When I moved it
to enter, it made such a sound that I thought the house was
falling about me. The marquis, to pass the time, climbed up
also with eight or ten Spaniards, and because this veil made
the room so dark, with our swords we cut it down and the
room became quite light. . . . About the walls were images
of their gods. . . . The marquis, at the sight of the blood of
sacrifice sighed and cried out, "Oh God, why dost thou permit
the devil to be so greatly honored in this land? Lord, let it
appear good to thee that we serve thee!"
Calling his interpreters, he began to speak to the people,
for at the sound of the bells many priests had surrounded them.

[56] MacNutt, op. cit., I, 260-262.

"God, who made the heavens and the earth, made you and us and everybody and gives that which you need. If we are good he will take us to heaven; if we are evil we will go to hell, as we shall explain further when we understand each other better. I desire that here where these idols stand there shall be placed the image of God and his Holy Mother, and that you bring water and wash these walls and take all these things away." The people laughed, as if such a thing could not be done and said, "Not only this city but the whole world have these for gods; and the people esteem their fathers, mothers, sons, or daughters as nothing in comparison with these, and they will die sooner than do so. Already they have taken up their arms and will die for their gods."

The marquis at once despatched a soldier to the palace with orders to guard Montezuma carefully, and to send thirty or forty soldiers. To the priests he replied: "Well pleased am I to fight for my God against your gods which are nothing"; and before the Spaniards arrived, angered at certain words which he heard, he seized an iron bar and began to strike the idols of stone. I swear by my faith as a gentleman and before God it is the truth, it seemed to me that the marquis with a marvelous leap threw himself upon the idol and with the iron bar struck at the eyes of the figure, breaking away thus the golden mask it wore, crying, "Shall we not do something for God?"

The people sent word to the emperor who besought Cortés to allow him to come thither and that meanwhile he should do nothing to the idols. The marquis sent to bring him under heavy guard, and on his arrival, he told us to put up our images on one side, leaving the other to the pagan gods. The marquis was unwilling. Then Montezuma said, "Well, then, I will try to have done that which you wish, but you must give us the idols that we may carry them to any other place we desire." So the marquis consented saying, "See, they are but stone; believe in God who made heaven and earth; and by His works, know the Master." The idols were then taken with great skill and care, and they washed the walls of the rooms. . . . The marquis set up two altars.[57]

[57] Andrés de Tápia, "Relación sobre la Conquista de México," in García Icazbalceta, *Colleción de Documentos*, II, 586. Alfredo Chavero thinks it probable that the temple in which the destruction of idols took

Then follows a curious story, one which evidently was current during the early years of the conquest, for it is mentioned by other writers. It was doubtless appealed to by the early preachers of the gospel as one of the proofs of the truth of the Christian religion. Tápia writes that a few days later, when the altars were finished and mass had been said, Indians came to Cortés complaining that the lack of rain was destroying their crops. Since the Spaniards had taken away the gods to whom they were accustomed to pray for rain, he, Cortés should have the Christian God send the needed showers. Cortés replied reassuringly that it would rain and "charged all of us to pray for water. The next day we organized a procession to the tower where the altars were placed and said mass. At that time the sun was shining brightly, but when we returned home, it was raining so hard that the water covered our feet as we walked through the court." The author adds, "and the Indians marvelled greatly."[58]

Unfortunately, we have no certain knowledge as to the date of Tápia's narrative. Like that of Díaz del Castillo, it may have been written several years later, when this story, possibly arising out of a tradition bearing some resemblance to the story as told, or possibly being only a pious fabrication of the early religionists, was current. The author simply gives it a setting such as the story seems to require for its best effect. The important thing regarding such stories is not their truth or falsity, but the fact that they became current and were accepted as true by a credulous people who found nothing impossible in them and were practically affected by them in their attitude toward Christianity.

place was not the great temple, but another, probably Tlillan where he found many idols. With this "guess" of his own, he follows Tápia in the rest of his narrative.

[58] Andrés de Tápia, *op. cit.*, p. 587.

Which one of the accounts of Cortés and the idols is to be credited as true, it is difficult to say. The fact that Cortés wrote within a few months, at most, from the time the events occurred, while Díaz del Castillo wrote many years later, would incline one to follow the conqueror. Corroboration of the fact of the destruction of the idols by Tápia adds weight to the narrative of Cortés. The latter wrote, however, with at least one eye to impressing the King with his own importance. Also it puts a strain on one's credulity to believe that, as he states, "they all wore happy faces," while their cherished shrines were being violated. On the whole, the account of Díaz del Castillo seems much the most reasonable of the three.

But if the Spaniards felt happy at seeing their own sacred emblems on the temple, the effect on the Indians was quite the opposite. From the time of their erection, according to Díaz, a storm began to gather over the heads of the Europeans. The gods, Huitzilopochtli and Tezcatlipoca, were very angry. They declared, through the priests that they would leave the country, since they had been treated with so great contempt. They would not dwell together with the cross and the Virgin. They would consent to remain only if the insulting foreigners were killed. When this was communicated to Montezuma, he called Cortés and told him with great sadness what the gods had said and warned him, if he valued his life and that of his followers, to leave Mexico at once.

At about this time, an expedition under Narváez, sent out by Velázquez of Cuba to take Cortés, appeared on the coast. Learning of it, the general marched at once with the greater part of his army to meet him, leaving Alvarado with a small garrison to hold Montezuma and the palace. Although outnumbered many times over, the doughty little company under Cortés overcame the rival band and won over the greater part of them to his own cause. But, while rejoicing at this success, he was dismayed to receive word from Alvarado that the Spaniards had been attacked by overwhelming numbers and that immediate help was necessary. With the increased force recruited from the army of Narváez, Cortés hurriedly marched back to the capital. His total force now amounted to thirteen hundred men, ninety-six horses, eighty cross-bowmen, and a like number of musketeers. In addition, he was accompanied by two thousand Tlascalans.

Stories differ as to the occasion of the attack upon the Spaniards in Cortés' absence. The Mexicans asserted that, without any provocation, Alvarado and his soldiers had fallen upon a company of chiefs who were celebrating a feast in honor of Huitzilopochtli, for which they had secured permission from Alvarado. The Spaniards maintained that the Mexicans had risen up in arms to liberate their king and to revenge the insult to the gods of setting up the cross and the Virgin in the temple. Several Mexicans had tried to overthrow these sacred emblems but had been unable to do so, which fact caused great wonder among them. Whatever the cause, the results were disastrous. The Indians were no longer to be held in check. Even Montezuma's influence over them was not sufficient to restrain them, and they beset the palace of the Spaniards with such fury and in such numbers that the conquerors were able to hold them back only with the very greatest difficulty. Even the death of Montezuma[59] from wounds received at the hands of his own people

[59] There exists a persistent tradition that Montezuma was baptized before his death. Is it true?

An elaborate discussion of the matter is presented by Don José Fernando Ramírez, whom Chavero characterizes as one of Mexico's greatest historians, in an article entitled, "Bautismo de Moteuhzoma II, Noveno Rey de México," published in the *Boletín de la Sociedad Mexicana de Geografía y Estadística;* 1a epoca, tomo X, 1863. He indicates the very meager support which the tradition enjoys, but four references

while he was seeking to quiet them, did not serve to make them hesitate in their attack.

At last, Cortés resolved to cut his way out of the city and seek the open country where he would at least have a better chance at victory. The night of the attempt is still known as the "noche triste" or night of sorrow. Although the Spaniards escaped from the city, they paid a fearful price in the number killed and captured, while almost all were wounded. In addition, all their cannon and powder were gone and most of the treasure which they had sought to carry out with them was lost. A little later, Díaz states that their whole force consisted of only four hundred and forty men, twenty horses, twelve cross-bows, and seven muskets.

This study is not concerned with the retreat to the coast; the reinforcements that came to them by sea; the building of ships and carrying them over the mountains to launch them upon the lake in which the capital was situated; nor with the fearful siege which, by land and water, the Spaniards laid to the city. The resistance of the Indians was admirable. Few examples of greater courage and endurance will be found in the annals of human warfare. Only one event,

in all being found in the early sources, Tezozomoc, Muñoz Camargo, Ixtlilxochitl and one other. Against them he arrays the testimony of practically all of the principal early sources discussed in Appendix I, Cortés, Díaz del Castillo, Sahagún, Gomarra, and others. Gomarra does make the explicit statement that Montezuma had requested baptism on the day when the chiefs assembled to declare their allegiance to the Spanish crown, but that the Spaniards wished to defer it until Easter day, when it would be solemnized with much greater pomp. Before it could be consummated came the attack of the Indians, and in the stress of circumstances it was not performed.

Torquemada, who was most anxious to record every victory for the Faith, however, will not admit the truth of the tradition. He quotes Herrera, *Historia General de las Indias,* as saying that just before the death of Montezuma, they urged insistently that he allow himself to be baptized, but that he refused saying, that for the half hour of life that remained to him he did not wish to separate himself from his gods. (Torquemada, *Monarquía Indiana,* I, 523.)

however, stands out as of any importance to the religious phase of the conquest.[60]

The issue of the siege was by no means clear for a long time. Because of the numerous canals and bridges in the city, its capture was very difficult. Finally, the only means of taking it seemed to be the demolition of buildings one by one as they were taken, and the filling up of the canals. Little by little, the Spaniards moved into the city, though resisted with the greatest stubbornness. Every white man who was captured was sacrificed before the war-god. As they penetrated further into the city, they came so close to the temple that they could see their comrades slaughtered before the altars to the droning of war-drums.

The Indian allies of Cortés began to tire of the long-drawn-out siege. Most of their share in it was the hard labor of demolishing the buildings, while the besieged Indians taunted them, declaring that they would be the very ones who would be obliged to rebuild the city. Finally, after an almost disastrous defeat of one division of the army which was nearly cut to pieces in one of its raids, the allies began to desert and to steal away back to their own provinces. The beleaguered Indians by subtle propaganda had almost convinced them that the gods of Mexico would overthrow the foreigners. Then the priests overstepped themselves, giving out an oracle that in ten days Huitzilopochtli would deliver the city.

So long as the oracles were indefinite, they had tremendous influence and were very difficult for the Spaniards to counteract. However, with a definite date set, it was a comparatively easy matter to get their allies to hold out for the

[60] Ixtlilxochitl, *Decimatercia Relación de la Venida de los Españoles,* bound with Sahagún, *Historia General de las Cosas de Nueva España,* Vol. III, p. 74, says that while in Tezcuco during the siege, Tecocotzin who was the first to be baptized in Tezcuco, died. Apparently Cortés and Díaz del Castillo were too much engrossed in military affairs to note the religious progress being made at this period.

stipulated period, and when it was seen that the war-god had not fulfilled his promise, it became easy to convince them that the prophecy had been a mere trick of the idols to delude them. Subsequently, this failure to make good their promises was used to very good effect in proving the falsity and deceitfulness of their gods, in whose existence even the Spaniards appeared to believe, though they thought of them as evil spirits. Thus were the allies induced to return, and the destructive siege went on to its victorious conclusion, leaving Cortés master of Mexico.

AFTER THE FALL OF MEXICO

Although it was not given to Cortés to rule for a long period the land which his courage and persistence had won for the crown of Spain, he did lay the foundations for orderly government, and what is of more importance for this study, he did take real steps toward the conversion of the Indians to Christianity. Already he had written in his first letter to Charles V of his desire for the conversion of the natives. He had requested that the emperor seek to secure the interest of the Pope in the task which he well knew would be difficult and would call for more than the mere force of arms. In this letter which bears the date of July 10, 1519, he wrote:

Now let your Royal Highnesses consider if they ought not to prevent so great an evil and crime (human sacrifice), and certainly God our Lord will be well pleased, if, through the command of your Royal Highnesses, these peoples should be initiated and instructed in our Very Holy Catholic Faith, and the devotion and hope which they have in their idols be transferred to the divine omnipotence of God; because it is certain that if they served God with the same faith and fervor and diligence, they would surely work miracles.

It should be believed that it is not without cause that God, our Lord, has permitted that these parts should be discovered in the name of Your Royal Highnesses, so that this fruit and merit before God should be enjoyed by Your Majesties, of having instructed these barbarian people, and brought them through your commands to the True Faith. As far as we have been able to know them, we believe that, if there were interpreters and persons who could make them understand the truth of the Faith and their error, many and perhaps all, would shortly quit the errors which they hold and come to the true knowledge; because they live civilly and reasonably, better than any of the other peoples in these parts. . . .

Your Majesties may, if you deem proper, give this account as true to Our Very Holy Father, in order that diligence and good system may be used in effecting the conversion of these people, because it is hoped that great fruit and much good may be obtained; also that His Holiness may approve and allow that the wicked and rebellious, being first admonished, may be punished and chastized as enemies of Our Holy Catholic Faith, which will be an occasion of punishment and fear to those who may be reluctant in receiving knowledge of the truth; thereby, that the great evils and injuries they practice in the service of the devil, will be forsaken.[61]

Soon after the fall of Mexico, though just how soon we do not certainly know, since the document bears no date, Cortés issued a *requirimiento* to the Indians of the country as to their attitude toward Christianity. It is rather long, but, since the writer has found no translation of it in English, it seems worth while to give almost the whole of it here. It was the common custom for the notary or clerk who accompanied the expedition to read such a formal *requirimiento* before taking possession of any land in the name of the king. It made no difference that the Indians could not understand a word of it, since it was given in Spanish. Indeed the reading sometimes took place when there was no one present to hear; yet all scruples were apparently satisfied in this way, and if the Indians refused to submit, they were dealt with as rebels against royal authority.[62] Whether the

---

[61] MacNutt, *op. cit.,* I, 164-5.   [62] *Ibid.,* p. 178.

religious *requirimiento* of Cortés was delivered in this way, is not certain, but probably it was, though it was the custom of Cortés to use interpreters in his own religious dealings with the people.

The document here translated was found by the present writer only in a seventeenth century work, *Teatro Eclesiastico* by González Dávila. It seems strange that it has not been reproduced in some of the many collections of documents that have appeared both in Spain and in Mexico. Yet it bears all the marks of a genuine work of Cortés, and must have been issued shortly after the fall of Mexico. It reads in part as follows:

Representing His Majesty Charles V, etc., I, his servant, notify and make it known to you as best I can, that the living and eternal God, our Lord, created the heavens and the earth, and man, and woman from whom you and we and all men in the world are descendants, as well as all those who shall come after us. However, because of the multitude of generations issuing from these in the five thousand years since the creation of the world, it was necessary that some should go one way and some another, and that they should be divided into many kingdoms and provinces, since they could not all maintain themselves in one.

God, our Lord, gave charge of all these people to one called St. Peter, that he should be lord and superior of all men in the world and that they should obey him, and that he should be the head of all the human race, and should love all men of whatsoever land, religion and belief. To him he gave the world for his kingdom, ordering his seat to be placed in Rome, as the best place suited for the ruling of the world. He was, however, permitted to establish his seat in any other part of the world and to judge and govern all peoples, Christians, Moors, Jews, Gentiles, and of whatsoever other sect or creed they might be. This man is called the pope, which means wonderful and great Father, governor of all men. He and his successors have been so accepted.

One of his successors, as lord of all spiritual matters, made a donation of these islands and New Spain to the Catholic monarchs, Ferdinand and Isabella and their successors, so that they now belong to them. Other islands have received and obeyed their majesties willingly and without resistance, and likewise have obeyed the religious men sent to preach and teach them our Holy Faith. All of them, without reward or other condition, became Christians and are now such. Their majesties received them gladly and benevolently, and ordered that they be treated as their other subjects and vassals. Now, you too must do likewise.

Wherefore, as best I can, I urge you and require you that you seek to understand and obey what has been told you. Take such time as may be reasonable for deliberating over it and understanding it; recognize the church as superior in the world and the pope as superior in matters spiritual and the king and queen as lords and sovereigns of this land; likewise consent that the priests declare and preach to you their doctrine.

If you do this you will do well, and will fulfill an obligation. Their majesties and I will receive you with all love and charity and will allow you to have your wives and children and your lands freely, without serving as slaves . . . and we will not compel you to become Christians, unless, after being informed regarding the truth, you desire to be converted to our faith as all your neighbors have done. Moreover their majesties will give you many privileges and show you many kindnesses.

But, if you do not do this and put impediments in the way, I swear to you that by God's help, I will come among you powerfully and make war upon you everywhere and in every way that I can, and I will subject you to the yoke of obedience to the church and their majesties. I will take your persons, your women and children, and will make slaves of them and sell them or dispose of them as their Highnesses shall command. I will take your possessions and will damage you as much as I can, as vassals who do not obey or wish to acknowledge their sovereign, but resist and oppose him. And furthermore, I protest that the damage and death which you suffer thereby shall be your own fault and not the fault of their Majesties, nor mine, nor the knights who accompany me. Of all I say and require of you, the scribe who writes this shall be my witness.[63]

---

[63] González Dávila, *Teatro Eclesiástico*, I, 3-5.

Possibly the crowning act of the Conqueror in his zeal for the conversion of the Indians was his reception of the first group of Franciscan friars who came to Mexico to begin the Christianization of the natives, the first ecclesiastics directly commissioned for this purpose. According to Mendieta who tells the story, when the first twelve priests arrived in Mexico, they proceded to the capital and were received with great honor by Cortés, who,

kneeling on the ground in front of one after another, kissed their hands, followed by the other captains and cavaliers. This act has been the subject of many paintings in New Spain, and has been told to the eternal memory of so great an act, the greatest which Cortés performed, not as any human man, but as an angel of heaven by whose means the Holy Spirit operated in laying a firm foundation for His Holy Word. . . . It was Cortés' greatest act, for in it he overcame not others but himself.[64]

After the new arrivals had been properly lodged, Cortés turned to the native chiefs and spoke to them in substance as follows, still in the words of Mendieta:

They must not wonder at what they had seen, that he, being captain general, governor, and representative of the emperor had acknowledged obedience and subjection to these men who had arrived in poor and despised habit from Spain. "For," said he, "we who have power and dominion and govern others, . . . though commissioned by the emperor, really have it from God himself. However, this power which we have is limited; it extends only to the bodies and possessions of men . . . , but the powers which these men have is over immortal souls, each of which is more precious than anything in the world. These priests have come from God to teach you the way of salvation. Wherefore, reverence and esteem them as guides of your souls, messengers of the great God, and your spiritual fathers. Hear this doctrine, obey them, and seek to make others do so, for this is the will of the emperor and of God himself."[65]

[64] Mendieta, *Historia Eclesiástica Indiana,* III, 211-12.
[65] *Ibid.,* pp. 211-12.

We have, in this chapter, traced the activities of Cortés relating to the conversion of the Indians, from the time of his arrival in the country until shortly after the fall of Mexico. During this whole period Cortés stands out alone as the dominant personality. While always considering himself as representative of the emperor, his acts were, nevertheless almost, if not quite, untrammelled by governmental interference. But after the fall of Mexico, a different régime began. Although he was still for a number of years the outstanding figure of Mexico, his rule was no longer personal but controlled, in good part, through the representatives appointed by the Council of Indies which governed all the over-seas colonies of Spain. It is, therefore, no longer proper to record simply the attitude of Cortés toward the problem of conversion, but that of the government. It will be inevitable, however, that the name of Cortés appear frequently during the earlier years of its progress, and that important documents written by him be cited and quoted at length.

Chapter V

THE EARLY MISSIONARIES—THEIR CHARACTER AND METHOD

THE CHARACTER OF THE EARLY MISSIONARIES

There has already been frequent occasion to mention the two representatives of the church who accompanied Cortés in his conquest of Mexico, Father Bartolomé de Olmedo and the licentiate, Juan Díaz. Of the latter we know but little. His activities seem to have been confined chiefly to the work of chaplain to the Spanish army, though, as once noted, it was probably he rather than Olmedo who baptized the Tlascalan chiefs. Olmedo, though more often than not yielding the place of spokesman to Cortés in dealings concerning religious matters with the Indians, did now and then appear in the character of evangelist to the natives. Prescott paid him high tribute. He wrote:

He afforded the rare example, rare in any age, of the union of fervent zeal with charity, while he beautifully illustrated in his own conduct the precepts which he taught. . . . It is scarcely too much to say that his discretion in spiritual matters contributed essentially to the success of the expedition as did the courage and sagacity of Cortés in the temporal. He was a true disciple in the school of Las Casas. His heart was unscathed by that fanaticism which sears and hardens wherever it touches. He had come out to the New World as a missionary among the heathen and shrank from no sacrifice for the welfare of his poor benighted flock to whom he had consecrated his days. He combined an enthusiasm controlled by reason, and a quickening zeal, tempered by the mild spirit of toleration.[1]

It was inevitable, however, that the task of conversion should pass out of the hands of the conquerors, and that the

[1]Prescott, *History of the Conquest of Mexico* (Philadelphia, 1876), I, 271.

church should undertake the evangelization of the people. Cortés himself recognized that this must be done. We find him writing early to the emperor, urging that missionaries be sent out to carry on the work that he had begun. In his fourth letter to Charles V, he writes at length of his desires in the matter and indicates that he has written earlier letters asking for help, but with very little result. His statement is in part as follows:

Every time I have written to your majesty, I have mentioned the readiness that exists among some of the Indians here to be converted to our Holy Faith and become Christians, and I have pled with your majesty to send us religious workers of proper life and conduct. And since, up until this moment few have come, I again urge that you will at the earliest moment fulfill our desires. It will be a great service to our Lord and will satisfy your own wish as a good Catholic. . . .

Instead, however, of sending prelates for the administration of orders and of worship, as I previously asked, it has seemed best to me to do otherwise. Send, your majesty, to this land many devout monks who are zealous for the conversion of the Indians. Let these build monasteries and let the tithes be paid them for their upkeep and the support of their work, and what is left over, let it be used for churches and ornaments in the cities where the Spaniards live. . . . If bishops and prelates come, there would be the same wasting of funds in pomp and vices or in their legacies to their children or relatives. And since the natives had in their time, priests who conducted their rites and ceremonies, and these were so honorable and chaste, that if any other thing were practiced they suffered the death penalty; now if they see the power of the church and the service of God in the hands of the canons and other worthies, understanding that these were ministers of God, and should see them practicing vices and profanations such as in our time they are accustomed to practice in Spain, it would bring discredit upon the faith and make it a byword. The damage would be so great that no amount of preaching could overcome it.[2]

[2] MacNutt, op. cit., II, 213-16.

Before this, however, as news of the vast empire which had come under the power of Spain spread throughout the land, the zeal of many priests and friars for serving the church led them to offer themselves for service in Mexico. But, so careful was the monarch who was perhaps but little less zealous than they, that three years were spent in consultation and deliberation before the first missionaries with papal sanction and powers reached Mexico, though three Flemish monks, without waiting for official action, did actually arrive in New Spain. Among them was Fray Pedro de Gante, recognized today as the father of education in Mexico. His work we shall have occasion to mention later.

Another Flemish Friar, Joan Clapión, and Fr. Francisco de Angeles, both distinguished churchmen, desired to go and asked permission of the emperor. Then they approached the pope and sought the concession of rights and privileges which former popes had already given to monks who had gone to preach to other heathen peoples. Pope Leo X accordingly issued a Bull of April 25, 1521, in which he authorized the Franciscan monks who might go to the New World to preach, baptize, confess, absolve, marry, and administer the sacraments of the eucharist and extreme unction, in the exercise of which they were not to be hindered by any dignitary of the church. He likewise authorized them to exercise certain privileges belonging peculiarly to bishops, even the ordination of priests "de primera tonsura," and the lesser orders.

The death of Leo X shortly after the publication of the Bull, brought Adrian VI, a Spaniard, to the Holy See. He issued a Bull in which he granted even larger powers than his predecessor had given. He gave them authority to exercise all the functions of the episcopacy which did not require specific episcopal ordination, providing no bishop were accessible.

The heads of the Orders were to have the full authority of the Pope himself in matters relating to the conversion of the Indians. An even greater extension of power was granted by Paul III in 1535, which made it licit for the mendicant friars to exercise these special functions even in the near proximity to bishops, provided the bishop gave his consent.

But though Clapión and Francisco de Angeles had secured the necessary authorization to go to Mexico, neither of them was permitted to carry out the plan. Death claimed Fr. Clapión, while his companion was elected general of the Franciscan Order, and so was unable to go. Instead, Fr. Martín de Valencia, provincial head of his order in San Gabriel, was chosen to lead a company of twelve friars—in imitation of the first company of twelve disciples—to plant the Faith in the new continent. Fr. Francisco de Angeles, as general of the order, gave them a solemn commission in which he declared: "I send you with twelve companions, for this was the number which Christ took in his company for the conversion of the world. . . . You are called of the Father to labor in His vineyard, not as hirelings for wages, but as sons of the great Father, seeking nothing for yourselves but the things of Jesus Christ. Go then and labor . . . as true sons of the Father."[3]

The chosen group spent a month in the convent of Sta. Maria de los Angeles, conferring with the general, and performing spiritual exercises, in preparation for the fulfilment of the great commission. On January 25, 1524, they embarked for Mexico, where they were received auspiciously by Cortés as already noted,[4] and began their great task of transforming a pagan people into Christians. The journey of the friars from the coast to the capital took them through many populous cities. The Indians were naturally very curious and crowded around them everywhere, so different

---

[3] Mendieta, *op. cit.*, pp. 203-204.   [4] See *ante*, p. 128.

were they from the Spanish soldiers who had passed that way. They marvelled at the friars' poor garb and said to one another, "Who are these poor men? What kind of clothing is this they have on? These are not like the Christians of Spain." They kept repeating over and over a word in their language, *motolinea, motolinea*. One of the friars, Toribio de Benevente, inquired of a Spaniard the meaning of the word so oft repeated. "It means poor," replied the Spaniard. "Then," said Fr. Toribio, "that shall be my name henceforth." So all through his life he signed himself Toribio Motolinia. It was the same Motolinia whom we have quoted so often throughout this study. His action was characteristic of the whole group.

Probably no happier choice of a leader could have been made than that of Fr. Martín de Valencia, a truly apostolic figure. He was a man of mature years and of proved character and capacity. He had passed through some profound religious crises in which his faith had seemed to be slipping, and he had found himself. He was an ascetic, utterly inconsiderate of himself. He was exceedingly humble and unwilling to be raised above the level of his fellow friars except in the degree of his service. It is told of him that while he was provincial superior of his Order in Spain, before hearing the confessions of his brethren, he first made a public confession of his own sin. Kneeling in the midst of the group he rebuked himself for his faults, and throwing off his habit, lashed his body severely and humbly kissed the feet of the other friars. They could thus see the *cilicio*[5] which he always wore. This same humility he observed likewise among the Indians, disciplining himself in their presence before applying the discipline to them.

On another occasion it occurred to him to make a visit to his friends and relatives in his native town. But as he neared

[5] A rough hair shirt worn as a means of mortifying the flesh.

the village, he fell to thinking what a vain thing it was to make such a visit. Holding that it was a worldly impulse which had lured him to make the journey, he resolved to humble himself and to make himself despised by his fellows as a penance for his weakness in yielding to the temptation. To do this he took off his robes, and partly naked, attired only in his underwear, he tied a rope around his neck and had a companion lead him thus like a criminal through the streets of the town, past the homes of his relatives and the friends he had intended visiting. Then, after going to the church, he returned to the monastery whence he had started, having earned the censure of relatives and friends.

Already past fifty years of age when he arrived in the New World, he never acquired a free use of the native languages, but with the little he knew, asserts Mendieta, he did more than others, because of the example of a holy life which he afforded. So great was his devotion, that he desired above all else the privilege of martyrdom for the faith. He longed to pay with his life the price of evangelizing unbelievers. Not even the vast opportunities which Mexico opened up to him satisfied his desire to serve. He wanted to go on to distant China and plant the faith there. He died, however, after ten years of untiring labor in Mexico, and so great was his reputation for saintliness that a number of legends and traditions grew up about him. His love of poverty was so great, so the story goes, that when his friends went to replace an old board on his coffin by a new painted board, such a noise was heard in the sepulcher that they hastily put back the old one. Some thirty years after his death, on opening his sepulcher, as they had often done before, the coffin had disappeared, and its whereabouts since that time, no one knows. The pious friar, Mendieta, who himself desired to look upon the form of the great saint which tradition claimed had not been affected by decay, thinks that the Lord may have taken it away in displeasure at the irreverence of those who kept desiring to open the grave.[6]

A modern writer states that today hundreds of thousands still make their way every year to Sacro Monte, where, in a cave, Fr. Martín used often to go for prayer and meditation. "Unwashed garments, articles of clothing torn from the body, human hair pulled out of the head in exalted frenzy, lie spread out on the trees and bushes where the spirit of the saint in passing will pause to give them blessing."[7]

When one recalls the state of the clergy in Spain during the period of the conquest, and the character of Valencia and his companions who were men of much the same type as their chief, he cannot but feel that the choice of the first missionaries was fortunate. Doubtless they were of a sort that modern evangelical Christianity no longer holds as ideal. They were narrow and fanatical. Their conception of religion was faulty. But, in holiness of life, in unselfishness of purpose, and in devotion to duty, they have not been surpassed in any period.

About eight months after the coming of the twelve, came another group of Franciscans who founded a monastery in Cuernavaca. After that, scarce a year passed that others did not come out, and as they came, other convents were opened. In 1526, the Dominicans began to come, and in 1533, the Augustinians. Numerous monasteries were soon scattered over the country. An old history of the Augustinian order describes the character of the priests which they sent out as missionaries:

For so holy a work, priests were sought who eagerly hoped to suffer martyrdom or any other adversity for the name of Him whom they went to preach. . . . These holy men began to preach, confess and baptize. They founded the Order in

---

[6] Mendieta, *op. cit.,* V, 13.
[7] Quinn, *Beautiful Mexico,* p. 359.

New Spain, not with buildings of stone, but with penitence, fasting, and discipline. In the beginning they wore no shoes but only sandals and poor coarse black robes, and they went about preaching, forgetful to provide for their own necessities.[8]

Perhaps, since he was himself a Franciscan, the high tribute which Mendieta pays to the character of the early Franciscan monks may need to be discounted. He asserts that the example of the lives of these early preachers supplied the lack of miracles that accompanied the work of the primitive apostles. According to this author, the purity of their lives and the holy customs they practiced, seen by the Indians, were sufficient to make them believe that the friars were truly messengers from heaven. They saw in them great mortification of the body, for they went barefoot and almost naked, with their coarse habits torn and worn, and slept with a stick or a bundle of grass for a pillow, covered only by an old *manta*. Their food was *tortillas* and *chile, tunas,* and ground-cherries, and they lived in very humble dwellings, in vivid contrast to the habits of the secular clergy who lived in abundance and dwelt in palaces. They were without thought for themselves, humble, inviolably chaste, and lived in love and charity among themselves and with others. "This was what the Indians esteemed most highly, for they seemed to be qualities of men from heaven rather than from earth."[9]

The people saw the persecution and insults which they received at the hands of the governors and the great patience with which they bore all these things for the love of God. They saw that some were offered bishoprics and honors, but refused them, and preferred to continue in their humble state. For these and other reasons, the Indians were so satisfied with the life and doctrine of the friars that they did not hesitate to put themselves wholly into their hands and to be

[8] *Crónica de la Orden de los Ermitaños de San Agustín,* p. 119.
[9] Mendieta, *op. cit.,* p. 250.

governed by their helpful counsel and direction, loving them as if they were their fathers and mothers. When asked why they preferred the Franciscan fathers, they replied:

Because they are poor and barefooted as we are, and they eat our food; they sit on the ground with us; they converse humbly with us; they love us as their own children. Therefore, we love them as our fathers.[10]

The author admits in the next paragraph that the Augustinians and Dominicans were also barefooted and ill clad, but for some reason the Franciscans seem to have won a deeper place in the hearts of the Indians than any of the other Orders. This is the testimony of many early writers, some of them not belonging to the Order. Don Martín Cortés, in a letter to Philip II, in 1563, writes:

Without depreciating any of the other Orders, that of the Franciscans has continued here without stain and is a great example. The Indians esteem them most highly, and all want Franciscan priests rather than those of other Orders. They more easily secure their obedience because of their poverty. They have no income nor other benefits.[11]

Mendieta has filled many chapters with cases of Indians refusing to allow the Franciscan padres to be taken away from them and others, either secular priests or members of other mendicant orders to be substituted for them. There is probably some exaggeration in the accounts, but there is without doubt also some truth. One case will serve as an illustration.

By agreement between the Franciscans and another order, the village of Guatinchán was to pass into the hands of the latter, the Franciscans retiring from the field. The

---

[10] Mendieta, *op. cit.*, p. 250.

[11] *Colección de Documentos Inéditos Relativos al Descubrimiento Conquista y Colonización de las Posesiones Españoles etc.* (referred to hereafter as *Colección de Documentos Inéditos*), IV, 457.

provincial of the order went to take over the work. But meanwhile, the people had heard of the proposed change and when the two priests presented themselves at the door of the priest's lodging, the door was locked. They went to the church and said mass. In the meantime, the chief Indian of the village ordered the porter to go away so as not to have to open. The friars went out into the city to try to talk to the people. On seeing them approach, every one fled. They returned to the lodging, broke the lock, and went in. Next day, they found all the ornaments taken out of the church. Arguments and commands had no effect upon the Indians. The priests succeeded in catching the porter and two others, bound them hand and foot, and threatened to hang them if they did not consent to their coming to the parish. The Indians remained steadfastly opposed to it. The padres persisted, declaring that the Franciscans had abandoned them. "Nevertheless, we will not be disloyal to them," was the reply.

The Indians refused to bring them any food or drink. They agreed among themselves to attend mass at a neighboring village where there was a Franciscan monastery. They even appealed to the viceroy, who referred them to the Franciscan provincial superior. This official, having given his word to the other order, would not yield to their entreaties. They wrote letters and sent delegations, but to no purpose. "Only send us one of your robes which we can keep as a sign that it is your village," they begged, "so that no other friars may enter, and in time, when more friars are available, you may have compassion on us again." Seeing that their wish was not to be granted, they determined to abandon the village entirely and to settle in another where there was a Franciscan monastery. Eight hundred families sought to enter the village of Tecali. Finally, after much delay, and an appeal to the bishop of Tlascala, the authorities agreed to forego the plan of exchange, and the Franciscans again took over the care of the village.[12]

The early bishops and prelates were likewise, for the most part, men of high character. Mendieta writes of them:

Bishops came, it is true, but the emperor furnished, as Cortés had urged, men who were poor and humble and as free from care for the things of this world as those who came under their direction. This so wise provision of unworldly prelates and true priests, made at the suggestion of the good captain Cortés, was, after God himself, the whole cause and instrument of the conversion of the Indians with so good a foundation. Had priests come in whom existed sin and the love of money, who doubts that there would have been no true Christianity established?[13]

The Franciscan friars at least were opposed to drinking. Mendieta declares that they always held it a vice to drink wine. On one occasion, the guardian of the convent in Mexico returned with thanks a gift of wine from the archbishop Zumárraga. On another, Martín de Valencia rebuked the same archbishop because he carried wine along with him to give to the friars on one of their trips. He would only allow the wine for the sacrament to be kept in the monastery.[14]

On the Franciscans, Dominicans, and Augustinians fell the burden of the early pioneer misionary work.[15] It was not until nearly fifty years after the arrival of the Franciscans that the first representatives of the vigorous newly formed Jesuit order appeared.

[12] Mendieta, op. cit., III, 183-5.
[13] Ibid., p. 185.
[14] Ibid., pp. 254-55.
[15] It is true that there were a few Mercedarians in Mexico in the early period, indeed, Bartolomé de Olmedo was a member of that order. In 1530, on his return from Spain, Cortés brought with him twelve Mercedarians, but they were not well received, and after a comparatively short time they went to Guatemala. It was not until near the end of the century that they succeeded in founding one of the monasteries in Mexico proper. See Cuevas, op. cit., II, 322-24.

The Jesuits entered Mexico in 1572, a company of sixteen. At first they were very poor and without resources. Before long, however, they found a wealthy patron and were soon established in their own house in the capital. In 1576 they founded the College of St. Peter and St. Paul. Reinforcements arrived from Spain, and by the end of the century a substantial building for the school was completed which still stands after over three hundred years. Later, schools were founded in Michoacán and Oaxaca. Their work in the early years was largely with the Spaniards and their descendants. Their intention, they declared, was to train ministers who, knowing the native tongues, would be able to work more effectively than those from abroad. Later, they began to acquire the language and to make it a requirement for ordination. They observed two methods of work with the Indians, either organizing centers from which they reached the Indians, or sending missions to aid the clergy of the different parishes who did not know the language of their constituency. They were in great demand for this service.[16]

In 1585, by order of Philip, eleven friars of the order of the barefoot Carmelites arrived in Mexico, took possession of the Ermita de San Sebastián, and founded there a convent. This was done in 1586.[17]

Of the work and character of the secular priests who began to arrive in considerable numbers in the late thirties, we shall have more to say in a later chapter.[18] Unhappily, they were not the equals of their colleagues of the regular clergy, either in character, or in activity.

THEIR METHODS OF WORK

By what methods did these early missionaries hope to achieve the conversion of the natives? By force, like the

---

[16] Cuevas, *Historia de la Iglesia en México*, II, 350-1.

[17] González Dávila, *Teatro Eclesiástico*, I, 38.

[18] *See post*, p. 215 ff.

archbishop Ximenes, among the Moors a generation earlier?
Or by the slower, more effective method of securing voluntary acceptance of the faith, as used by Talavera? Obviously, the quicker way lay through the method of compulsion,
and the excessive zeal of some of the ardent missionaries
must have made them chafe under the limitation of the
voluntary mode, but a fair examination of the evidence
would seem to indicate that while there was some employ-
ment of pressure, particularly of a negative sort, the earlier
workers were disciples of Talavera rather than Ximenes.

If we seek an expression of the theory on which the
better of the missionaries tried to work, we may take the
word of Valencia. Speaking to the friars who were about
to separate into companies and go to different centers, he
urged them to see to it that the example of their lives and
customs be the chief method of preaching, "in order to convert to the Creator, those souls which are blinded by idolatry
and sunk in terrible vices."[19] Or the statement of Las Casas
might be taken:

> The only way of doing this (converting the Indians) is by
> long assiduous and faithful preaching, until the heathen shall
> gather some ideas of the true nature of the Deity and of the
> doctrines they are to embrace. Above all, the lives of the
> Christians should be such as to exemplify the truth of these
> doctrines, that, seeing this, the poor Indians may glorify the
> Father and acknowledge Him who has such worshipers, the
> true and only God.[20]

This has a truly evangelical ring to it and would be ap-
plauded by most Christians of today. That they did not
always realize their ideal, is abundantly evident, particularly
the ecclesiastics who came later, but one cannot read the
stories of the first missionaries without feeling that their
lives must have made a tremendous appeal.

[19] Mendieta, op. cit., p. 216.
[20] Quoted by Prescott, op. cit. (Philadelphia, 1874), I, 272.

The chief actual methods used throughout the whole process were four: teaching, preaching, the suppression of idolatry, and the general use of force and authority. The first two blend so closely that it is impossible to treat of them separately. The latter two, while not identical, are nevertheless closely related, but they will be considered in separate sections.

Valencia struck the keynote of his own program and that of his order when, in an address to the Indians assembled on the occasion of Cortés' reception of the first Franciscan group, he said:

God has brought us here from a distant land, not to seek gold, and silver, nor any other temporal interest, but your salvation. Wherefore, beloved brethren, it is necessary that you put your young children into our hands that they may be taught, for they are without serious occupation, while you are engaged in many duties. Furthermore, they, being but children will understand more easily the doctrine we teach. Afterward they will aid us in teaching you what they have learned.[21]

This came to be almost the invariable custom on entering any new village or city. They well knew the difficulty of converting the adult, and they understood perfectly, as the Roman Catholic church has always understood, the advantage of training the child during his most plastic period. Already, Pedro de Gante, the Flemish monk, and his companions had undertaken to teach a few children of the principal families in the city of Tezcuco, but without the prestige and backing of Cortés, only a small number had been under instruction. With the official reception of the twelve, the Christian religion received a public sanction that contributed greatly to the success of the work of conversion.

According to Mendieta, there were, all told, when the twelve arrived in Mexico, seventeen clergymen. Two were

[21] Mendieta, *op. cit.*, p. 214.

acting as chaplains to the army, three were Flemish priests who had already begun their work in Tezcuco. These, Valencia as official prelate, called together for conference, and for fifteen days they were together, conferring regarding the work they were to undertake. Valencia, with his customary humility, desired to give up the leadership of the group, saying that he had discharged his commission in leading them thither, but he was elected over his protest by the unanimous vote of the entire company as head of the church in Mexico. It was decided to break up into smaller groups and begin work in various centers. Accordingly, Valencia and four other friars remained in the capital, while other groups of four each went to Tezcuco, Tlaxcala, and Guaxacingo.

Immediately on reaching these centers, the priests selected suitable sites and ordered the construction of low buildings in which there should be a large room where the children might be taught and might sleep, with other smaller rooms for service of various sorts. The Indians obeyed the order with alacrity, though "rather in obedience to order, for they remembered what Cortés had commanded and did not wish to displease him."[22]   When the buildings were ready, the chief Indians were instructed to bring their children and place them in the school. Most of them did so, but some, instead of bringing their own children, substituted for them the children of their servants or slaves. In doing so, writes Mendieta, they really deceived themselves, for the children of the poor people there educated, learned to read and write and became later on mayors and governors over their former lords.[23] They gathered from six hundred to a thousand in each school where they were cared for by old men and fed with provisions brought by their mothers who likewise looked after clothing them. The padres practically lived with them, and for the sake of example, performed their devotions before them.

[22] Ibid., p. 217.   [23] Ibid., p. 217.

The school day began with matins, which all the pupils were of course expected to attend, since the principal instruction they were to receive, especially in the early years, was religious. After matins they taught the children until the hour of mass, and again after mass until the noon meal hour. After eating, they rested awhile and returned again to study until late afternoon.

The first things the schools taught was that which they considered that a Christian ought to know; how to cross himself and to kneel properly, the Lord's Prayer, the Ave María, the creed, the Salve Regina—all in Latin, for the priests did not yet know the vernacular and had no interpreters.

"What they could, they taught by signs," says Mendieta, although one wonders just how they managed to make all that he mentions intelligible by means of signs, viz:

That there was but one God instead of many, as their fathers thought; that their own gods were evil and hostile, deceiving mankind; that there was a heaven above, a place of glory and happiness, the dwelling-place of God; that there was a hell of fire and of infinite pain and torment, where dwelt the spirits which their fathers held as gods, and where all who worshipped them would go to be tormented; that the image of the crucifix was God in his earthly form which he took in order to redeem those who believe and obey; that the image of the woman was the Mother of God; how this Mother should be honored and reverenced as advocate and mediator through whom to obtain from God that which was best.[24]

On one occasion, according to Cuevas, one of the fervent missionaries, an old man, gray and bald, probably Valencia, was standing with others out in the blazing mid-day sun, earnestly teaching the people with signs and speaking in a loud voice in a language which his hearers did not understand. The chiefs standing by, watching him intently, said,

[24] *Ibid.,* p. 218.

"What is the matter with these poor unfortunates who are talking so loudly? Find out if they are hungry, sick, or crazy. . . . Let them talk, for some form of insanity must have overcome them. . . . At midday or night, when all are happy these seem to mourn. Without doubt their affliction must be very great, for they do not seek pleasure, but only sadness." "But," says the chronicler, "although they said this of the venerable friar and of all others because they did not understand them, at last God touched the hearts of many, and they were converted and received the water of baptism."[25]

Besides trying to teach the children, they assembled groups of adults in the courtyard and attempted to teach them the rudiments of Christianity. The Indians permitted this chiefly out of respect for the power of Cortés. They learned to say the prayers in Latin, taught by some of the more advanced pupils in the schools. But, as might naturally be expected, little fruit came of this, for the people understood nothing at all of what was told them, and they continued their idolatrous practices.

The priests realized that they would be able to do but little until they acquired the language, so they set themselves to learn it. There were as yet no grammars or dictionaries, nor were the languages even reduced to writing. Such writing as the Mexicans practiced was picture writing. It was therefore no mean task to which these men set themselves. In order to learn it they took to playing with the children. When they heard a new word or sound they would write it down and confer together as to its meaning, trying thus to make up a dictionary and get the construction. But many times when they thought that surely they had found the right meaning and construction, they discovered next day that they were mistaken. It was a long tedious process, but with the

[25] Cuevas, *Historia de la Iglesia en México,* I, 180.

help of the older boys they were making fair progress when they found an easier way out of their difficulty. There was a Spanish widow in the city with two children who had from infancy been thrown with those who spoke the Indian language and had thus learned it naturally. Spanish, however was used in the home, so that the children became accustomed to use both with equal ease. At the earnest request of the friars, one of the children was allowed to go and live with them and serve as interpreter. Through him they were accustomed to preach to the people, and the boy himself eventually became a priest.[26]

Helped forward in this way, some of the priests made rapid progress in learning the native tongue, and within six months time were able to make themselves understood when they attempted to preach. Some of them became very proficient in the use of the languages and both spoke and wrote them with comparative ease. They were now in position to do effective work.

At first their time was almost exclusively taken up in the building of schools and learning the language, so that they did little outside the centers they had chosen to occupy. But the sons of the chiefs who had come, some of them from distant cities, and learned the doctrine, were sent back that they might spread the news of what they had learned regarding the law of God and that they might teach their parents, relatives, and dependents who were ordered to come together on certain days, as in the towns where there were monasteries. Thus the instruction spread rapidly through the country, and because of what the students were able to teach them, people began to come to the centers, asking that the foreign priests be sent to their villages to teach the new doctrine.

As reinforcements came out from Spain, new centers were occupied, monasteries built, and vast circuits of visita-

---

[26] Mendieta, op. cit., pp. 219-20.

tion established in connection with each. The educational work was perforce restricted to these centers in the beginning; but as the years passed and the number of priests increased, and as the pupils under instruction were graduated and fitted to teach others, the doctrine was carried to the most distant parts of the land.

Though at first the major part of the instruction was religious, it was not confined wholly to that, but included, as we have seen, reading and writing. However, the material of instruction in these subjects was chiefly religious, and the end almost wholly so. Music was taught, but not music for its own sake. Rather it was taught as an aid to learning certain parts of the religious material which was considered desirable and to prepare those who might help in religious services. Very soon also they added manual training, special rooms being constructed where instruction in carpentry, masonry, and other trades was afforded, likewise tailoring, metal-working, painting, weaving, and later also printing, in all of which the Indians proved themselves to be very apt pupils. Pedro de Gante's great school in the capital was the leader in this regard.

An interesting commentary on the success of the early schools is found in a letter from one, Geronimo Lopez, written to the king October 20, 1541. He writes:

Taking many boys into the monasteries in order to teach them doctrine, they likewise began to teach them to read and write. Because of their skill, which is very great, and for what the devil thought to gain thereby, they learned letters so well that it is a marvel to see them, and there are so many and such skillful writers that I cannot number them. By means of letter-writing they get to know everything from ocean to ocean very easily, a thing they could not formerly do.[27]

The achievements of the better and more capable students of the lower schools made evident the need for founding

[27] Quoted by Cuevas, *op. cit.*, I, 386.

higher schools. As early as 1533, a bishop, Ramírez de Fuenleal, wrote the king asking for help in opening such a school. He had already had the Franciscans begin the teaching of grammar to the more capable students, with such good results that, in his opinion, they outdistanced the Spaniards in both skill and capacity. "Without doubt," he writes, "within two years there will be fifty Indians who will know it and be able to teach it." All the instruction was to be in Latin.

The school was actually opened in 1536, under the name of Santa Cruz de Tlaltelolco, with sixty students. It flourished during the early years. Notable teachers were numbered among the faculty, Bernardino de Sahagún, whose writings the author has used so extensively, figuring among them. Splendid results were achieved. Graduates of the school became teachers in it and even teachers of the young candidates for the priesthood, taking the places of the older priests who were so constantly occupied in the spiritual care of the Indians. "Thus," says Cuevas, "the conquered Indians had become teachers of the conquerors, for since the Indians were not at that time admitted to orders, these youths must have been of Spanish blood, either sons of Spanish families or of Creoles."[28]

Unfortunately for this school, it acquired the reputation of being a source of heresy. An ex-student, a chief, Don Carlos Chichimectecotl of Tezcuco, was discovered seeking to inculcate certain heretical doctrines in his associates. He was brought before the Inquisition and was the first victim of the Holy Office to be burned in Mexico.[29]

This brought a great deal of opposition to bear upon the college. Geronimo de Lopez, counsellor of the viceroy quoted above, wrote in the same letter as follows:

Not content with teaching the Indians to read and write, keep books, play musical instruments, etc., they put them to

[28] *Ibid.*, p. 388.   [29] *See post,* pp. 316-18.

learning grammar. They gave themselves with such zeal to this that there are lads now, and every day there are more of them, who speak as elegantly in Latin as Tulio. And, seeing that because of increasing numbers the monasteries could not hold them, special schools were founded where they read science and books. From the first I protested against this, explaining the error and damage that might result from allowing the Indians to study science, and, particularly, allowing them to have the Bible and read it, since in this way many have been lost in Spain, and a thousand heresies have arisen due to a lack of understanding of that which they found. Indeed, they were not worthy to understand it because of their spiritual pride and arrogance. . . . When the Indians read of the sacrifices under the old law of Abraham, and that God permitted such, they will take it as a defense of like sacrifices today. Reading of the wives of David and others and other practices to which they were inclined, they will turn and apply the scripture to their own evil purpose, and no good will come of it. . . . Only eight days ago, a priest who had recently visited the college told me that while there he was surrounded by some two hundred students who in talking with him asked such questions regarding the scriptures and the faith that he was amazed and stopped his ears. The school he said was a veritable hell, and the pupils disciples of Satan. It seems to me that there is no remedy for this but to close the school entirely. If we do not, this land will become a cave of Sibyls, etc.[30]

Although the writer seems certainly to have been prejudiced against the school, he undoubtedly reflected the opinion of many of the people of Mexico, and he had no small influence on the final destiny of the institution. The result of such opposition was that its influence rapidly waned. Mendieta defended it as late as 1576, complaining that the effort seemed to be to take everything away from the Indians and to give it to the Spaniards.

The problem of the *mestizo* children, many of them illegitimate, early became a serious one. Don Luis Velasco,

[30] Quoted by Cuevas, *op. cit.,* I, 388-9.

writing to the king, Feb. 7, 1554, says that their number was increasing rapidly and that "all of them turn out so daring and so evilly inclined that they together with the negroes are to be feared."[31] He recommended shipping them to Spain for service in the army. Bishop Zumárraga, however, proposed the founding of a school into which they might be gathered and taught Christian doctrine and some useful knowledge. He sought the support of the king in the enterprise in a letter of Dec. 4, 1547.

So the school, called San Juan de Letrán, was established. It was not well supported, however, after the death of Zumárraga. A description of it in 1579 by the archbishop Moya y Contreras pictures it as in a pitiable state. He recommended that the Jesuits take it over, but they did not see fit to do so, on account of their very limited resources and reduced number of priests. As late as 1583, in a report to the *Oidores,* it was still continuing, and this group recommended that it be strengthened and linked up with the university.[32]

The girls were first gathered together, just as the boys, in the *patios* and taught the Christian doctrine, though they were kept apart from the boys. But, while the boys remained to learn reading and writing, the girls retired. Bishop Zumárraga felt that this was not enough; so at the archbishop's suggestion, the Colegio de Tezcuco for girls was founded in 1529 by the Franciscans. Returning from a trip to Spain in 1534, Zumárraga brought back a group of women teachers to whom he entrusted the education of girls in Mexico City in a day-school, being unable at that time to provide a boarding school. Apparently, however, these women were not a success, for in 1536, the archbishop wrote the emperor:

[31] Quoted by Cuevas, *op. cit.,* I, 391.
[32] Cuevas, *op. cit.,* I, 391.

After mature counsel as to the remedy for conditions here, we believe it is necessary to take the girls from their homes at the age of five or six and to put them in institutions where they can be reared by teachers. From our experience, it seems that the teachers should be nuns rather than laywomen.[33]

In a letter of Nov. 24, 1536, the good archbishop says that there is great need for the establishment of houses in every head of a district and in all the principal villages where the girls can be trained and indoctrinated and can be got out of the evil control of the chiefs.[34]

Cuevas quotes a letter written by Don Francisco de Velasco to the king, Feb. 1, 1558, in which he gives an account of the founding of the Colegio de Nuestra Señora de la Caridad. He says in part:

The rectors and the deputies and Charity societies of the City of Mexico, seeing the great necessity that the orphan daughters of Spanish and Indian parents be gathered together and indoctrinated, in order that their poverty and weakness might not offend God, founded, with the permission of the viceroy, a college called Nuestra Señora de la Caridad which is supported by the gifts of the societies of charity and friends. This has grown constantly, especially since your majesty by royal order commanded the viceroy to favor it, as indeed he has done. From this school, after they are taught what is suitable, many of the orphans marry who otherwise would be lost. There is provision in the school for the celebration of the sacraments; there are seasons during lent and other festival occasions; and some of the girls take part in the singing on feast days and in the service of the mass.[35]

This institution was at first only for the *mestizo* girls. There was, however, no school for the daughters of the Creole and Spanish families, so, finally, they too began to be admitted.

There were schools for the Indians and *mestizos* not only in Mexico City but throughout the country, though they

[33] Quoted by Cuevas, *op. cit.*, I, 401.
[34] *Ibid.*   [35] *Ibid.*

were less numerous elsewhere than in the capital. Cuevas mentions a number of schools for all three classes in Michoacán in 1543. The Colegio de San Nicolás was particularly for Spanish descendants who were in preparation for ordination to the priesthood. However the good bishop recognizing the debt owed to the Indians who, he says, did most of the work of constructing the buildings, ordered that those whose parents might wish to send them there be received gratis and taught everything that the others were taught.[36]

Though the Jesuits came much later than the other three orders, they were still early enough to make a distinct contribution, particularly through the educational work which they everywhere used so effectively. They had two kinds of schools, one in which the Spanish and Indians alike were taught doctrine, reading, writing, etc. "But," writes a Jesuit chronicler,

besides this, we have two seminaries for Indian boys only, chosen from among the sons of chiefs and the most capable, for it would be neither possible nor proper to take all. These are educated in some part of our monasteries, a master being in charge of each group. The purpose of this is to train the sons of the chiefs and leading men in all good discipline, for, since they will later govern villages, their proper instruction is necessary, in order that their example and teaching may bear fruit among the people. Also, if there are any who are capable and of such proven virtue that they might become priests and ministers of the doctrine, they will be of very great help in the instruction and conversion of the people. We try to have the more capable of them study Latin, as now four promising boys are studying in our school in the capital.[37]

On January 25, 1551, the University of Mexico was founded under the direct auspices of the Church. It was confirmed by Pope Paul IV who gave it the statutes by which the University of Salamanca was governed. It had a de-

[36] *Ibid.,* p. 399.
[37] Quoted by Cuevas, *op. cit.,* II, 352.

partment of theology with a Dominican friar as professor, and a department of Bible with an Augustinian as teacher. Indeed, the very founding of the university was due, in part, to the need of training the sons of the Creole families, that is, native-born, pure Spanish families, for the priesthood.[38]

Formal instruction in other than doctrine was probably confined largely to the centers where there were monasteries, but the schools for doctrinal instruction seem to have been widely scattered, for, after a few years, there were Indians in considerable numbers who were able to act as *doctrineros* or teachers of doctrine, although they were not admitted to orders.

At first, the Indians were reluctant to bring their children to the priests, and some, as we have seen, substituted other children of the poor for their own. Bishop Landa of Yucatan gives an interesting account of conditions there which reflect the general situation throughout Mexico. He writes:

The manner of indoctrinating the Indians was gathering together the young children of the chief people and putting them in houses built near by the monasteries. There all lived together and the parents and the relatives brought their provisions. . . . The governor and the judges provided agents to aid the priests by gathering the Indians to be taught and punishing those who lapsed into the old life. At first, the Indians brought their children reluctantly, thinking they were to be made slaves, as had been done by the Spaniards in some cases. For this reason they sometimes substituted slave children for their own. But when they understood the plan better, they gladly brought them.[39]

According to the system of *encomiendas,* by which the land and Indians were distributed among the Spaniards, it became the duty of the *encomendero* to provide for the indoctrination of the Indians under his charge. While not

---

[38] *See further, post* p. 277.
[39] Landa, *Relación de las Cosas de Yucatán* (Paris, 1864), p. 100.

always effectively applied, there were definite penalties for those who were remiss in this duty. This system made it at once possible for the priests to extend their work just as far as their limited forces would permit. While theoretically obliged to attend the doctrine schools, practically, many of the Indians did not do so and had to be won.

The first Apostolic Assembly, in 1525, ordered all governors of Indians to call the neighboring Indians early on feast-days and to take them in procession, led by the cross and reciting their prayers, to the church. There they were to hear mass and be taught by the priest the rudiments of the faith. Likewise the boys and girls were to go every day to the church, conducted by some adult, in order to learn the doctrine and at the same time, music.

The common people seemed at first not to take kindly to the new faith and fled from contact with the priests. Finally, however, the skilled teacher, Pedro de Gante, found a way to draw them. He writes:

By the grace of God, I began to understand them and to see how they must be won. I noted that in their worship of their gods, they were always singing and dancing before them. Always, before a victim was sacrificed to the idol, they sang and danced before the image. Seeing this and that all their songs were addressed to the gods, I composed very solemn songs regarding the law of God and the faith, how God became man in order to free humanity, and how he was born of a virgin, Mary, who remained wholly pure and without stain. Likewise, I gave them certain patterns to paint on their shawls for the dances as they were accustomed to do, according to the dances and songs which they sang. Thus they were dressed, gaily, or in mourning, or for victory.

Then when Christmas time drew near, I invited every one from a radius of twenty leagues to come to the festival of the Nativity of our Redeemer. So many came that the *patio* would not hold them all, and they sang, the very night of Nativity, "Today is born the Redeemer."[40]

[40] Códice Franciscano, *Nueva Colección de Documentos,* IV, 221-5.

His pupils scattered everywhere carrying his teachings. The Franciscans as well as the other orders and the secular clergy adopted his method also.

The priests at many points sought to make use of already existing habits and interests to accomplish their ends. They found in the organization of the villages a system which lent itself well to the work of converting the natives. They organized the people into groups of twenty and one hundred under captains who were responsible for seeing that they fulfilled their religious as well as civic duties. Each captain was instructed as follows:

1. To compel his group to hear mass and the sermons on Sundays and to observe feast-days properly.

2. To see that new-born children were brought for baptism and to inform the priest when any adult was to be baptized.

3. To see that those to be confirmed appeared when the bishop was to arrive.

4. To see that adults confessed during Lent, if possible, but at least once during the year, and to inform the priest of any who refused to do so. Likewise, to see that the sick confessed.

5. To see that there was no fraud in marriages.

6. To inform the priest in case of any separation of man and wife.

7. To inform the priest of any man and woman living together without having been married.

8. To inform the priest of loose sexual habits on the part of either single or married men.

9. To give notice of any who had run away from another village, in order that they might be returned.

10. To notify the priests of cases of habitual drunkenness, and the houses where such practices were permitted.

11. To discover cases of witch-craft, superstitions, or return to infidelity.

12. To be careful that all those under his charge knew the doctrine, informing the priest of any who refused to learn it.

Innumerable good results followed this system, according to the writer of the *Códice Franciscano,* and many evils were avoided, for the people "were as wax to receive the impression of any doctrine, good or evil, which might be given them." Moreover they were so new and weak in their faith that if their ministers had not attended them with great diligence they would have fallen away and forgotten it.[41]

At the end of a half year the friars were able to speak reasonably well in the Indian tongue, and with the help of the better students, they had soon translated parts of the Christian doctrine into the native languages and put it to music so appealing that it greatly attracted the people. The adults were gathered into *patios* and taught by the older boys. They became very enthusiastic about it. According to Mendieta, they crowded together as herds of sheep in the houses and *patios* for three or four hours at a time. Moreover, wherever one went by day or by night, he could hear the chanting of prayers and the commands of God.

The priests used the boys as interpreters when they went out into the villages to teach and to preach; and the boys, on their own account, argued with eagerness against the evil of idolatry and other pagan rites, declaring their faith in the one true God.[42]

The older Indians especially had difficulty in learning the prayers and other rites. They found it necessary therefore to employ some system of mnemonics. Mendieta describes their method:

[41] *Nuevos Documentos para la Historia de México,* II, 81.
[42] Mendieta, *op. cit.,* pp. 224-6.

Some counted the words of the prayer which they were learning with pebbles or grains of corn, representing each word or phrase by a pebble or grain, thus: Our Father, one grain; which art in heaven, another; and so on to the end of the prayer. . . . Others used a different method, more difficult but more curious; that of choosing words which in their own tongue corresponds somewhat with the pronunciation in Latin, and representing them on paper by the picture symbol, for they had no letters. For example, the native word which sounds like *Pater* is *pantli* which means "little banner." So, to remember *Pater,* they picture a little banner. For *noster* the native word most nearly like it in sound is *nochtli,* the name of a fruit which the Spanish call *tuna,* the fruit of the cactus. *Pater noster,* therefore, is represented by a banner, followed by a tuna, and so on.[43]

Some, in preaching and teaching, used a very fruitful method which conformed to the native custom of using paintings. They would print on a cloth representations of the articles of faith, or the ten commandments, or whatever else they desired of Christian doctrine. When, for example, the teacher desired to preach on the commandments he hung up the painted cloth and with a pointer indicated what he wished to teach.[44]

THE CONTENT OF INSTRUCTION

The content of the instruction given the Indians is found in the catechism included in the *Códice Franciscano.* There were other like catechisms in circulation but this by Fr. Alonzo de Molina was adjudged to be the best and an effort was made to have it used universally by restricting the circulation of others. We present here a summary of its contents.

It begins with instructions as to making the sign of the cross; then follow the Apostles' Creed with brief explanations, the Lord's Prayer, the Ave María, and the Salve Regina. It then details what a good Christian ought to

[43] *Ibid.,* pp. 245-6.   [44] *Ibid.,* p. 249.

know, namely: the Articles of Faith, fourteen in number, seven relating to the divinity of Christ and seven to humanity; the Ten Commandments, three relating to God and seven to man's relations with his fellow men. The first three are given as follows: "1. Thou shalt love the Lord thy God with all thy heart. 2. Thou shalt not take His name in vain. 3. Thou shalt sanctify or keep holy the feast-days, doing no work or servile labor thereon."

The five commandments of the Mother Church follow: 1. To hear mass on Sundays and feast-days. 2. To confess during Lent. 3. To receive the body of Christ at Easter time. 4. To fast whenever the Mother Church requires. 5. To pay tithes and first-fruits.

The seven sacraments are enumerated and briefly explained; then the venial and mortal sins are defined and the means indicated whereby the sinner might receive absolution. Seven mortal sins are catalogued and the seven corresponding virtues pointed out. In addition, seven theological and cardinal virtues are listed, faith, hope, and love being rated as theological; justice, prudence, courage, and temperance as cardinal. Instruction in works of mercy follows, seven corporal and seven spiritual works being given. The works of mercy are feeding the hungry, giving drink to the thirsty, clothing the naked, visiting the sick, redeeming the captive, giving lodging to travellers, and burying the dead; the spiritual works are giving wise counsel, punishing and correcting those who err, comforting the sad, pardoning injuries, enduring them with patience, suffering with patience the weakness of neighbors, teaching the ignorant, and praying to God for all those who do one evil.

The seven gifts of the Holy Spirit are wisdom, understanding, counsel, courage, knowledge, piety, and fear of God. These are to be asked of God in prayer constantly. Then is added a list of the corporal senses, seeing, hearing, tasting, smelling, and feeling which were given man by God to be used for his glory and not in evil deeds. The powers of the soul are three: memory, understanding, and will. The enemies of the soul are the world, the flesh, and the devil, the flesh being the greatest because we cannot rid ourselves of it.

Following this come the eight beatitudes, then the list of the gifts of the glorified body, a statement of the obligations of god-parents, and the general confession. The confession is as follows:

I, a sinner, confess to God, to Holy Mary, to St. Peter, St. Paul, St. Michael the Angel, to St. Francis, and to all the saints, and to you, father, that I sinned in eating, drinking, in laughing, in playing, in mocking, in murmuring against others, and not bettering my life. The good I would do, I did not; and the evils I would not, I did. For all this I repent and confess my fault which is great. I renounce the devil and give myself completely to our Lord God, and supplicate the most holy Virgin, she who is our advocate and intercessor, that she beg her precious son Jesus Christ to pardon all my sins, having mercy on me; and you, father, please on your part absolve me.

That those desiring baptism might know what to answer, the questions asked of adults at baptism are given. This simply asks regarding belief in the Apostles' Creed, phrase by phrase, with these additions: "Do you earnestly repent of your sins and desire to lead a new life? Do you give yourself completely to God? Do you wish to receive baptism with all your heart?" A brief admonition for those who have just been baptized is included:

Dearly beloved son, our Lord has shown you many mercies, for he has cleansed you and pardoned all your sins and has adopted you as a son. Now you are a member of the Holy Church and are free from the sins that grievously afflicted you. Therefore, be grateful to your God and love Him with all your heart. Give thanks, adore Him, and be joyful. Be glad and rejoice in Him and have a care to fulfill all that to which you are now as a Christian obligated. Learn well and commit to memory all the articles of faith and the commandments of our Lord to live according to them. If you do that, you will please your Lord and will deserve his grace here in this world. After your days are ended here, He will take you to his royal palace in heaven that you may rejoice forever with Him.

The catechism ends with a suggested blessing for use at the table, and for the giving of thanks after eating. The statement is made that the above doctrine was for the Indians who could read and for those who wished to read it at home, or for the children to study in school, where every day they had to say the greater part of it. But it was not taught in the church, nor was more than the substance of it required of those who were to receive the holy sacrament, that is, the part which it was felt that every Christian should know, such as the Per Signum Crucis, Ave María, Credo, Salve Regina, the fourteen articles of faith, the ten commandments, the five commandments of the church, the seven mortal sins, the seven sacraments, and the general confession.

All this is taught, continues the document, and all Indians who are to receive any of the sacraments are held accountable for it. However, in the case of the old and the untutored who had spent many days trying to learn the doctrine but had not succeeded, the priests were to be content if they knew how to cross themselves, say the Pater Noster and the Ave María, though they must confess the articles of faith at least before the priests could hear their confessions or administer to them the sacrament of matrimony. Some such concession was necessary that they might not live together illicitly for lack of some one to marry them.[45]

It has been commonly thought that the conversion of the Indians was really only nominal and that, while there was some attempt at indoctrination, this consisted chiefly in the

---

[45] Códice Franciscano, *Nueva Colección de Documentos para la Historia de México,* II, 50-61.

memorizing of certain prayers and responses and statements of doctrine. Color would be lent to such an idea by the above-quoted catechism. However, Cuevas charges that Protestants are responsible for this calumny, while as a matter of fact, the friars sought to relate religion very definitely to the most intimate details of life. He finds proof of this in a part of the confessionary of Fr. Alonzo de Molina, written about the middle of the sixteenth century. The questions, which doubtless reflect graphically the customs of the people at the time, were to be asked by the teachers or *doctrineros*. They are found in the comment on the seventh commandment. We do not translate the document fully nor literally, but choose here and there questions which serve to indicate the general character of the procedure.

Have you stolen anything such as shawls, chickens, sheep, cattle, or perchance a horse; or gold, or silver, feathers, plumes, or jewels? Have you taken any corn from another's field? Have you planted another's field or have you taken anyone's squashes, or beans, or peppers? Have you cut wood from another's timber?

And when you sell or buy anything, do you cheat or deceive your neighbors? Perhaps you have not used your office for the good of the city or to favor the poor, but have sought only to enrich yourself, and have thus stolen from the poor, the miserable, and from little children. And when you have gone on a journey, perhaps you have failed to take enough provisions and have stolen corn or peppers or other eatables.

When you bought good *mantas* to sell, did you mix them with others of inferior grade or torn ones? You who sell cocoa, did you mix the good with the bad? Did you whiten green beans with white earth to make them look ripe and of good quality? The wax that comes from Campeche (in Mexico), did you sell it for wax imported from Spain? You who sell *tamales,* perhaps you put in but little meal, put a lot of beans inside them and wrapped them with many leaves so that they would look big. You who make pottery, do you bake it well? Do you put in sufficient wool so that it will not easily break?

You medical men, have you studied medicine and the art of healing or have you only pretended to know the herbs and medicinal plants which you give the sick, and have you thus caused people to grow sick and die? Possibly your medicines are old or adulterated?

"Thus," says Cuevas, "in paternal and very apt form, they ran through the whole of the ten commandments, in this way, forming the moral judgments of the people."[46]

Probably, however, this represents the indoctrination at its best rather than the general practice. When one considers the vast number of converts within the first quarter of a century, in comparison with the very inadequate number of priests, he cannot but suspect that there was, of necessity, much less thoroughness than the best of the early Christian leaders would have desired.

THE DESTRUCTION OF IDOLS AND TEMPLES

One has but to recall the enormous number of temples and shrines and the numerous feasts in the religion of the Indians to see the difficulty which the missionaries faced even with the prestige of the conquering army to support them. There were visible reminders of their own religion before the eyes of the natives constantly, and although Cortés had commanded the cessation of human sacrifice, the numerous priests and others connected with the native cult still continued to practice openly most of their rites and secretly, even to sacrifice human life upon their altars. They were not particularly averse to the worship of the God of the Spaniards, the cross, the Virgin Mary, or their other holy objects. They would gladly have incorporated them bodily into their system. It was the exclusive claims of Christianity that aroused opposition. The Spanish priest with his cruci-

[46] Cuevas, *op. cit.*, II, 198-9.

fix, the Virgin, and the saints, could not brook the images of the Indians.

The missionaries were naturally very much pleased with the progress of the boys in the schools and their eagerness to preach and teach the new doctrine to the people. The apparent eagerness of the Indians to learn the songs and to take part in the feasts was gratifying, but the priests felt that this was mere external compliance rather than a voluntary approach to Christianity, and a genuine forsaking of their idols. It is true that human sacrifices were almost gone and were performed only secretly in caves or in the forests. The priests urged upon Cortés a vigorous punishment of all who continued to practice it, but the enforcement of the law was in the hands of the lay Spaniards, most of whom were so engrossed in their efforts to exploit their new possessions that they were indifferent to what was going on, and did little to stop it so long as it was not publicly done.

As time went on the priests came to feel that they were losing time and working in vain so long as the temples and idols remained undisturbed. Therefore, after conference, it was agreed to begin destroying them in the different sections of the country and not to stop until every temple and idol had been razed to the ground. They were resolved not to be deterred in this even though it might cost them their lives.

They began the work of destruction in Tezcuco, not far from the capital, where there were some magnificent temples. This was in 1525. Later those of Mexico City, Tlaxcala, and Guaxocingo followed, and gradually, throughout the whole of the occupied territory, the temples and shrines were demolished. It was done by the priests with the help of their pupils, the sons of chiefs for the most part, at a time when, according to Mendieta, those who might have opposed it were occupied otherwise.

ROMAN CATHOLIC CHURCH BUILT UPON THE SUMMIT OF AN ANCIENT PYRAMID AT CHOLULA, MEXICO.

Thus fell the walls of Jericho with shouts of praise and joy from the faithful children, while those who were not of that number stood by frightened, amazed and heart-broken (literally, "broken the wings of the heart"), seeing their temples and gods fall to the earth. Against this heroic act some tried to argue, but the priests replied with many and excellent reasons for what they had done.[47]

Cortés was among those who raised some objection. He made the suggestion that they ought to preserve some of the temples as relics, but though his suggestion was made "gently and without insistence," the priests were unwilling to do so, fearing that a relic would be dangerous and that the Indians having it to remind them of their past, would be less easily won to the new faith. Others censured the missionaries severely on the ground that such action might provoke a rebellion on the part of the Indians, but the priests held strictly to their purpose, and the work of destruction went steadily forward.

Mendieta defends this destruction of temples on several grounds. One of the chief defenses lay in the fear which it put into the Indians. Far from leading to revolt, this demonstration of fearlessness on the part of the Spaniards was the very thing needed to stifle the disposition to revolt, which, in the absence of Cortés on a southern expedition, was growing. On the spiritual side, which was the special interest of the friars, he contends that, seeing their principal shrines destroyed, they weakened in their following of idolatrous practices and the door was opened for the easy suppression of what remained. So great was the cowardice and fear which this occasioned, he asserts, that thereafter it was only necessary for one of the priests to send a child with his rosary or some other sign to bind and bring to him anyone caught in idolatry. This incredible submission and the re-

[47] Mendieta, *op. cit.,* pp. 227-8.

spect which they felt for the priests was necessary for the advancement of Christianity, in his opinion.

Cuevas, a modern Jesuit, writing in 1921, declares:

It has been lamented with impiety and exaggeration by various ancient Christian writers and by many modern ones. In regard to the temples and idols, the glory of having destroyed as many as they could ought not to be denied to the missionaries.[48]

The destruction of the temples carried with it the destruction of many invaluable ancient writings of the Indians which would have made the work of the historian of ancient Mexico infinitely easier than it is. But Archbishop Zumárraga, influenced probably by the example of Ximenes in destroying a generation earlier the magnificent literary treasures of the Moors, lest its existence prove an obstacle to their Christianization, refused to allow the preservation of these ancient writings, and countless thousands of valuable codices were consigned to the flames. Cuevas attempts to exonerate the church from this charge, but his efforts are not convincing.

It was no easy task to which the missionaries set themselves. It was easier to break down the physical temples and objects of worship than to uproot the cherished beliefs and practices of the people. Naturally the native priests exerted every possible opposition to the destruction of their cult. Mendieta says of them:

The Indian priests had no words or reason with which to contradict the preaching of the servants of the Lord who taught the way to heaven, but in order not to lose their interests, their prestige, and their authority, . . . they sought to lead the people as they had been accustomed to do and to conserve their ancient rites, ceremonies, and sacrifices.

The Christian priests, however, sooner or later found out everything that was going on, for the converts who were loyal told them. . . . The very children went home and found idols,

[48] Op. cit., I, 203.

and came and told the priests where they were to be found.
The friars thereupon went and took away the idols and either
burned or broke them.[49]

To convince the children in the schools of the truth of
Christianity and the falsity of their own gods was comparatively easy. Indeed, it was not long before they were
quite active themselves in destroying idols. Taken from
home and kept under the constant influence of the priests, it
was inevitable that they should forsake the religion of their
parents. Mendieta gives a number of interesting accounts of
how they responded to the new teaching.

He relates the story of a priest of Ometochtli of Tlaxcala, who attempted to frighten a group of boys from the
monastery school by pretending to be a god. They fell to
arguing with him, and as he appeared more and more angry,
one boy cried, "Let's get rid of this devil," and threw a stone
at him. Others, seeing this, picked up stones to throw also.
The priest started to run away but tripped and fell, "God
permitting it because of his sins." The children fell upon
him with stones, and in a moment he lay dead. They were
proud of what they had done. "Now," they declared, "the
people of Tlaxcala will see that he was no god but a liar and
a devil, and will see that God and St. Mary are good, for
they helped us to slay the devil." And, indeed, it did have
a deep effect. The people were stunned by what had happened. The boys returned to the monastery boasting proudly
of what they had done. The priests desiring to punish them
asked who killed the man. "All of us," they cried. "He was
not a man but a devil, and God and St. Mary helped us give
him the punishment he deserved." There is no record of
any punishment being given them.[50]

Not a few of the children thus trained paid for their new
convictions with their lives. Mendieta relates the story of

---

[49] Mendieta, *op. cit.*, p. 233.   [50] *Ibid.*, pp. 234-36.

the martydrom of several children whose parents, angered by their activities against the gods, slew them. The "Niño Cristobal" was cruelly kicked and beaten to death by his father because he had destroyed certain idols and spilled several casks of wine. Traditions as to the miraculous preservation of the child's body soon grew up. He was considered one of the first martyrs of the faith in Mexico, and his memory was long cherished.[51]

Two Dominican friars, passing through the capital, visited the Franciscan monastery. Seeing there the large number of boys well instructed in religion, they besought Valencia that they be allowed to take two of the boys to assist them in their work in the new district to which they were going. With Valencia's consent they called for volunteers, and two young Indians, sons of prominent chiefs, responded.

In order to prove them, Fr. Martin talked to them and presented the dangers and difficulties involved, possibly even death. But the boys, far from being frightened, replied, "Father, we have thought of all that, and we are ready to go and do whatever they desire of us. If it please God that our lives be taken, shall we not give them for the love of Him who first died for us? Did they not crucify Peter and behead Paul?" So they set out and came to the region of Tepeaca where there were still a great many idols. Fearlessly they entered into the houses in search of the forbidden images. At the end of three or four days, the inhabitants were so angry at them that they set a trap for the zealous young reformers, and, having locked them in a house, set upon them with clubs and beat them to death.[52]

THE USE OF FORCE AND AUTHORITY

After the foregoing description of the destruction of temples and idols and the rigid suppression of their charac-

[51] *Ibid.,* pp. 240-41.   [52] *Ibid.,* pp. 242-43.

teristic sacrifices to the gods, it may seem idle to inquire regarding the use of force and authority in the conversion process. Yet there is a real sense in which the Catholic apologist can say that they were not compelled to become Christians. To be sure, Mendieta recounts approvingly the story of the use of authority in destroying idols and temples. It did serve to intimidate them and to render them more susceptible to the entrance of the gospel among them, but they were not obliged to accept it. We quoted in a previous chapter[53] the *requirimiento* issued by Cortés, in which he stated that they would not be compelled to accept Christianity. "They (the priests) will not compel you to become Christians, unless, after being informed regarding the truth, you desire to be converted to our faith, as all your neighbors have done," but they were obliged to allow the new religion to be preached and taught them without hindrance and "to recognize the church as superior in the world and the pope as superior in matters spiritual." Yet, technically, they were not forced to become Christians.

Whether or not the lash was used on all Indians under instruction before they became Christians by baptism, and whether it was ever used as a means of inducing decision favorable to baptism, is not certain; but it is quite evident that the friars, even the much-beloved Franciscans, made frequent use of the whip in dealing with the Indians. They were charged by the Spaniards with great severity in their treatment of the natives. Their practice is illustrated by an account in the Franciscan Codex.

At daybreak the Indians are gathered into the patio of the church whither they are brought by the tribunes or centurions in charge of the groups. There they are counted and those who are recalcitrant about coming when they are obliged to are given half dozen lashes over their clothing, since they are in the church—outside they are given lashes on the bare back

---

[53] *See ante,* pp. 126-27.

when they make any mistake or do their common tasks wrongly. This is the punishment they have always known, even for very light offenses. To take this away, in the temporal as well as in the spiritual government, would be to take away the only way of controlling them, for they are like children, and to control them properly it is necessary to do just what the school-masters do when children fail to get their lessons or get into mischief—give them a half dozen lashes.[54]

A sentence from Bishop Zárate, in a letter to the king in 1551, whether justly or not, charges the friars with the custom of beating the Indians. He declares that the Indians in some of the villages do not treat him as bishop, "nor do they dare to," he says, "lest they be beaten by the friars, as they are accustomed to beat and mistreat many."[55]   In a reply of Mendieta to the criticism of the Spaniards that the Indians were less harshly reprimanded than they, he indicates their custom of whipping the natives:

You say that we reprimand you more than the Indians. How can that be, for them we not only reprimand by word of mouth, but we also whip them as children. And, seeing that we do it in love and for their good, they not only endure it patiently but thank us for it.[56]

The council of 1539, taking cognizance of the criticisms against the friars of cruelty to the Indians, brought by Span-iards who had no thought for the welfare of the Indians, but desired only to trouble the priests, passed an order to the following effect: that in the evangelization of the Indians, they must not be put in stocks, nor beaten, particularly grown men. In the monasteries there should be no stocks nor prisons, nor other means of punishment than such as were considered legitimate for school masters to employ. "To do otherwise is to usurp the powers of government and to lay

---

[54] *Códice Franciscano* (Edición, García Icazbalceta), pp. 66-8.
[55] Quoted by Cuevas, *op. cit.,* I, 340.
[56] Mendieta, *op. cit.,* p. 316.

a heavy yoke upon the Indians which will produce hatred toward the gospel rather than love."[57]

Apparently a royal order was given, forbidding the practice of punishing the Indians, though such an order has not come under our observation, for Mendieta, writing to the Commissary General of his order in 1562, declares that he does not see how the king can have declared the friars without authority to punish or correct the Indians, or to have a hand in their affairs, when it is very clear that to take away such power is to undermine the force of their preaching and the doctrine of Jesus Christ, and the proper administration of the sacraments, for, he writes, "These people are so low and so miserable that if one has not all authority with them he has none."[58]

The total impression made upon one of the early writers, not so much perhaps by the work of the missionaries, but by the total conversion process, is registered in the observation of Dorantes de Carranza:

Although the ends were good, the means used were greatly mistaken, for to preach the gospel with the sword in hand and shedding of blood, is a fearful thing, and it seems to human judgment that their descendants are now paying penance for it, for hardly any of them will be found who are not begging or wandering about the country or even abroad. Although we do know that the saints aided them in some battles, and even the queen of heaven herself. Who can understand this, for the secrets of God and his judgments are inscrutable.[59]

The conclusion to which one may fairly come, it seems, is that, unquestionably, the pressure of authority played no small part in the conversion of the Indians, but that the part played by it has been overstressed. We shall see in a later

---

[57] Cuevas, *op. cit.*, II, 197-98.
[58] *Nueva Colección de Documentos para la Historia de Nueva España,* I, 6.
[59] *Sumaria Relación de las Cosas de Nueva España,* p. 17.

chapter how, as the years passed, the priests received less and less support from the secular arm, and yet the conversion of the Indians went forward. Doubtless force and authority played an important role in the opening years of the religious conquest, but it dropped more and more into the background as the movement gathered momentum from the increasing numbers who came under the influence of the more constructive features of missionary endeavor, namely, preaching and, even more, education.

Perhaps there is no better way of making clear how the early priests went about their work than to give here at some length an account of the activities of one of the most distinguished pioneer missionaries, Pedro de Gante. The following extract is from one of his own letters, written to his friends in Ghent many years after his coming to Mexico.

We are distributed in nine convents, living in houses which the natives built for us, separated from each other seven, ten, or even fifty leagues. So we work for the conversion of these infidels, each one according to his strength and spirit. My duty is to teach day and night. In the day I teach reading, writing, and singing; at night I read the Christian doctrine and preach. Because the land is so extensive and populated with an infinite number of people, and because the friars are few for the teaching of such a multitude, we take into our houses the sons of the chief men in order to instruct them in the Catholic faith that afterward they may teach their parents. These boys learn to read, write, sing, preach, and celebrate the divine office, according to the custom of the church. Of these I have in my charge close to five hundred or more in this city of Mexico, for it is the principal center. From this number I have chosen fifty or more of the more sagacious, and each week I teach them separately what they are to preach on the Sunday following. It is no small task for me to work thus day and night, fortifying them and arranging their sermons for them. On Sundays they go out to preach in the city and all the territory round about for a distance of four, eight, ten, twenty, or thirty leagues, setting forth the Catholic faith, and with its teaching, preparing the people for baptism.

We go out with them, destroying idols and temples in one section while they are doing the same in another. Thus we are raising up churches to the true God.

In this manner we use our time, undergoing all kinds of labor, day and night, that this infidel people may come to the knowledge of the faith in Jesus Christ. I, myself, by the mercy of God . . . have erected more than an hundred houses consecrated to the Lord, churches and chapels, some of them magnificent temples. Each time I sally forth, I have enough to do and more in destroying idols and rearing temples to the true God.[60]

ACCOMMODATION OF CHRISTIAN TEACHING AND PRACTICE
TO INDIAN IDEAS AND CUSTOMS

One of the most interesting questions that arises in this study is as to how the Christian faith, coming into contact with the native faith was itself modified. While, in a later chapter, an attempt is made to sum up the permanent influences of the native beliefs and practices on Roman Catholicism, certain cases of deliberate accommodation properly belong in this study of the method of the missionaries.

We have already quoted the statement of Pedro de Gante as to his method of attracting the people who were at first hesitant about receiving the new doctrine. He explicitly says that he took advantage of the singing and dancing which always accompanied their sacrifices and that he himself composed songs regarding the law of God and the faith. Whether he means that he composed the music, or merely the words to accompany music with which they were already familiar, is not clear, though probably he gave them the music also. He would hardly have risked perpetuating the music associated with their own cult, lest their attachment to it be thus kept alive. The thing that mattered was the adoption of their custom of associating the music and the dance with religion. He further appealed to their love of

[60] Quoted by Cuevas, *op. cit.*, I, 159-60.

adornment by giving them designs to paint on their *mantas,* as they were accustomed to do in their own feasts. So successful was this method that his pupils scattering everywhere carried it with them, and the other priests, both regular and secular likewise adopted it.

Evidently such methods proved not to be wholly advantageous, for we find the *Junta* of the church, meeting in 1539, legislating against certain abuses which had grown up in the cult, abuses which neither they nor their successors have been able to eradicate, if we may accept the statement of Cuevas, a modern Mexican Jesuit. A summary of the action of the council is as follows:

> Since the Indians of these parts are very much inclined toward the dances which have come down from paganism, and since it is necessary to avoid the appearance of evil, we order that when they dance, they must not use anything which will cause suspicion. They shall not sing any songs which have not been first examined by the priests, who must endeavor to prevent anything apart from the Christian doctrine. They must not dance before daybreak nor before high mass, but only after Hours until vespers, and when vespers ring, they must attend, leaving off dancing. Any infraction of these rules is to be punished according to the will of the priests who have them in charge.[61]

Article IV of the council's action says that Indians shall not hold feasts in which there is dancing, or eating, or costumes, or Castilian wine, nor shall there be joint feasts of neighboring parishes, for such feasts have resulted in drunkenness and fights and even the death of some of the Indians. Article IX says that since there are sufficient bells to call the people to service, there should be no need of other profane methods such as dances, races, or like spectacles, for these things distract the heart from quiet and devotion.

[61] Quoted by Cuevas, *op. cit.,* I, 430.

It should be noted that not all accommodation to Indian customs and practices came with the official approval of the church. This was, in some cases, precisely the thing which the church did not desire, but which it was ultimately driven to accept or tolerate through inability to control the situation. The practice of the church in Yucatan appears in a letter of instruction from Bishop Francisco de Toral to the priests of his diocese:

Do not allow the Indians to dance at night under any conditions, not even at feast-times. In the daytime, after the principal mass, they may dance in the *patio* of the church at festival times, provided that the priest first examine the words they are to sing in the dance, signing it with his name so the Indians will know that it is proper and holy. Let the Christian doctrine be the first to be given them in writing for the dance. . . . When this has been learned and sung many times . . . other sacred and holy things may be given them. . . . Do not permit them to wear their ancient costumes in the dance. Men must not dress as women or as devils as they formerly did, nor must they sing their songs during the dance or elsewhere, for all these things tend to bring back their old thoughts and lead to idolatry.[62]

In the matter of feasts and fasts, the church made certain concessions in favor of the Indians, chiefly because of the poverty and misery in which they lived. For example, in the rules adopted by the first council of Mexico, we find forty-two feast-days beside Sundays required of the Spanish Christians, while but twelve are required of the Indians. The list of those from which they were exempted includes but two of the more important days, namely, All Saints and Corpus Christi. Both of these in later times became very important for the Indians also, so evidently some subsequent rulings were made. The ones the Indians were held to observe were the following:

[62] Quoted by Cuevas, *op. cit.*, II, 490.

All Sundays	The Assumption of Our Lady
The Circumcision	
The Resurrection	The Birth of Jesus
The Holy Spirit	The Epiphany
The Feast of the Holy Sacrament	The Ascension
	The Annunciation
The Purification of Our Lady	The Nativity of Our Lady
	The Feasts of St. Peter and St. Paul

But one feast appears here which is not included in the longer required list, namely that of the Holy Sacrament. The Indians were obliged to fast only at Nativity, Resurrection, and the Fridays during Lent. On such days the Spaniards were supposed to exempt them from service.

One other special concession to the Indians was their exemption from the Inquisition. This was due to the theory widely held at one time that the Indians were of a lower order of humanity and therefore incapable of the Faith, a theory which was relied upon chiefly to excuse the cruelties inflicted upon them. This opinion was debated by thirteen sages of the University of Salamanca, and it was finally resolved that such an opinion was heretical and that any one who defended it pertinaciously must be put to death by fire as a heretic. This exemption did not operate in the earliest times, however, for the fact is that a number of Indians were condemned to death by the Inquisition. A fuller discussion of this appears in a subsequent chapter.[63]

In an appendix to the reports of the Provincial Councils, the editor has published a list of what he describes as the privileges of the Indians. It should be noted, however, that he wrote late in the eighteenth century and that not all he mentions were effective in the earlier period, notably that relating to the right of ordination.

[63] *See post*, pp. 267 ff.

For the contraction of matrimony with blood-relatives there is no impediment up to the second grade inclusive.

It is forbidden to work only on days of two crosses, which are Sundays and the days indicated in the calendar.

They have only nine days of fasting in the year, the seven Fridays of Lent, the Nativity, and Resurrection Sunday.

If they fall into idolatry, heresy, or like error, they are not denounced to the Holy Office of the Inquisition but to the diocesan bishop, and they have a judge for their affairs in the Royal Tribunals.

They may be ordained *in sacris,* admitted to the seminaries, and promoted to ecclesiastical dignities and public offices; and those who are pure, without taint of infection or hated sect, even though they be not *caciques,* may have all the prerogatives, dignities, and honors which, in Spain, those of pure blood enjoy.

The *Caciques* may ascend to high positions, secular and ecclesiastical, and enjoy the honors conferred on the nobles of Spain.[64]

Just a little indication of the way in which missionaries must often have yielded to Indian desires and customs is found in a brief note regarding the Chichimecs, quoted by Cuevas:

The Chichimecs, before they would consent to being converted to Christianity, had exacted that a cross be stationed there, of the same color and shape that had been seen by one of their old men. So the builder, Juan de la Cruz, formed one from a stone of three colors, white, red and purple.[65]

That they were allowed to continue their practice of making offerings before images, appears in the work of Motolinia who says that on the Feast of Kings they offered wax, incense, doves, partridges and other fowls hunted especially for that day, before the figure of the Virgin and Child in the manger which had been set up in the church.

[64] *Concilios Provinciales,* p. 391.
[65] Cuevas, *op. cit.,* I, 150.

SUMMARY

Cuevas, commenting on the vast number of baptisms reported by Motolinia, says that every sort of sophism has been employed in the attempt to explain them, since they cannot be denied. He attacks vigorously the statement that the Indians received baptism in order to escape evil treatment at the hands of the whites. But this, he declares, is to shut the eyes to what actually happened, for the Indians, as a matter of fact, did not better their social situation by baptism. He writes:

Nor is it true that the conversion was the result of conquest, for during the first four years after the conquest the masses were unaffected, no one urging them nor paying attention to them except to see that they did not perform their sacrifices before the eyes of the conquerors. On the other hand, the priests were looked upon with disfavor by a great part of the conquerors, yet it was after their coming that most of the conversions occurred.

To suppose that they were baptized without understanding what they were doing, is to rate the Indians lower than the facts warrant, and is to conceive falsely of the missionaries.

The real fact is that they were attracted, some by the good example of others, some few by the conversion of their old lords, and all were helped to it by comparison between their old cruel religion and the Christian religion, all sweetness and gentleness. But the true and chiefest motive was none other than the impulse and grace of the Holy Spirit, an impulse and grace which we, the faithful, feel and understand but which the apostates rightfully have lost and therefore hate.[66]

While unable to follow the author in supposing that all the vast multitude understood what they were doing, nor to rate the Christianity of the period as all sweetness and gentleness, we do believe that there is reason in the rest of his statement.

Another Jesuit, José Acosta, who wrote before the end of the sixteenth century, reports that a priest in New Spain

[66] Cuevas, *op. cit.*, I, 192-3.

told him of having asked an old Indian chief when he first arrived there, how it happened that the Indians had received so quickly the law of Jesus Christ and forsaken their own without proof, investigation, or discussion. The old Indian replied:

Do not think that we have accepted the law of Christ so inconsiderately as you have imagined, for I say to you that we were already so weary and discontented with the things which the idols required of us that we had tried to leave them and find another law. And since what you preached to us seemed to us to be without cruelty, well adapted to us, just, and good, we understood that it was the true law and so received it very willingly.[67]

Acosta thought that he found confirmation of this in one of the letters of Cortés to the emperor, where he tells how ambassadors came to him from Michoacán while he was at Coyoacán, asking that he send those who could teach them his law, for they wished to abandon their own, since it no longer seemed good to them.[68]

The fact is, of course, that no simple explanation of such a complex phenomenon as the conversion of a race is possible. A wide variety of contributing circumstances rendered it possible. We turn to a consideration of some of the factors, both favorable and unfavorable, affecting the process and its final outcome.

[67] Acosta, *Historia Natural y Moral de los Indios,* II, 85.
[68] *Ibid.*

CHAPTER VI

CONDITIONS FAVORING AND HINDERING CONVERSION

The task of converting a great nation from its pagan faith to Christianity would necessarily be fraught with a host of very serious difficulties. On the other hand, such a transformation could hardly have been wrought in so brief a period, had there not been also a great many conditions favoring it. The purpose of this chapter is to consider what were the favorable and what the opposing factors.

FACTORS FAVORING CONVERSION

Those factors which favored the ready acceptance of the new faith by the Indians were at least four, *viz:* (1) the similarities, real or apparent, between the two forms of religion; (2) the high character of the early missionaries; (3) the support and coöperation of the government, both imperial and local; and (4) the character of the Indians.

Over against such favoring factors were at least five which hindered: (1) the hostile or indifferent attitude of the Spanish inhabitants toward the conversion of the Indians; (2) the evil example set by the Spaniards; (3) the gross mistreatment of the Indians; (4) the lower moral character of the priests who came later; and (5) the conflict between the religious orders and, even more, that between the secular and regular clergy. We proceed to a more detailed discussion of each of these.

In the case of the first two favoring conditions, namely, the similarity between the religions and the character of the early priests, it will suffice to refer to the discussion in chapters three and five, where they are amply treated. The third, it will be well to document rather fully, for undoubtedly the favorable attitude of the imperial and vice-royal government was of very great help to the earlier missionaries.

By the very terms of the Bull of Alexander VI dividing the new discoveries between the Spaniards and the Portuguese, the conquest of these lands carried with it the moral obligation to Christianize the Indians who might be found there. Their conversion became a duty which the monarchs, it must in fairness be said, made a real effort to perform. Again and again in the correspondence between the officials and priests of New Spain and the king of Spain with reference to converting the Indians and providing for their spiritual care and direction, the appeal is to the discharge of his moral obligation, or literally the "discharging of his conscience."

Las Casas, the tireless defender of the Indians, made much of this obligation when addressing himself to the king regarding the condition of the Indians, temporal as well as religious. On one occasion he wrote the king, setting forth a number of propositions touching the whole theory of the right of possession and the consequent obligations thereby entailed, which he purposed discussing before the king. We do not give them all, but it will be worth while to note the more important ones. They are as follow:

1. The pope derives from Christ his power and authority, extending over all men in matters of salvation and eternal life, but this should be exercised differently over infidels and those who have had a chance to become believers.

2. This prerogative of the pope puts him under solemn obligation to propagate the gospel and offer it to all infidels who will not oppose it.

3. The pope is obliged to send capable ministers for this work.

4. The pope may exhort and even oblige Christian princes to this work, by money and authority to remove obstructions and to send true workers.

5. The pope may distribute infidel provinces among the Christian princes for this work. In this distribution, the instruction, conversion, and interests of the infidels themselves should be held in view, not the increase of honors and titles, riches and territories of the princes.

6. Any incidental advantages which princes may thus gain are allowable, but temporal ends should be wholly subordinate, the paramount objects being the extension of the church, the propagation of the Faith and the service of God.

7. Neither native rulers nor subjects should be deprived of their lands for idolatry nor any other sin.

8. No tribunal or judge in the world has a right to molest these infidels for idolatry or any other sins, however enormous, before they have voluntarily received baptism, unless they directly refuse, oppose and resist the publication of the gospel.

9. The kings of Spain are bound by the law of God to choose and send fit missionaries to exhort, convert, and do everything for this cause. They have the same power and jurisdiction over these infidels before their conversion as the pope has and share his obligation to convert them.

10. The means for the establishing of the Faith in the Indies should be the same as those by which Christ introduced his religion into the world, mild, peaceful, and charitable; good examples of a holy and regular way of living, especially over such docile and easy subjects.

11. Attempts by force of arms are impious, like those of the Mahometans, Romans, Turks, and Moors; they are tyrannical and unworthy of Christians, calling out blasphemies, and they have already made the Indians believe that our God is the most unmerciful and cruel of all gods. The Indians will naturally oppose the invasion of their country by a title of conquest and will resist the work of conversion.

12. The kings of Spain are bound to reënforce and establish those Indian laws and customs which are good, and such are most of them—and to abolish the bad, thus upholding good manners and civil policy. The gospel is the method for effecting this.

13. The devil could not have done more mischief than the Spaniards have done in distributing and spoiling the countries in their rapacity and tyranny, subjecting the natives to cruel

tasks, treating them like beasts, and persecuting especially those who apply to the monks for instruction.[1]

Such ideas, of course, while representing the opinion of many of the clergy of the day, by no means represented all, for Las Casas was considered a wild radical by many of his contemporaries, and found very severe opposition to many of his ideas among his colleagues. Such reforms as he proposed were radical, for they would affect the income and the properties of the church as well as that of individuals. It is possibly just because of this that he was so bitterly fought from within the church itself. It is of interest to note that it does not occur to him to question the ultimate right of the pope to dispose of the new world. He is concerned rather with the conditions under which the right should be exercised.

However much one may be convinced that Las Casas was given to exaggeration in his description of the treatment of the Indians by the Spaniards, modern readers cannot but appreciate the good sense and truly Christian spirit he shows, particularly in his notions as to how the gospel should be introduced. His condemnation of the use of force in conversion and his estimate of such methods was in direct conflict with the thought of many of the rulers and clergy of his day. The fact that he so specifically condemns it, is a sure indication that undue use of force was still being practiced when he wrote.

An even more thoroughgoing statement comes from a Dominican priest, prior of a monastery, whom one of the *visitadores* quoted in a letter to King Philip in 1550. Apropos of the question of the right of the emperor to tribute, he said:

[1] Quoted by Justin Winsor, *Narrative and Critical History of America,* II, 32.

His majesty has nothing here beyond what the pope has given him, and the pope could give the land to no one save for the spiritual good of the Indians. The day when it has a government and is instructed in the things of the faith, the king will be obliged to give the country over to the natives.[2]

It is not likely that such doctrine found large favor at court, nor is it probable that such a view was at all widely current among the friars. We have nowhere else found such a suggestion.

At the risk of some degree of duplication, we will quote here, in whole or in part, a number of communications from the Spanish kings bearing on the conversion of the Indians. These are presented chronologically, interspersed with other material from diverse sources, reflecting the general attitude of the government to the conversion task.

Not a little space has already been given to the religious interest of Cortés in the natives. In a previous chapter a long letter of his to the emperor regarding the need of priests was quoted. His earliest specific reference to the obligation of Spain to Christianize the Indians appears in his letter of July 10, 1519; that is, before the fall of Mexico City. He wrote then as follows, referring to human sacrifices:

Now let your Highnesses consider if they ought not to prevent so great an evil and crime, and certainly the Lord will be well pleased if through the commands of your royal highnesses these people should be initiated and instructed in our very Holy Catholic Faith; and the devotion, faith, and hope which they have in their idols should be transferred to the Divine Omnipotence of God; because it is certain that if they served God with the same faith and favor and diligence, they would surely work miracles.

It should be believed that it is not without cause that God our Lord should have permitted that these parts be discovered in the name of your royal highnesses, so that the fruit and

[2] *Colección de Documentos Inéditos,* IV, 370.

merit before God should be enjoyed by your majesties of having instructed these barbarian peoples and brought them through your commands to the true faith. As far as we are able to know them, we believe that if there were interpreters and persons who could make them understand the truth of the faith and their errors, many and perhaps all would shortly quit the errors which they hold and come to the true knowledge, because they live civilly and reasonably, better than any of the other people found in these parts.[3]

In 1523 the king addressed a lengthy letter of instruction to Cortés regarding the treatment and conversion of the Indians, in which the royal will is set forth touching the obligation which he feels for the indoctrination of the natives. In the course of it emerges the question which was to cause the crown so much difficulty, the matter of the *repartimientos,* or the distribution of lands and Indians among the Spanish colonists. It will be noted that in this letter such a plan was prohibited, and in case action had already been taken looking toward it, it was to be revoked. But to order a thing done was easier than to enforce the ruling. Care must be exercised in working with these government sources to remember that they do not always reflect what was actually done. More often rather they are of value as indicating what was not practiced. The long distance by which the royal council was removed from the scene of action made the execution of their orders exceedingly difficult to secure. The letter is in part as follows:

Having learned from your reports and those of others who have been there that the natives of New Spain are more intelligent and capable than those in other islands; and, since therefore, they are more apt for conversion to our Lord and for being instructed and living in the Roman Catholic faith as Christians, in order that they may be saved, which is our principal interest and intention; and since we are obligated to help them to this end, I hereby charge you as well as I may that you

[3] MacNutt, *Letters of Cortés to Charles V,* I, 164-5.

make your chief care the conversion and indoctrination of the Indians which are under your own rule, and that you exert all your powers that the natives of New Spain be converted to our Holy faith and instructed in it, that they may live as Christians and be saved.

Since you know how subject the Indians are to their lords and so faithful in following them, it would seem that the best method of going about it would be to begin by indoctrinating the chiefs first; besides it would hardly be wise to try all at once to urge that all the Indians become Christians and thus perchance have them take offense at it. However, go over the matter there with the priests and people of good life who live there, study it with much earnestness, using whatever moderation seems best. . . .

Since from reports from there, it appears that the natives have idols before which they sacrifice human lives, eat the human flesh, and practice abominations contrary to our Holy Catholic Faith and natural reason; and that when they go to war they sacrifice and eat their captives, thereby offending greatly our Lord, you are to notify them and warn them that they are no longer to do so under pain of dire punishment.

In doing this, try every way to help them to see how fearful an offense it is against both God and man to eat human flesh. In order that they may have flesh to eat, let there be continual importation of cattle, so that stock shall become plentiful and there shall no longer exist any excuse for such an abomination. Likewise warn them that they must have no idols nor temples for them of any sort. After you have warned them and notified them many times, punish with serious public penalties those who refuse to obey, using whatever measure of moderation may seem to you just to employ.

In view of the long experience with the *encomienda* system in Cuba and the other islands resulting almost in the extinction of the natives, due to the ill treatment and severe labor imposed upon them by the Spanish Christians, and in view of the fact that this has constituted a serious obstacle to the conversion of the Indians . . . we ordered the theologians, monks and doctors of good and holy life to assemble together with the Council and to discuss the matter.

In the light of this discussion, it has seemed to us in good conscience that since God created these Indians free and not subject, we cannot order their distribution by *encomienda* or *repartimiento* among the Christians. Wherefore, I command you that you make no such distribution in Mexico, but that you allow them to live in freedom as our vassals live in Castile. If, before the receipt of this, any such allotment has been made, revoke it at once, freeing the Indians from the power of those to whom they have been allotted, allowing them complete freedom. In order that they may retain their liberty, take away their vices and the abominations in which they have lived. Give them to understand the mercy which we have shown them and the desire which we have that they be instructed and well treated so that with a better will they may come into the knowledge of our holy faith. . . .[4]

He further exhorts the Spaniards to treat the Indians fairly and honestly in commerce and in all mutual relationships. Cortés is required to bring about love and good feeling between the races. To this end he stresses the necessity of keeping any promises given them. Only thus is their confidence to be won. He continues:

You are to prohibit the Christians from making war upon them and doing them any harm, or taking anything from them without paying for it, for fear that they rise up in rebellion. Rather you shall punish severely those who treat them ill or do them harm without your express order. In this way the Indians will come into more contact with the Christians which is the best way to bring them to the knowledge of our holy faith, which is our chief desire and intention. One hundred converted in this way are worth more than one hundred thousand by any other.[5]

That the king was in error in expecting the contact between the Christians and natives to aid in the conversion of the latter will appear a little later. Indeed, such contacts came

[4] *Colección de Documentos Inéditos,* XXIII, 354 ff.
[5] *Ibid.,* XXIII, 354 ff.

to be considered one of the chief hindrances to winning these Indians to Christianity.

In two other documents, one bearing the date of 1524 and the other without any date, both relating to the government of certain villages, an interesting light is thrown upon the religious requirements put upon Spaniards as well as natives. To his lieutenant, Francisco Cortés, in the village of Colima, Hernando Cortés wrote:

You are to have care in punishing blasphemy, gambling, and all other public sins; and that you may be justified in what you do, give orders at once that no one dare say evil of God nor of his glorious mother or the saints, and that no one play at dice or other forbidden games, and that any one incurring in such faults be punished. . . .

Since the principal reason why we relieve the natives of that region from service is that they may be brought to a knowledge of our Holy Catholic Faith and abandon their idolatries and superstitions, above all, notify them in a language which they understand that henceforth they must have no more idols and that they must perform none of their rites and ceremonies which they formerly practiced, especially that they kill none in sacrifice, as they were accustomed to do formerly, under pain of death. Give each chief to understand that he must enforce this order, and if evidence is found of its having been disobeyed, he shall suffer the penalty for permitting it to occur.[6]

It is interesting to note his order that these instructions be given in a language the Indians could understand. This was a step forward beyond the former custom of reading a *requirimiento* in Spanish. In this as in his former orders, he fixes the responsibility for its execution upon those who had the authority to execute it. He would not seek out the individual offender but would make the chief responsible for what happened in his group.

The undated document reads in part as follows:

[6] *Ibid.,* XXVI, 151.

On Sundays and feast-days, the inhabitants and all who may be in the village shall attend mass in the principal church, entering before the reading of the gospel and remaining until the priest says, "Ita Missa est," and gives the benediction, under penalty of a fine of a half peso gold. On said Sundays and feast-days, nothing of any sort shall be sold from the time the bell calls to mass until it is all over, nor shall any store or office be open during that time, under penalty of a fine; one-third of it to go to public works; one-third to the officer who reports it; and one-third to the work of the church.[7]

In 1524 Cortés issued several important orders to the people of New Spain relative to the proper government and treatment of the Indians. Large sections of the various documents have to do with religious problems. These we quote or summarize. It will be remembered that in January of that year the first group of authorized Franciscan missionaries arrived. The orders may, therefore, be considered as given in support of the work these men had just begun to do, and they doubtless had a wholesome effect in two directions; first, in disposing the Spanish conquerors to receive the friars and lend them support; and second, upon the Indians whose high respect for the great military prowess of Cortés would dispose them to give heed to whatever he might order in matters religious as well as other things. Religion came to them with the weight of the Conqueror's prestige behind it. Part of the document reads thus:

Since as Catholics and Christians our principal intention ought to be the honor and service of God, and since the motive of the Holy Father in giving to the emperor the rule of these lands and the profit from them was that the people be converted to our Holy Catholic Faith, we, therefore, require that all persons who have *repartimientos* of Indians be obliged to take away all their idols and warn them against further idolatrous practice, and that they refrain from all sacrifice of human life to their gods. Failure to comply with the order will on first

[7] *Ibid.,* XXVI, 180.

offense be punished with a fine, the second offense with a double fine, and the third offense with the loss of the Indians.

Whosoever has Indians, if there be chiefs in their villages, shall bring the sons of said chiefs, and if there be a monastery shall give them into the hands of the priests that they may be instructed in the Holy Faith, and shall there provide them with food, clothing and other necessities. In case there be no monastery there, they shall be given to the village priest or to the person charged with such instruction. If there be no great chief in the village, then let the sons of the leading men of the place be brought as above directed.

When no priests or friars are available, let the mayor hire some person, the most capable and worthy possible, to take charge of the instruction of the children, the salary to be paid by the person having the *repartimiento,* in proportion to the number of the Indians. Failure of the officers to do this will result in their loss of office.

In order that all the natives shall share in the word of the Lord, I require that every person having a *repartimiento* of more than two thousand maintain in the village a priest or friar who shall instruct them in the Holy Faith, forbid their ancient practices, and administer the sacraments of the church. Wherever this is not done, provided that a priest be available, the *encomendero* shall lose his Indians.

Since there are many who have but few Indians and could not afford to maintain a priest alone—besides, there are not enough of them—I require that they combine together, those who live within a league or so of each other, and provide a priest, paying him to look after all their Indians as above indicated. Failure to obey the order will result as in the previous article.[8]

If the legitimacy of their general methods of conversion be admitted, the reader cannot fail to recognize the high practical wisdom of Cortés in this order. Such a plan systematically and effectively enforced would provide for the indoctrination of the whole country as it was gradually occupied, the responsibility for conversion resting upon those who

[8] *Ibid.,* XXVI, 140-2.

were profiting by the distribution of the Indians. In the case of sections which were not distributed among the Spaniards but remained under their native lords, it became the direct obligation of the king through his agents to see to the indoctrination of the people.

As a paper program it was admirable. As a matter of fact it broke down at many points; first, because of the lack of a sufficient number of priests or persons properly prepared to give the instruction ordered; second, because of the resistance of the *encomenderos;* third, because of the half-hearted coöperation of the local officials in attempting to enforce the order. Distance from the capital and the difficulties of communication made close supervision next to impossible. Besides, it must be remembered that the indoctrination of the Indians was but one interest among many, and to many of the Spaniards, perhaps even to Cortés himself and his successors, a minor one; if indeed, the whole idea of obligation may not have been considered as merely nominal, which the issuance of an order quite as well as its fulfillment would satisfy.

Cortés himself, probably more genuinely interested in religion than his fellow conquerors, continued so long as he was in authority to insist on the duty of conversion. Another order which, while bearing no date, probably belongs to a period not much later than the one above cited, goes into still greater detail regarding the matter of instructing the Indians and reiterates the threat of punishment in case of failure to carry out his orders. He begins with the customary exhortation to convert the Indians and continues:

In places where the Spaniards are served by the natives, images of Our Lady shall be set up and each morning before the Indians go to work they shall be required to appear there and to hear the things of the faith and be taught the Lord's prayer, Ave María, or Salve Regina, so that they shall come to know and receive the Holy Faith. Failure to comply with this order will be penalized by a fine of six pesos gold. The Spaniards and others who have Indians shall be held responsible for destroying their temples or other sanctuaries which they may have and provide a church for their village with altar and images where they are to come and ask God to give them the light of salvation and other temporal goods. If within six months after receiving the *repartimiento* this has not been done, the *encomendero* shall be fined, and at each subsequent visitation a like fine shall be assessed.[9]

While many of the Spaniards failed to follow his orders, many others did so quite faithfully. Indeed, it ought in fairness to be said that some of them were, like Cortés, very much interested in the indoctrination of the Indians and went beyond any legal requirements to bring it about. Throughout the whole extent of Latin America it is still a common custom for the big estates to maintain some measure of responsibility for the religious life of their Indians. Many of them have chapels, some, well-appointed churches, and the larger ones maintain a priest, though usually the *padre* visits the chapels only at stated intervals. The writer has himself frequently seen such chapels in Bolivia, South America, where very much the same practices were common among the Spaniards in relation to the Indians. Many of the modern books of travel on Mexico contain mention of such estate churches, and some of them describe the ceremonies and customs witnessed at special seasons of the year. Typical of these may be cited the description of the *Hacienda San Gabriel,* in *Mexico as I Saw It,* by Mrs. Alec Tweedie.

The village containing nearly three thousand souls belongs to the *hacienda.* . . . There is no church in the village. That, like everything else, belongs to the *hacienda* and is attached to the house. These churches are extremely quaint and have steeples and domes. Some of such private places of worship are quite beautiful and contain rare treasures that have been

---

[9] *Ibid.,* XXVI, 167.

in the family for generations. There is a private entrance to the sacred edifice from the house leading to a gallery used by the owners. The priest comes from the next village to celebrate mass on Sundays, holidays, and days of obligation, when all the villagers attend the various masses, for the church could not hold three thousand at once, although it certainly accomodates seven or eight hundred, there being no seats. The proprietors of the *hacienda* pay the priests and doctor, though the latter receives a little extra for attendance from outside. Practically, however, the land-owner has to look after the spiritual and bodily needs of his people.[10]

The viceroys who succeeded Cortés in the government of Mexico were, in general, favorable to the cause of converting the Indians. Perhaps none surpassed Don Antonio de Mendoza in his attention to this. Two royal documents of instruction to Mendoza on assuming charge of the government, reveal the attitude of the Spanish sovereigns, and at the same time reflect what must have been the state of affairs in that period. The first was written in 1535, apparently before Mendoza departed for Mexico, the latter soon after his arrival in 1536. To understand the detailed instruction which the king gives as to ecclesiastical procedure, it is necessary to remember how very jealously the royal house guarded the prerogatives in relation to the church which it had gradually acquired through resistance to the encroachments of papal power. While Spain was perhaps the most Catholic of nations, and Ferdinand and Isabella had been honored with the title of Catholic Kings, no nation was more consistent in its avoidance of papal interference within the national church. Although, theoretically, Spain held Mexico and the other New World colonies as a papal grant, she exercised every care to keep papal influence there at a minimum, just as in the mother country. We, therefore, find the royal court dealing in what would ordinarily be considered

[10] P. 339.

purely ecclesiastical matters to be handled by the ecclesiastical authorities.

The earlier of the two documents referred to reads in part as follows:

First, before all else, on arriving in that land and understanding something of what is going on there, inform us of the progress that is being made in spiritual matters as well as dynastic, especially in regard to the building of temples for holy worship and in the conversion of the native Indians . . . etc.[11]

Continuing, the king orders the confiscation of articles of gold and riches in pagan temples, the instruction of natives in monasteries, the building of monasteries without great burden to the natives, the sending out of good priests. He discusses further the matter of tithes, and finally whether for the conversion of the Indians it is better that the Spaniards be required to live apart from them.[12]

The second document we give in greater detail:

First of all, be careful to seek the best and most successful methods for the conversion of the natives of that land to our Holy Catholic Faith, for besides being obligated to the task out of gratitude to God for having in these days given the land to the crown, we are sure that it is the best way to secure their love and loyalty to us as their sovereign and to ensure that they live in peace, respect and perfect obedience.

Wherefore you will give orders that the monks who dwell there be distributed to live in the provinces and villages where there is less knowledge of our Lord God and greater need for the doctrine. To do this best you will not permit two monasteries to be built close together except for reasons that seem to you to benefit the service of God and the Indians.

Command likewise all those who have *encomiendas* that they exercise care in the indoctrination of their Indians as they are under obligation to do, and provide that in the villages where

[11] *Colección de Documentos Inéditos*, XXIII, 426 ff.
[12] *Ibid.*, XXIII, 423.

the tribute warrants it and there are priests who are able to do it, they be employed and paid by those who collect the tribute. Where this is impossible, order that some of the Indians who have been taught the doctrine by the priests teach it to others. . . .

Provide further that where there are priests or those who teach, there be certain hours for instruction and that the Indians attend, being careful to see that an hour be chosen which does not interfere with their hours of labor, and that the instruction be free. Strictly prohibit the Spaniards and chiefs from hindering the Indians being taught, punishing those who do hinder them. We are informed that in the mines there are many Indian slaves, and there is no reason why they should lack the faith. See, therefore, that in the mines or on the farms, or wherever they are, they be instructed, for it is not just that simply because they are slaves, they should lose, along with their liberty, their right to know God, which is so important for them.

Since in order to advance the conversion of the natives, it is very important that the priests and monks apply themselves to learning the Indian tongue and that they reduce it to some sort of a system easy to learn, always favor those who have set themselves to learn it, in order that others may be stimulated to join them. In the churches of the city and the schools for Spanish children it seems that it would be wise to do some teaching in the Indian tongue, so that those who are to become priests and monks or hold public office in the villages may know how to teach and confess the Indians and understand how to deal with them, for they are so numerous that they cannot at present be required to learn our language.

Already, it seems, the king had forbidden the importation of books which might have a bad effect on the Indians who could read them, but without success. He again finds it necessary to prohibit such importation. The discord among the priests he considers a major evil and urges that all differences be set aside so that Christianity may seem to present a united front to the Indians. He urges that con-

ferences of leaders be held regarding their problems, offering
if necessary to ask help for them from the pope.   He adds:

> Since you know how, even in Christian countries, public
> sins greatly corrupt the good customs of the people, it must be
> even more harmful in a land where the faith is but newly
> planted.   Wherefore, be very diligent in restraining and pun-
> ishing public sins of the Spaniards, for they are a great obstacle
> to the preaching of our Holy Catholic Faith which we so much
> desire to root in the hearts of the people.
>
> In order that the work of the prelates and priests who de-
> sire the conversion of the Indians be effective, and that the
> hatred which they cherish toward the Spaniards on account of
> ill treatment may not lead to the hatred of our Faith, which is
> preached by Spaniards of the same race and color as those who
> use them ill, you will use the utmost diligence to see that the
> Indians are well treated.[13]

Again in 1550, the king, writing instructions to a new
viceroy, reiterates his feeling of obligation to continue the
work of conversion, and in dealing with the various problems
involved, reflects the situation at the time he wrote.

> First, in recognition of the great mercy of God in placing
> us as king over so many and such great provinces as our Indies,
> we are under obligation always to see that the Indians of said
> provinces know and serve God and leave off the infidelity and
> error in which they have lived, that His Holy Name be exalted
> and known in all the world and the natives reap the rich fruit-
> age of their holy redemption; for this is the principal end and
> aim which we entertain.   We charge you, therefore, that you
> be exceedingly active in the conversion to Christianity of said
> Indians, that they be well instructed in the things of our Holy
> Catholic Faith and gospel.   Wherefore, inform us whether
> there are sufficient ministers to teach them the doctrine and to
> administer the holy sacraments of the mother church which
> they are prepared to receive, and if there are not enough, com-
> municate it to the prelates of the church and let us know what
> your opinion is that we may order whatever is necessary to be

[13] *Ibid.,* XXIII, 454-60.

done, lest for lack of teachers and ministers the Indians suffer damage to their souls and consciences. . . .

And, since we are informed that the chief fruit thus far in the conversion of the natives is due to the friars who live among them, call together the principal priors and other prelates of the orders and command the building of monasteries, of course with the permission of their diocesans, in the place where the need is greatest and where there is the most notable lack of teaching; commanding the friars to exercise great diligence in the salvation of souls. Encourage them to go forward with the work, making the monasteries centers rather for the teaching of the Indians than places of spiritual retreat for the members of the Order. Likewise, see that monasteries be not built one over against another but at a distance of some leagues apart, in order that the gospel be heard most conveniently by all the natives.[14]

Though many other similar documents might be cited, these will suffice for illustration of the attitude of the imperial government toward the conversion of the Indians. There is, however, one exceedingly interesting letter of instructions by Philip written July 13, 1573, that is, some fifty years after the conquest, suggesting a method of dealing with tribes which have not received the Christian message. This, it should be said, was not addressed specifically to Mexico but was a general order effective there as elsewhere throughout the Spanish dependencies. It is preserved in the Code of Laws for the Governing of the Indies.

In places where the Indians do not receive the Christian teaching peaceably, the following order should be used.

Get the chief of a neighboring tribe which is at peace to try to draw the hostile Indians over into his territory on the pretext of some diversion or other, and let there be preachers and some Spaniards and friendly Indians present. Then, when the proper moment arrives, let them teach the Christian doctrine. In order that the people hear them with greater veneration, let them be solemnly robed and with the cross in their hands. Let

[14] *Ibid.*, XXIII, 520 ff.

the Christians listen with the very greatest respect and veneration, for the infidels seeing this will imitate them.

If it seem wise, in order to attract their attention and admiration more effectively, music of singers or minstrels may be employed to draw the Indians together, as well as other means that may soften and pacify them. Even though they seem to be pacified and ask for a teacher, be careful, asking first that they send their children to be taught—these will serve as hostages—and urging them to build churches first where ministers may go and teach and preach. By such means and others they can be won gradually and taught without any one suffering any injury.[15]

In consideration of the expense and dangers incident to the conquest and the conversion of the new found lands, the pope had, in 1501, conceded the tithes to the king of Spain, that is, the tenth part of the produce of field and flock, a sum which ordinarily belonged to the bishops, clergy, and the charitable work done by the church.[16] Cuevas holds that this wrought serious hardship to the church, impeding as it did the free administration of its income. As a matter of fact, however, the king conceded to the church almost the whole of the tithe. The pinch came principally, however, in the fact that the control of these funds gave the king a very direct control of the church and clergy.

That the king tried conscientiously to carry out his obligation with reference to the conversion of the Indians, seems evident. Bishop Zumárraga, the first bishop of Mexico,

---

[15] *Recopilación de Leyes de Los Reinos de las Indias,* Libro I, titulo i, ley 4.

[16] The legal definition of the tithe is given in the *Recopilación de Leyes,* Lib. 1, titulo 16, under date of 1501; "We command that in all the Indies, Islands and Mainland the tithe and first-fruits be collected and paid in the following form. 'He who harvests wheat barley, rye . . . corn . . . oats, etc., shall pay as a tithe one measure for ten *(de diez medidas una)* and if there be other things that are not measured he shall pay as tithe one for each ten *(de diez una),* which tithe shall be paid entire without first taking out the seed, the rental shares or any other expense !' etc."

warmly defends the monarch against any charges of profiting at the expense of the church and of failure to do his part toward the religious task of converting the natives. He writes:

The king who undertook the enterprise of reducing these regions to his dominions and therefore, to the bosom of the church, merits the powerful support of the latter. . . . It is only just to say that during the early years, the *patronato* was a heavy charge upon the king, one which he nobly bore. He worked with zeal and interest in the founding of these churches; chose worthy prelates and supported them energetically in the correction of abuses; and attempted with great enthusiasm the conversion of the Indians, sending out constantly new missionaries. The concession of the tithe with the obligation of providing properly for the churches was not a profit to him, but a heavy loss to his treasury, for the product of the tithe was not sufficient to meet the expense, and the king supplied what was lacking. Later, when the tithes provided more than necessary, he returned the product to be administered by the church, reserving only the two ninths and even this he drew upon whenever some worthy need presented itself.[17]

Astrain, in his *Historia de la Compañía de Jesús,* grows sentimental as he reflects on the part Spain's sovereigns played in the great drama of conversion. In almost poetic language, yet, doubtless remaining true to the essential facts of the case, he writes:

The king supplied to the missionaries a sacred chalice and sacred ornaments for the celebration of the mass; paid for the wine employed in it; and provided the oil for the lamp of the holy sacrament. This tender solicitude of the ancient Spanish state for the preachers of the gospel cannot but inspire tender devotion. When the Augustinian friar raised his altar yonder on the rocky coasts of the Philippines; when the Franciscan prepared to say mass in the deep forests of the Paraná; when the Jesuit built an humble thatched chapel in the swamps of the Marañón; in all these cases, the missionary opened his box, took

[17] Quoted by Cuevas, *op. cit.,* II, 59-60.

out the ornaments given by the king of Spain, and when, after celebrating mass, he left on the humble altar of wood the crucifix, the king of Spain lighted and kept burning the lamp which in those solitudes was to burn constantly.[18]

Perhaps quite enough has been said to establish the fact of the consistent support of the royal court in propagating the faith in Mexico, and of the support of Cortés and his successors who governed the land. It may be an open question as to whether or not this should be considered as a factor favoring the genuine spiritual conversion of the Indians, but that it was a tremendous factor in the Christianizing process as it was actually carried on, there can be not the slightest doubt; and it is of this that we are writing. The following opinion from an early document, whether representing the exact truth or not, reflects the opinion currently held among the people who were in the midst of it.

The people here are so simple and of such low intelligence that from what we have been able to judge, if the government rested with them, the coming of the gospel would have profited them little in this land, for it would have fallen to the ground.[19]

A fourth factor favoring the rapid acceptance of the faith was the character of the Indians themselves. Mendieta, the Franciscan friar who himself was one of the leaders of the work in the latter part of the sixteenth century, has a long chapter in his *Historia Eclesiástica Indiana,* in which he details the qualities of character which disposed them to take over the new faith. He gives it as his judgment that never in the world has a nation or a generation of people been discovered who were more disposed or better prepared for the salvation of their souls than the Indians of Mexico.

Among the conditions and qualities which favored their salvation, he rates first the fact that they were a meek and

[18] Quoted by Cuevas, *op. cit.,* II, 60.
[19] *Colección de Documentos Inéditos,* IV, 506.

peaceful people. He cites the statement of a bishop to the effect that in twenty or more years of living among them, he had not seen an Indian quarrel with another one, save once. The cause of their gentleness, he thought might be their phlegmatic temperament, though it was also a virtue taught among them. How greatly different they were from the Spaniards! So great was their meekness that even chiefs accepted humbly the rebukes of the priests who learned of the evils they had committed, and in penance either lashed themselves or allowed others to lash them, and thanked them for it afterward.

Their simplicity, he considered a second favoring quality. How else could they have taken the Spaniards for gods and received them as angels, although they came with arms? Did they not think that horse and rider were one and that the friars were not as other men, but that they were born thus? Did they not esteem glass beads above gold? This quality made them easy victims of unscrupulous exploiters who preyed upon their lack of discrimination. Moreover, they readily pardoned any injury done them. No Indian felt himself so highly offended that a priest could not, with a reasonable amount of persuasion, get him to pardon the offender.

A third quality was their poverty and contentment with it, for they were without the vice of avarice and the desire to accumulate great treasure. Naturally this commended them to the Franciscans to whom poverty was, according to Mendieta, the treasure of treasures. The food of the Indians was the simplest; their dress meager, so poor as to have shamed the supposed poverty of St. Francis. Surely, thinks Mendieta, the world has seen no poorer, more contented people, nor people less disturbed by covetousness and avarice, which is the root of all evil, nor a people more liberal with what they had.

A fourth quality was their humility. Even important chiefs would sweep the church or allow themselves to be whipped as children.

A fifth quality was their obedience. No novitiate of any religious order could surpass them in this. White or black, little or great, high or low, every one commanded them and they would obey all. Yet under all their ill treatment they were patient. Subjected to every sort of exploitation and humiliation, they endured all with unbelievable patience. "When I consider the unending labors and injuries and troubles to which these people are subject," cries Mendieta, "I cannot help wondering why it is that they do not flee to the mountains and caves like wild tribes. . . . The shepherd carries off a son, the cartman a daughter, a negro the wife, a mulatto insults him, and beyond this comes another *repartimiento* which sends him to the mines where he wears his life out."

And finally, declares Mendieta, they approached death with a resignation and conformity to the will of God that was truly remarkable. "The Lord's will be done," they would say, and without inquietude or fear or regret would yield up their spirits. "Not only from adults," writes the pious friar, "but from children also, I have heard in their last moments such things as have caused me to marvel and to rejoice, for I seemed to see them flying heavenward." The reason why they surpassed other Christians in this was, he thought, the fact that they were less attached to properties and other earthly things, and had deeply impressed upon their hearts and memories the thought of the brevity of life. He might have explained it more accurately on the basis of the hardness of their present life and the appeal of the future life with its promise of rest and happiness.[20]

Acosta, also an early writer, and one who had seen the actual process of conversion, joins Mendieta in stressing the

[20] Mendieta, *op. cit.,* pp. 437 ff.

submissive character of the Indians as a reason for their ready acceptance of the faith. The quaint old English of the translation made in 1604 gives something of the flavor of the Spanish original.

It hath also been a great help to induce the Indians to receive the law of Christ, the subiection they were in to their kings and lords and also the servitude and slaverie they were held in by the divell's tyrannies and insupportable yoke. This was an excellent disposition of the divine wisdom the which draws profit from ill to a good end and receives his good from another's ill, which it hath not sowen. It is most certain that no people of the West Indies have been more apt to receive the gospel than those which were most subject to their Lords and which have been charged with the heaviest burthens, as well of tributes and services, as of customs and of bloodie practices. All that which the Mexicaine kings and those of Peru did possesse, is at this day most planted with the Christian religion, and where there is least difficultie in the government and ecclesiastical discipline.

But he adds:

The Indians were so wearied with the heavy and insupportable yoke of Sathan's lawes, his sacrifices and ceremonies whereof we have formerly spoken, that they consulted among themselves to seek out a new law and another god to serve. And therefore, the law of Christ seemed good unto them and doth at this day seem just, sweete, clean, good, and full of happiness.[21]

We may note the testimony of at least one more writer of the early period in confirmation of what has already been said. Bishop Vasco de Quiroga writes of them in 1531:

This people know not how to resist anything they are ordered to do . . . and are so docile that the Christian teaching can be impressed upon them if diligence is used, for they are naturally humble, obedient, indifferent to the world and to

[21] Acosta, *Natural and Moral History of the Indies* (Markham edition, London, 1904), II, 530.

nakedness, going barefoot and bareheaded, with long hair, as
the apostles were accustomed to go.   They are as a smooth
board or soft wax.   Wherefore, I offer with the help of God to
produce here a kind of Christians like those in the primitive
church.[22]

THE HINDRANCES TO CONVERSION

We turn now to the hindrances, and passing over those
natural difficulties incident to the conversion of any people,
note the special factors which added to the difficulty of the
task.   Of the five mentioned in the introduction to the chapter, the first three center in the Spanish lay inhabitants, the
latter two in the priesthood which was also, of course, very
largely Spanish in the beginning.

If it were true, as stated in an earlier chapter, that the
Spaniards regarded themselves as crusaders engaged in a
holy task when they penetrated into the heart of Mexico and
took possession of it for the crown of Spain, it is equally
true that most of them seem to have felt that their crusaders'
task ended with the political conquest and did not extend to
the propagation of the faith among the subdued peoples.   It
is probably true that whatever religious zeal was manifested
during the conquest was largely due to Cortés himself and
the constancy of his own emphasis upon the religious conquest.   One gets a new conception of the Conqueror's own
conviction as he realizes how much indifference, not to say
actual disfavor, his religious efforts must have inspired in
his followers.   But, whatever interest they may have had
seems to have faded out almost immediately upon the occupation and distribution of the land and Indians among them.
While it would not be fair to say that none of them aided in
the conversion process, it is certainly true that many of them
failed utterly to coöperate with those who were attempting
to Christianize the natives.   As the century advanced and
large numbers of Spaniards came, inspired wholly by a spirit

[22] Quoted by Cuevas, *op. cit.*, I, 312.

of adventure or a desire for gain, the priests complained bitterly of the active opposition they met in their efforts.

Let two quotations suffice to illustrate this, one from Mendieta who represents the central section of Mexico, and one from Bishop Landa of Yucatan. Frequent references of the same sort occur in other writings of that period.

Apparently, when Cortés lost the government of Mexico, the representatives of the church lost the support and favor of the Spaniards. This continued until the coming of bishop Ramírez de Fuenleal. During this time, the Spaniards were extending their dominion in every direction and lived without restraint, each doing as he wished and falling into every vice. They treated the Indians shamefully, imposing unbearable tribute upon them and forcing them to give service in building their houses in the cities.

The priests, seeing how seriously this interferred with the acceptance of the faith by the Indians, preached against such vices and sins as the Spaniards committed publicly and reprehended them with great Christian liberty. This aroused their ire. Fearing lest the friars would report evil of them to Spain, they used every effort to prevent communication, and did all they could to discredit the representatives of the church before the government at home. Finally through the friendship of Spanish merchants, letters were gotten to the queen, and within a few months a new president and council were sent out.[23]

Bishop Landa writes that Fr. Jacobo de Testera, a Franciscan, came first to Yucatan and began to teach the children of the Indians, but that the Spanish masters were unwilling to allow them time from their work to learn the doctrine. Because of this Fr. Jacobo returned to Mexico City. Later, from Guatemala and Mexico other friars were sent who took up residence in Campeche and Merida, under favor of the governor. A monastery was constructed in Merida and the priests sought to learn the language. Finally, it was reduced to writing and Fr. Luis de Villapando wrote a treatise on

[23] Mendieta, *op. cit.*, pp. 311-13.

Christian doctrine in it. However, there was much opposition on the part of the Spaniards who thought only of tribute and profit; and on the part of the Indians who sought to continue in their idolatry and drunkenness. The fact that the Indians were scattered through the mountains made it especially difficult.

The Spaniards were troubled at seeing monasteries built. They sought to make the Indians afraid of the Christian teaching, and twice they burned the monastery and church at Valladolid, so that the friars were obliged to live among the Indians. When the natives rose in revolt against Spanish ill-treatment, the Spaniards charged the priests with having incited them to rebellion. Investigation proved that at the time of the uprising, the priests had not yet arrived in the particular province where it occurred. By night the Spaniards watched the friars, trying to take them in some sort of a scandal with the Indians in order to discredit them, and finally they ceased to give them alms.[24]

It will be remembered that the possession of an *encomienda* carried with it the obligation to indoctrinate the Indians, yet Diego de Robles writes in 1570 that there is no *encomendero* anywhere who gives any attention to it.[25] Mendieta declares that the Spaniards did everything possible to discredit the padres before the Indians and make it impossible for them to secure the punishment of the Indians for such things as the ecclesiastical court was empowered to punish, and further that they made it impossible to oblige the Indians to assemble together for instruction. Evidently, from this statement, the friars were accustomed to rely to no small extent on the pressure of authority in order to get the Indians together for their teaching.

Chief among the hindrances to the conversion of the Indians was the evil example of the Spaniards. It is only

[24] Landa, *Relación de las Cosas de Yucatán,* pp. 94-96.
[25] Quoted by Cuevas, *op. cit.,* II, 33.

necessary to recall the make up of the army of conquest to understand how real a difficulty this was. Adventurers, many of them, inspired, partly at least, by a greed for gold, unscrupulous in their methods of getting it, and morally, exceedingly vicious, it is little wonder that their example hindered the progress of conversion. Some insight into the character of the early Spanish settlers is found in one of Cortés' own letters. He writes to the effect that if all the Spaniards who were already there and who were to come were like the friars or were interested principally in the conversion of the Indians, their conversation with them would be profitable, but since the reverse was true, the effect would be otherwise, for he says, "It is notable that the greater part of those who come out are of the baser sort and extremely vicious." If these were to be permitted to move about freely, the Indians would rather be converted to their evil ways. . . . If only there were enough workers for so great a harvest, he would hope for the establishment of the church in the land in a very brief period.[26]

The pious hope of the king expressed in the letter quoted on page 187, that contact between Spaniards and Indians would result in the spread of Christianity, was in fact not borne out. On the contrary, we find writers, both lay and clerical, declaring in the latter half of the century that such mingling of the races was a great evil and urging that steps be taken to bring about a separation. Mendieta, the most forceful of such writers, says:

So great has been the damage to the conversion of the Indians from the fact that the Spaniards and Indians live together that it can hardly be calculated. Not only the Spaniards but the negroes, the mulattos and *mestizos* of various degrees of mixture, by their daily contacts with the Indians, infect them with their vices, not only of words but of shameful practices of every sort which separate men from the love of God and the

[26] Quoted by Cuevas, *op. cit.*, II, 22.

respect of men. If formerly the Indians committed wrong, they did so secretly, but now they have learned not only to do so without shame but even boastingly.

What Indian in their times of infidelity would have dared steal another's wife away and openly go off with her? It would have cost him his life to have done so, nor could he have fled where he would not have been found out.

Formerly the Indians dared not steal; now they have become bandits under the example of the Spaniards and others. Before the Spaniards or those trained by them came to the villages, the houses were without doors, nor was there fear of losing anything even though all should go away to the church. Now, not even doors and locks are sufficient protection, for the thieving Indians climb over walls or break open doors, so that it is necessary for half the people to miss religious services in order to guard the houses.

But, asks one, do not these Indians and servants of the Spaniards attend mass? Not unless they choose, for being servants of the Spaniards they think they can do just as they choose, without anyone being able to order them.[27]

In a memorial through which the chiefs and natives of the City of Mexico seek redress at the hands of the king, we read:

On account of the different conditions and treatment which the Indians and Spaniards enjoy, the frequency of ill treatment of the slaves and servants on the part of the Spaniards, and especially on account of the vices and offenses against God our Lord which the Spaniards, negroes, *mestizos,* and other Indians reared by the Spaniards invent every day, we pray you that the natives and Spaniards be not allowed to live together in the same sections. When they do, they commit many evils, and many illegitimate children are born of adulteries, while the good name of the police and even of Christianity itself is corrupted. Wherefore, we beg your majesty to provide that the Spaniards and Indians live apart.[28]

[27] Mendieta, *op. cit.,* pp. 501 ff.
[28] García Icazbalceta, *Nuevos Documentos para la Historia de México.* IV, 186.

Father Mendieta writing in the latter part of the century has already begun to hark back to the good old days when the Indians in the first flush of enthusiasm for the new religion were faithful in the observance of its feasts as they no longer seem to be. He draws an interesting picture of a feast-day before the corrupting influence of the Spaniards had made itself felt among the Indians.

The night before the feast, the captains of hundreds and of twenties went about among the group for whom they were responsible, reminding them that they should retire early in order to rise early next day for the feast. Again at two or three o'clock in the morning they went about awakening the people and calling them to assemble for their march to the church. When they had come together, they were formed in lines, men and women separately, and marched with a banner at the head of the column, singing songs or reciting the doctrine, to the church. The good father is deeply moved by the memory of it. It was a sight that caused tears of excessive joy to see what the Lord had wrought in this group of Indians who so recently had been engaged in abominable pagan practices.

Reaching the church, they assembled by groups in the *patio* where they were counted, the roll called, and the names of the absent noted. These for failure to appear would later be given half a dozen lashes on the back. Here, before the sermon, one of the older pupils would stand before the group and repeat the Christian doctrine which the people repeated word for word after him, going over the whole of it sometimes twice. Then the preacher ascended the pulpit and preached for more or less an hour. The sermon ended, and the order regarding fasting and other observances having been given, mass was celebrated and the people were dismissed to their homes.

This, however, was before the Spaniards had mixed much with the Indians. With this mingling, the Indians, noting the indifference of the white men to religious practices, became likewise careless until, says Mendieta, "Even though a minister break his head trying to get them together, only those come who so desire, and that not before ten o'clock in the morning or later. Then, before the service can be concluded, they get hungry and want to leave. Yet, the minister does not dare punish them, unless the civil rulers be very favorable. No longer do they call the roll, and when the doctrine is repeated only a few devout women respond. Men, it seems, do not repeat a word, unless the minister himself is present and leads the service.'"[29]

Mendieta felt that the great mistake was in not requiring the Indians and Spaniards to live quite apart from each other. This, no longer possible to require, would have been easy, he thinks. He says:

I remember when many of them, chiefs as well as humbler folk, applied themselves with great diligence to learning to read and write. . . . Then, they besought us with insistence to provide ministers for them and entered into their religious exercises with great enthusiasm; but now we cannot get their children into the schools, nor do they apply themselves to learning. They prefer to be mule-drivers and cartmen, shepherds, farmers, or servants to the Spaniards in order to be free thus from the heavy toll exacted of them in enforced service. Those who do remain in the villages have so much to do to live and work their little fields that they require the service of their children from infancy, forgetting to teach them to know God and to try to serve Him.[30]

One of the serious obstacles to the conversion of the Indians was the drunkenness which, common enough among the Indians, was aggravated by the Spaniards who at first drank the native *pulque* but later introduced Spanish wine

---

[29] Mendieta, *op. cit.,* p. 496.   [30] *Ibid.,* p. 508.

and beer. A letter of one Juan Herrera, to the king on May 15, 1544, tells of establishing a brewery in Mexico City. He says that the natives like beer better than *pulque* and that, judging from the success of the first establishment, a hundred such could be profitably introduced.[31]

In 1529 Bishop Zumárraga had obtained from the royal house a decree against the manufacture and distribution of *pulque,* but like most royal decrees of the time, it remained a mere paper order and had little practical effect. It reads in part as follows:

I am informed that the Indians of New Spain make a kind of wine which they call *pulque* . . . , with which they become drunken, and in this condition return to their old ceremonies and sacrifices. Rendered furious by this drink they lay hands on one another, kill each other, or commit other unspeakable evils by which our Lord is greatly offended. To remedy this situation, it is necessary that the cultivation of the plant from which the drink is made be prohibited. Therefore, we command that you look to the matter, fixing such penalties for an infraction of the law as may seem proper to you—not however a mere fine—and advise us of what you have done that we may consider it. Meanwhile, let whatever you have ordered be obeyed.[32]

The royal legislation regarding *pulque* had little practical effect. Diego de Robles wrote in 1570 of the difficulty of getting officers to enforce the law. He says, "Care must be taken that the *alguaciles* be not robbers who do nothing more than make the rounds of the *pulquerías* and collect hush-money from the proprietors, never going inside or making any report of the true conditions."[33] Mendieta declares that one of the greatest evils wrought by the Spaniards was through the wine which they taught the Indians to drink. Most of the Spaniards living in the villages were tavern-

[31] Quoted by Cuevas, *op. cit.,* II, 28-9.
[32] *Ibid.,* II, 29.
[33] *Id.*

keepers, he avers. The evils which flowed from this were many; fights and killings; many innocent women were slain; and frequently the Indians sold their very clothing for money with which to buy wine. Women sold themselves for it. Chiefs even mortgaged their properties to the Spaniards and, unable to redeem them, became of necessity their servants.

Although the Indians have been charged with being much given to drunkenness before the coming of the Spaniards, Zurita one of the *visitadores* of the king insists in one of his reports that the Spaniards and friars were mistaken in making such a charge. His opinion, based on information got from the older Indians, is that the cause of such frenzied drinking in later times was to be found in the fact that the native judges had lost their old time authority and that the Spaniards were unable to control them.[34] But, while the defense is probably warranted in part, the fact is that drunkenness was common before the conquest and that it was only aggravated by the coming of the Europeans.

The evil wrought by the Spaniards through their loose sexual habits was very great. In this regard the level of Indian morality seems to have been higher than that of the so-called Christians. Witness the declaration of Mendieta quoted above.[35] But not alone by their own illicit relations with the natives did they corrupt them. Impelled by their insatiable desire for wealth, they overrode every law and custom designed to maintain high standards of sexual morality. Mendieta complains that they corrupted the marriage relation by obliging Indians to marry to suit their own convenience. The result was frequently unhappiness, separation, and sometimes bigamy, it having been discovered that in some cases the Indians whom they had obliged to marry were already married and had families in other villages.

[34] *Colección de Documentos Inéditos,* II, 51.
[35] *See ante,* p. 208.

One great evil that the Spaniards wrought by their example was to discredit the word Christian, for it was used, not only at first but for a long time, as the term for the white man as over against the Indian. It was still the custom in vogue eighty years after the conquest when Mendieta wrote. At first it was natural enough and had no evil effect, but after many years of effort to Christianize the Indians, the continued use of the term in that sense could only result in discredit not alone to the word Christian but to Christianity itself. The *mestizo* also was called Christian. If the white men and *mestizos* were called Christian, then why should not the Indian assume that he was not Christian? When the evil character of those who named themselves Christian was so apparent, it was not strange that the natives should say, "If these are Christians, then we do not want to be Christian." Thus they came to abhor not only the name Christian but also the name of Christ himself.

"If you think this is not true," says Mendieta, "go to the Chichemecas for example and tell them the Christians are coming. At once they fly to the mountains with cries of alarm, as one who cries, 'thief, thief!' or 'the enemy!' To the priests they say, 'we welcome you, but do not bring any Christians with you.' Even when they complain of one of the priests who has proved to be unworthy, they say, 'he is like a Christian.' " Fr. Rodrigo de la Cruz offers a similar testimony. He says:

Thus among the poor Indians, when a friar happens to approach, someone says, "Here comes a Christian," but another who sees better says, "No, he is a priest." And if one asks an Indian, "Are you a Christian?" he replies, "No." The Mexicans who best understand the things of God do not call the Spaniards Christians, because they see that they do not act like Christians; but they call them *Castiltecas*.[36]

[36] Quoted by Cuevas, *op. cit.,* II, 23.

We do not consider it necessary to document the declaration that by their evil treatment of the Indians, the Spaniards greatly hindered the Christianizing process. That they did mistreat them terribly needs no extended proof. It is a matter of common knowledge. But, while many matters of common knowledge are in reality misrepresentation, this one is abundantly borne out by even a cursory reading of the historical documents of the period, whether lay or clerical. That there may have been less ill treatment than is commonly supposed, is possible. We have stated elsewhere our opinion that Las Casas did overstate his case; but after discounting the worst of his declarations, there still remains a sad, sordid story of exploitation which resulted in the destruction of countless thousands, not to say millions of lives. It may even be true, as some recent Nordic historians have admitted, that after all the Spaniards were no worse than the English or the Dutch or the French. But that only detracts from the once high estimate of these latter whose shortcomings have generally been minimized by writers of history. None can deny that the Indians of New Spain were cruelly mistreated under the *encomienda* system, and under that of forced labor in the mines which amounted to slavery.

It is no defense, as some have thought, to say that the Spaniards were less ruthless than the emperor Montezuma and his predecessors in their treatment of subject tribes. This may be perfectly true, but it does not justify the Spaniards who were a supposedly Christian people, nor does it disprove in any way their own cruelty. Perhaps no brief word of proof of the cruelty of the Spaniards could be more effective than that of Zurita who quotes a noted priest as recounting an agreement on the part of the Indians of Oaxaca either to have no access to their wives or other women, or to seek some means of avoiding conception, or of causing miscarriage in case of those already pregnant;

because, they said, they could not pay the tribute exacted of them. They did not wish to have children, lest their offspring suffer in the same way they themselves had suffered.[37]

Given this mistreatment as a fact, there can be no doubt that it seriously handicapped the missionaries who tried to demonstrate the superiority of Christianity over the pagan faith. If today the industrial system of the occident as applied in the oriental countries constitutes an obstacle to the acceptance of Christianity by those peoples, it is easy enough to understand how the Spanish exploitation would have hindered the conversion of the Indians, even though the Christian gospel as proclaimed at that time was not conceived as now in social terms.

We have noted as one of the favoring factors in the Christianizing process the high character of the earlier missionaries. Unfortunately, the character of the later priests, so far from aiding, proved in many cases a hindrance. Not that all of them were bad, for consecrated and worthy men, particularly among the religious Orders, continued to find their way to Mexico. The testimony of many writers is, however, that the later arrivals left much to be desired in the matter of character. Motolinia, himself one of the original twelve, sets their attitude in contrast to that of the earlier workers. He charges that some of them lacked perseverance; some preferred only to preach to Spaniards, despising and disliking the Indians, and being unwilling to endure the discomfort and hardship of ministering to them. Such priests he declares "are uncomfortable here and suffer torments until the land throws them off as dead bodies and unprofitable."[38]

But worse things were to be said of them than that they preferred to work among the Spaniards and that some of them returned home, unwilling to endure the hardships and

[37] *Colección de Documentos Inéditos,* II, 122.
[38] Quoted by Cuevas, *op. cit.,* II, 176-7.

difficulties of work in a new field.   Cuevas quotes from a letter which, on the basis of internal evidence, he thinks to have been written by Zumárraga, though bearing the signature of Las Casas.

Seeing every day the disorderly life of the clergy and the evil example which all commonly and for the most part show and have shown in this land, by which the divine things have been brought into great disrepute, I have sought to bring about a reform among them in so far as possible; but I confess at last that I have been able to do but little, for they are so many and so scattered, and I alone cannot be everywhere.   Since this results in harm to so many souls for whom I am responsible to God, I cannot but suspect that I am lost, and, therefore, I live a very uncomfortable life.   Thinking night and day of a remedy, it has seemed best to me that there is no other than to reduce all the clergy, particularly the beneficed clergy, according to the ancient canon law, and in this the other bishops concur.   I am determined to begin, if your majesty will support me in it, to require all the clergy to eat in a common refectory and sleep in a common dormitory, and that when one goes outside in the city he be accompanied by another.[39]

The letter and protests of the bishop that no priests be allowed to go out to Mexico without a royal permit, caused the government to make such a ruling.   By its provisions, any priest or monk desiring to go out must first present himself before his superior, and securing letters of approval, must then present himself in person to the archbishop of Seville.   It was further ordered that no foreign priests be allowed to depart for the Indies without the approval of his superior in Spain and the further approval of the Council of the Indies.[40]

But this proved rather an embarrassment than a help. A little later the bishops wrote Charles V that the actual result of the order was the practice of fraud of one sort or

[39] Quoted by Cuevas, *op. cit.*, II, 132.
[40] *Colección de Documentos Inéditos*, X, 46-8.

another in order to get there, particularly by the worst class of priests; and yet, when they arrived, the need was so great that, much against the will of the church authorities, they were obliged to make use of these priests though they were unworthy. They said, "We hold it a lesser evil that there be priests to administer the sacraments even though they be of an undesirable character than that the natives be wholly without sacraments, especially the holy rite of baptism." The bishops felt that if all the priests who wished to go out were permitted to do so, there would be some good ones at least among them and that the best could be received and the others rejected.[41]

The viceroy, Don Antonio de Mendoza, wrote in 1544: "The priests who come here are unworthy, and come out of self-interest. If it were not for what your majesty has ordered and for the necessity of baptism, the Indians would be better off without them. This is in general; some individual priests are good."[42] The bishop of Puebla in 1556 complained of the weaknesses of the priests and the scandal to which they gave rise, for they were, he said, priests who had fled from their former superiors. They came prompted by avarice rather than zeal for the faith, wherefore, being either ignorant or covetous, they did not deal with the things of the faith with the force or the purity and apostolic freedom necessary.[43]

It became necessary for the councils to take notice of their conduct, so we find the second and third councils prohibiting certain styles of dress which indicated luxury, extreme worldliness and extravagance. They were not to ride horses but mules, since horses were a luxury. Still later there were prohibitions regarding attendance at bull fights, masquerading, taking part in plays, going abroad in secular garb at night, serenading with music, and finally, carrying arms.[44]

[41] Quoted by Cuevas, op. cit., II, 133.
[42] Ibid.   [43] Ibid.   [44] Ibid., II, 134-5.

According to a letter of Fr. Juarez de Escobar, an Augustinian friar, to Philip II, the priesthood had evidently become engaged in business concerns to the detriment of the church, for he recommended that no minister to whom was entrusted the indoctrination of the Indians be allowed to engage in commerce, mining, etc., for, he said, "it is a scandal and evil example to the Indians. They ought rather to go two by two, live modestly, etc."[45] Further, the clergy, neither regular nor secular, ought to receive money for the administration of the sacraments, for, "besides smacking of simony, it works great injury to the Indians, since, if two *reales* is charged and the native has not that to give, he must remain without the sacrament; or requiring a *tostón* for marrying, the natives remain unmarried for lack of money; and the children die without baptism simply because the parents have not the four or five *tomines* which is charged for the rite."[46]

Other abuses are described in a letter to a member of the royal court by one Dr. Caceres. He complains that when the king has given money to bring out twenty-five priests, only six arrive, the rest of the money being used for other purposes; moreover, the priests designed for one place are sent to another. There are wandering priests who cause a great deal of trouble. This leads to the suggestion that priests be sent only with license and ordered to present themselves to the civil government of the country which should report back the arrival; and that after arrival in a certain place, they be not permitted to leave without government permission.[47] No priest, he thinks, ought to be allowed to remain more than two months in a place unless he intend to make it his fixed residence. After that time he should be obliged to submit to the direction of the local prelate or monastery.[48]

[45] *Colección de Documentos Inéditos,* XI, 206.
[46] *Ibid.*   [47] *Ibid.,* XI, 64-5.   [48] *Ibid.,* p. 76.

In another document bearing the date 1572, the need of regulating the building of churches is stressed, especially with reference to the secular clergy who "all desire to live with great show, trying to appropriate to their own uses the church funds, and then do not efficiently serve their parishes, being frequently absent, trying to enrich themselves and return to Spain."[49] In 1562, King Philip found it necessary to ask the Dominicans and Augustinians to observe their vow of poverty.[50] The archbishop reported in 1575 that there were one hundred and fifty-eight secular priests in his archdiocese. Of these seventy-eight were born in the country, seventy-one were from the peninsula, and nine were foreigners.[51] The general opinion seems to have been that those born in the country were more worthy than those from abroad, for they were trained chiefly by the monks, and were from families which were known and respected. They doubtless felt social pressure more keenly than those from overseas, which fact kept them on a higher moral level.

Cuevas thinks that conditions grew steadily better toward the end of the sixteenth century, due in part to the activity of the Inquisition and to the greater care given to the preparation of the priesthood. The founding of the University in 1555 was one of the chief influences in that direction.[52]

Of great importance, because of its bearing on the total problem of the conversion of the Indians, was the conflict between the regular and the secular clergy as to the administration of the parishes. According to canonical law, the secular clergy were by right the proper parish administrators. However, the circumstances under which the earlier work of conversion was carried on made it necessary that the friars

[49] *Ibid.*, p. 158.
[50] Gonzalez Dávila, *Teatro Eclesiástico*, I, 34.
[51] Cuevas, *op. cit.*, II, 138.
[52] *Ibid.*
Note. There were ninety-three laws which had to do with monks alone in the Code governing the Indies.

should exercise this function, since for years they were the only ones in New Spain. Furthermore, by an especial papal dispensation, the Franciscans, under Martín de Valencia, had been empowered to carry on the regular parish work. The other Orders, while having no definite authorization, followed the same practice which, of course, was sanctioned by every canon of common sense. The work must be done. The secular clergy were few in comparison to the rapidly increasing number of centers which were being evangelized. They could not possibly care for all of them, so for a quarter of a century the Orders continued their parish administrations. By the middle of the century, however, the secular group began to assert themselves and desired to take over the care of the parishes which the regular clergy had built up since the beginning.

Out of the charges and counter-charges made to the emperor appear some valuable facts regarding both sides of the controversy. It seems beyond question that, outside of the chief centers where the Spanish settlers and their descendants formed a considerable part of the population, the regulars had every advantage over the secular priests. In the first place, they were generally able to use the native tongue while many of the secular branch never made any attempt to acquire it. Many of the monks were learned men, masters of one or more of the native languages, authors of books, dictionaries, grammars, and catechisms. "Who," asks one of them, "who of the regular clergy has ever produced a book? Which of them does not seek out monks at special seasons to aid him in his confessions, because of his ignorance of the language?"

Then too, the character of the friars was much higher than that of the other group. While there were abuses among the Orders, the greatest evils were found among the secular priests. The latter, in general, were much more likely to be actuated by motives of self-interest than the former. The poverty and the humility of the mendicants greatly endeared them to the humbler Indian folk. The firm resistance offered by the Indians when it was desired to transfer certain parishes that were under the care of the Franciscans to others, indicates the hold which the humble brothers of the poor seemed to have upon the Indians.

This controversy, drawn out over a considerable period of time, could not but detract from the effort which should properly have gone into the conversion of the Indians. In a field too big for the combined secular and regular forces to evangelize, division, jealousy, and hostility between the groups inevitably interfered with the work. Perhaps of event greater adverse effect than that of loss of efficiency on the part of the priests engaged in strife was the spectacle presented to the Indians of rivalry and enmity among those who were seeking to bring them to the faith. Certainly the conflict of the priests must be charged with being an important factor in hindering the conversion process. Despite retarding factors, however, the work of Christianization went steadily on. We turn now to examine the results achieved by the various methods which were used to introduce Christianity into the land.

Chapter VII

RESULTS OF THE EFFORTS AT CONVERSION

NUMERICAL RESULTS

It is our purpose in this chapter to attempt to measure the results of the efforts put forth by the emperor, the conquerors, viceroys, local governors, and the missionaries who came to share in the conversion of the Indians to the Christian faith. We shall note, first of all, the actual numerical growth of the Christian community, in so far as it can be ascertained. We shall see the gradual increase in the building of churches, the founding of institutions, the introduction of the different sacraments and other ritual practices. We shall present cross-sections of the state of religion at various stages and try to evaluate in moral terms the effect of the preaching of the gospel among the natives. Two or three special phases of the total result will be treated in the following chapter on the developing native church, because it is assumed that the importance of the subject warrants its separate handling.

Obviously, any attempt to secure accurate statistics regarding the progress of the Christianizing process must meet with failure. Some estimates are not lacking, however, and some of these are presented, not because it is supposed that they are even approximately correct, but because they serve the purpose of helping to see how exceedingly rapid was the progress in the earlier years following the conquest.

The earliest estimate we have comes from a source which entitles it to respectful consideration, for no other knew more thoroughly what was being accomplished than Zumárraga, first bishop of Mexico. In a letter of June 12, 1531, only seven years after the entry of the Franciscans, he wrote:

We are very busy in the great task of converting the Indians. More than a million five hundred thousand of them have been baptized at the hands of our own Franciscan fathers. Temples of idols have been destroyed and more than twenty thousand idols ground to dust or burned. In many places churches have been built and the cross raised up and worshipped by the Indians. What seems most wonderful is that where formerly, in their infidelity, they were accustomed to sacrificing as many as twenty thousand human hearts, now they offer themselves not to evil spirits but to God, with innumerable sacrifices of praise, thanks to the teaching and excellent example of our priests, who are greatly respected by the children of the natives. Many of these converts fast and pray and discipline themselves with tears and sighings. Many of them know how to read and write and sing. They confess frequently and receive the holy sacrament with great devotion, and with joy preach the word of God to their parents, trained to do so by the priests. They rise at midnight for matins and are particularly devoted to Our Lady. They take the idols away from their parents and bring them to the priests, for which some of them have actually been killed by the parents and crowned by Christ in glory.

Each of our convents has a school alongside it and a dormitory, dining room, and chapel. The children are humble and obedient to the priests whom they love as fathers. They are chaste and quite clever, especially in painting, and have achieved a good heart before God.[1]

Another estimate is furnished by Motolinia who fortunately states the bases of his calculations. The numbers seem too well rounded to admit of very strict accuracy. The fact that his two different methods of counting lead to such different estimates does not tend to raise one's confidence in either one or the other. He says:

The number of baptized I count in two ways, one by the villages and provinces which have been baptized, the other by the number of priests who performed baptisms. There are at present in this New Spain a matter of sixty Franciscans, for of the other priests few have been given to baptizing, though some have—how many I do not know. Beside the sixty, twenty

---

[1] Quoted by Gonzalez Dávila, *Teatro Eclesiástico,* I, pp. 26-7.

probably have returned to Spain, having baptized many before their return, and another twenty have died who also baptized very many, especially our father Fr. Martín de Valencia, who was the first prelate in this country, and Fr. García de Cisneros, Fr. Juan Caro, Fr. Perpinán, and Fr. Francisco de Valencia, who baptized over ten thousand each. Of the sixty who are at present in the country (1536), I take out twenty who have not baptized, either because they are new or because they do not know the language. To the forty who remain, I attribute each one hundred thousand or more, for some have baptized two hundred thousand, some one hundred and fifty thousand, and some many less. Wherefore taking into account those baptized by priests who have since died and by those priests who have returned to Spain, there must be today about five million baptized.[2]

By villages and provinces, his count carries him to the astounding total of nine million. During Lent of the year 1536, in the single province of Tepeyacac by actual count, over sixty thousand souls were baptized.

Bishop Fr. Julian Garcés, of Tlaxcala, wrote to the king in 1541:

I baptize three days a week and confirm at the same time those whom I baptize. Every week I baptize three hundred and twenty or three hundred and thirty, never less than three hundred, and usually more.[3]

It is an easy matter to calculate that such a program of baptisms in a year would care for over fifteen thousand. In seven years he would have passed one hundred thousand, in ten years he would have reached one hundred and fifty thousand. It now seems well nigh incredible. Of course it can only be understood when one takes account of the method of indoctrination employed.

Gonzalez Dávila, writing in 1649 and having in mind not alone Mexico but the whole of Spanish America, declared:

---

[2] Motolinia, *op. cit.,* XI, Cap. iii.
[3] Quoted by Cuevas, *op. cit.,* I, 334.

So many there were who came to the obedience of the law of Christ and the worship of the cross that the Franciscans and Dominicans and a few secular clergy baptized more than ten million souls without counting what the others who served in the field did.

Commenting on Plutarch's characterization of Caesar's greatness, he says:

What would he say of the fame and the accomplishments of the renowned captains of our Christian doctrine, masters of the infallible truth who gave life thereby to innumerable kings and provinces and so many regions that it is difficult even to count them with exactness, who lived in the region of death, offering when necessary to do so for their salvation, their very life blood in martyrdom.[4]

A modern Jesuit becomes eloquent as he contemplates the work wrought by these doughty religious pioneers in the new world.

If the conquest of Mexico in the temporal sense is called an incredible heroic poem, the spiritual conquest, the founding of the Catholic church in the land of Anahuac is even more, the realization in history of the sacred poem of peace and love.

In only a quarter of a century, thousands of *teocallis,* bulwarks of Satan, and the most barbarous in the world, were reduced to dust. In a quarter of a century, with enviable zeal and method, eight millions of Indians were brought to profess, understand, and love the laws of government and truth condensed in the doctrine of the Catholic church; everywhere were raised up living institutions of charity, of instruction, and of sound and much to be desired justice.

And in this land, blessed by the Mother of God and fertilized by the blood of martyrs of both races, three religious orders with the enthusiasm of youth and a strong episcopacy, planted the gigantic, fruitful, and holy tree of the supernatural order, propagating the doctrine and sacraments of the Divine Redeemer of the world, Jesus Christ, our health; consoling thus, civilizing, and saving men and peoples. When this poem

[4] *Teatro Eclesiástico,* I, 3.

is seen to be an historic reality, well documented, one may well cry before all the world, and looking toward Tepeyacac, *"Non fecit taliter omni nationi."*[5]

During the first year of their residence in Mexico the friars were almost wholly occupied in learning the language and but seldom went outside of their monasteries to visit the surrounding villages. Unable as yet to preach in the native tongue, and having but few who could interpret for them, there were not many baptisms during the year 1524. First they baptized their pupils whom they had trained in the doctrine in their schools, some earlier, some later, according to their degree of progress in the faith. If those outside brought small children, these were baptized, for it was thought that on reaching the age of discretion, they would be Christians.

Adults from the outside were treated like the pupils. They taught them the Christian doctrine. When they had progressed sufficiently in this they were admitted to baptism. There were very few of these in 1524. In the case of the sick, less strictness was observed; enough that they showed complete faith, devotion, and contrition for their sins. In the earlier days, baptism was only by water and the sacramental words, for lack of oil and chrism. Later, those so baptized were recalled and these elements were employed.

It was not long before delegations began to come from outlying villages begging the priests to go and visit them. The calls soon became more numerous than they could possibly attend with their limited number of workers. As the missionaries became more proficient in the use of the languages they began to itinerate and to instruct the people for baptism. So great was the respect which the Indians had for the priests, that, seeing them and hearing their word, they

[5] Cuevas, *op. cit.*, I, 452.

at once brought their idols and destroyed them and set up crosses and began the work of building churches.

From Cuitlahuac the chief sent to Mexico City to ask Martín de Valencia to come to his village. He went, and none surpassed this chief in the number he assembled to hear the message. The chief spent most of the night talking with him and hearing the word of God. Next day he pleaded with Fr. Martín to baptize him, for he renounced the evil spirits which had until then deceived him and desired to be a servant of the Redeemer of the world. Seeing the devotion and the importunity of the chief and knowing him to be a man of much intelligence who understood what he was doing, Valencia catechized him and baptized him, giving him the name Don Francisco. This man gave proof of his Christianity, for as long as he lived, his village stood out above all others as an example of good government. He sent many children to the monastery in the capital and erected several churches.[6]

On another occasion Valencia, accompanied by another monk, went out to Xochimilco, one of the towns of the valley, where he was received with great honor. The people were assembled in great numbers to hear the message. So great was their belief in the example and holiness of life of the priests that, seeing and hearing them, they had no answer to make, except to bring their idols and publicly destroy them. They erected crosses and fixed certain sites for the erection of churches. They literally begged to be taught and to receive baptism. And while they were still in this village, representatives from yet other villages came begging that the priests visit them also.[7]

Motolinia gives a vivid description of the eagerness and enthusiasm of the Indians for the Christian songs and prayers in the early days. He declares that they filled the *patios* of the churches and schools, singing and learning the doctrine

---

[6] Mendieta, *op. cit.*, III, 261.   [7] *Ibid.*, p. 252.

for three or four hours at a time. On every hand, day and night, they could be heard singing and reciting the doctrine. The Spaniards were amazed at the fervor and the enthusiasm with which they learned it.[8]

BAPTISM

The description which Mendieta gives of the great numbers that came seeking baptism reminds one very much of the mass movements in India today. These people were not obliged to come. They were not driven to become Christians. It is true that idolatry was forbidden and that human sacrifice was banned, but little pressure seems to have been put upon them to make them Christian. We have already cited proof that the Spaniards were openly hostile to their conversion in many cases. Yet they continued to come. It became impossible for the priests to handle them with the care that ought to have been exercised. It is probable that they resorted to the custom of mass baptism, that is, the sprinkling of a whole group at a time with drops from the hyssop. It will be recalled that Archbishop Ximenes thus baptized the multitudes of Moors who, under pressure, sought baptism.[9]

Mendieta denies that there were wholesale baptisms in the early days. He says that one of the original twelve affirmed that no member of his own order did any such thing, and that he was sure that none of the other orders did so, for they were very careful in all that they did. Yet, in treating of baptism the first council in 1555 had the matter of mass baptism under discussion and agreed that henceforth it should be administered but twice a week, on Sunday morning and Thursday afternoon. The procedure of the early Catholic fathers was cited as justification for the practice of group-baptism. In a book prepared especially for the instruction and guidance of the priests to the Indians in a section on the

---

[8] Motolinia, *op. cit.*, p. 30.   [9] *See ante*, p. 12.

administration of the sacraments, it is specifically stated that "plural baptism is not allowable except under conditions of extreme necessity."[10]   It seems hardly likely that the matter would have come up for discussion, had there not been at least some who were practicing it.

Under the circumstances, it is not to be wondered at that abuses crept in and that, probably, very many were baptized who were in no way prepared to receive the rite.   In the first place, the number of priests was so small and their helpers were of such limited preparation that thorough indoctrination could not have been given to such vast numbers as received the sacrament of baptism.   In the second place, the fanatical zeal of the missionaries, their conception of the near magical powers of the rite, and their consuming desire to save souls, must have induced many of them to hasten the process unduly.   Cuevas, the modern Jesuit historian, with more partisan feeling than clear historical judgment, warmly defends the early priests.   He says:

It is a malignant injustice to suppose that those Franciscans, sufficiently expert in their duties and some of them very learned, should have labored so against their knowledge and their conscience, baptizing uninstructed neophytes. The difficulties, which being so rudimentary that they have occurred even to impious lay writers, must naturally have occurred to those instructed and sanctified apostles, and they must have given them the proper solution.[11]

But the action of the First Council specifically requiring certain very definite and careful preparation would hardly have been taken had there not been reason therefor.   The Council declared:

We command that no priest or monk administer the sacrament of baptism to any adult except he be sufficiently instructed in the holy faith, free from idols and the ancient rites, legally

[10] *Advertencias para Confesores de Indios,* Index, 1601.
[11] Cuevas, *op. cit.,* II, 187.

married, and having restored every thing wrongfully usurped. Let the chiefs be advised of this, that only with pure faith can they be converted to this Faith, and only thus will they receive the sacrament at their urgent request, unless in time of danger of death.[12]

Current criticism of hasty baptism is found in occasional letters of the period. Gerónimo López wrote the emperor in 1541 regarding the errors which he felt had been committed in the Christianizing process. He declared that some Indians were baptized repeatedly, indeed as often as the rite was offered, since they had no adequate idea of what baptism meant.[13]

In the early days the ceremony was performed only with water, for lack of oil and chrism, and was much less elaborate than that practiced in the old established churches. So many were seeking baptism that the missionaries very sensibly decided that it would be better to modify somewhat the formality of its administration than to turn the people away. But with the coming of the Dominicans, Augustinians, and secular priests, differences of opinion arose. Some wanted to limit baptism to only two days in the year. Those who held this doctrine were like the priest and the Levite rather than the good Samaritan, bitterly remarks Mendieta, "for they do not understand the work of converting the Indians; they do not learn the language; they do not love the people; they shrink from the nakedness and odor of the poor people and some even declare that they do not care to employ their years of study and preparation with beings so stupid and so bestial as the Indians."[14]

How could a priest attend to all the demands upon him, of marrying, confessing, catechizing, preaching to multitudes, and still baptize three thousand in a day, if he must

---

[12] *Concilios Provinciales*, p. 43.

[13] García Icazbalceta, *Colección de Documentos para la Historia de México*, I, 148.   [14] Mendieta, *op. cit.*, p. 268.

use the complete formal baptismal ceremony? "Who," asks Mendieta, "could furnish enough saliva to put on so many people, even if he drank constantly? What church or temple would hold such multitudes, for in that time there were but few buildings and it was necessary to baptize out of doors, and at times even without the lighted candle, for the wind would blow it out."[15]

The controversy was carried to the provincial council and thence to the pope who issued a Bull in 1537 declaring that the early missionaries who baptized without the full ceremony had not committed sin, given the peculiar circumstances that prevailed, which might be considered under the canon of urgent necessity; but that in the future, except in cases of urgency, the regular ceremony of the church should be employed, at least including four things: (1) That the water be properly sanctified; (2) that each be catechized and exorcised; (3) that salt, saliva, *el capillo,* and candle be used at least for two or three of the group being baptized together; (4) that oil and chrism be used. The interpretation of "urgent necessity" was still open to difference of opinion and some were disposed to consider the pressure of numbers in that category; but, generally, it was not so considered. The use of the whole elaborate ceremony naturally entailed much extra labor. Mendieta's description of the baptism and wedding of three thousand in a day is here introduced, as showing how the priests worked.

The Indians were placed in rows, properly paired. While they stood still, one priest passed along applying the oil of catechumens. On receiving the oil, they marched in order past the baptismal font, with lighted candles in their hands, and were there baptized by another priest; they then returned to their original place, where the priest who had administered the oil now administered, in order, the chrism. Meanwhile, the priest who had performed the baptism came down the line joining the couples in matrimony.[16]

There was a period of some months, while the whole question of baptism was under discussion, when no baptisms were supposed to be administered. Many came at that time seeking it, but none would perform the ceremony. Finally, in the convent at Guacachula, they could no longer bear to see the Indians turned away and began to baptize them. At first they came by two hundreds, then three hundreds, and so on until they were coming by thousands, some from a day's journey, some two, some four and even farther. They came, children and adults together, old men and women, sick and well. The old people who were baptized brought their children, the sons their parents, wives their husbands, and husbands wives. They were taught two or three days, though many of them had been instructed before they came. Many received the sacrament with tears. "Who would dare to say that they came without faith when they came from such distances?" says Mendieta. In five days the two priests claimed to have baptized fourteen thousand five hundred Indians. This continued for three or four months. So highly important was baptism in the minds of these missionaries that they trained Indian helpers who might perform the rite in case of serious illness or imminent danger of death, if no ordained priest was at hand.

CONFIRMATION

Confirmation was not practiced early in Mexico. It is, of course, ordinarily administered only by bishops, but the privilege of confirmation was granted to the friars by Leo X, in case no bishop were available. Motolinia seems to have been the only one who practiced it before the coming of the first bishop Zumárraga, according to the *Códice Franciscano*.

[16] *Ibid.*, p. 274.

CONFESSION

The practice of confession among the Indians was first introduced, according to Fr. Julián Garcés, in Tezcuco in the year 1526.[17] Once accustomed to confess, they were apparently very zealous in doing so, indeed the priests were quite insufficient in number to hear them all. Garcés says of them that in confession they had the simplicity of doves and that for purposes of confession, the whole year was Lent. He writes of their willingness to make restitution when ordered to do so. They far excelled the Spaniards in this respect. Confessors preferred to confess twenty Indians rather than one Spaniard. Sometimes they made their confessions in writing, which, it will be recalled, had been done in their confession to the pagan goddess.[18] Motolinia says that one time during Lent in Cholula, so many came desiring to confess that he was unable to hear them all. Finally he announced that he would only receive such as brought their confessions of sin in writing, in the peculiar form of picture writing which they employed. To his surprise great numbers of them came with written confessions so that in a very few minutes he was able to confess each one.[19]

Remarkable stories of restitution of large sums of money and lands and animals are recorded by Motolinia and Mendieta. Some even restored property rights usurped by their parents. Well does the writer ask, "Can any one doubt the sincerity of the first Aztec Christians?" Obviously, not that of the Indians of whom the stories were told. It seems quite likely, however, that the cases of faithfulness would be more freely recorded than those of remissness. They fulfilled their penances without remonstrance and, according to Motolinia, sometimes when they were not required to lash them-

[17] Quoted by Cuevas, *op. cit.*, II, 204.
[18] *See ante*, p. 70.
[19] García Icazbalceta, *Documentos para la Historia de México*, I, 122.

selves, they cried, "Why do you not discipline us?" for they held such to be a great favor, and many of them practiced it every Friday during Lent.[20]

The *Códice Franciscano* reports to the Royal Council of Indies the care with which the priests handled the numerous confessions which their very limited number was obliged to hear. Again, it is but just to observe that this probably represents theory rather than actual practice, or at best only the practice of the most conscientious and genuinely disinterested members of the clergy. If we are to credit the reports given in another connection, it is impossible to suppose that such practice was anything like universal. We do not quote literally, but summarize the statement of the Codex.

During Lent all the clergy who understood the native languages were relieved of all other tasks and were busied from early morning till night in confessing, except during mass and meal hours. Thus, they confessed from forty to sixty or more a day, for the Indians were more easily confessed, in their simplicity, than the Spaniards. Also, they were better prepared for it. The preparation ordinarily given the Indians was, first, an examination as to their knowledge of the doctrine; the Pater Noster; Ave Maria; Creed, Salve Regina; the fourteen articles of faith; the commandments of God, and the five of the church; the seven mortal sins and the general confession. If they did not know these they were taught them before they could confess.

Next they were taught the necessity and efficiency of the sacrament of penance by which sins were forgiven and the sinner made right with God. The three parts of it were, contrition, confession, and satisfaction. The order was, first, to remember the sins which had been committed and remembering them to feel contrition for having committed them, especially for having offended God who is so worthy

[20] *Ibid.*, Chap. V.

of love and honor; then, confession of the sins with the purpose of not committing them again, and, finally, the carrying out of the penance which the confessor might prescribe, making what restitution might be ordered.

The third step was to give them certain advice, such as telling them that if any sins had been kept back in former confessions or any penance not carried out, they should declare it without fear, since the priest was there to help, not to injure them; that they were to talk with the priest not of their troubles but only to confess their sins; and finally that they must not accuse others of any wrong nor try to put the blame upon them. These talks were given Sundays after dinner, when all those who were to confess the following week were assembled. They were then advised as to the day and hour when they were to appear for their confession.

The fourth step was the reading each day to those who came for confession, in order to aid their memories, of a list of the things in which people ordinarily commit sin, including the ten commandments and the mortal sins, pausing on each one to explain or to recall to their minds such acts as might fall under it. It was probably such a reminder from which we quoted on page 162.

Having made such preparations, it was possible sometimes for a priest to confess over a hundred in a day.[21] Although the great rush to confess was during Lent, some priests were kept busy all the year through, confessing many people every day, including the sick who were usually brought to the church, borne by the neighbors. The priests made it an almost invariable rule not to enter the homes of the Indians to hear confessions except in case of some of the more important chiefs. If too far to carry them to the church, the patients were usually at least carried outside the house for the confession.

[21] *Códice Franciscano* (Ed. García Icazbalceta), pp. 97 ff.

Mendieta tells of the extraordinary fervor of the Indians to confess during the early years. He says it frequently happened that on the roads a thousand or more Indians would follow the monks begging to be allowed to confess. Many women came, he says, some of them pregnant, and giving birth to their children on the way, and most of them carrying babies; old men and women came, tottering along with canes or crutches; some blind men were carried fifteen or twenty leagues in search of a confessor. Strong, well Indians came as far as thirty and even eighty leagues. Mendieta, writing certainly after 1554, declares that he himself witnessed such crowds on the roads as to make the friars lose patience at the delay, for they could not have attended to so many confessions without remaining several days. Yet neither arguments nor threats were sufficient to make the people go away. He tells of one priest who had to cross the lake in a boat and who was followed by many canoes full of Indians, some of whom leaped into the water trying to get to him first to confess. The pious friar is reminded of the crowds that surrounded Jesus when he walked through the country. Sick people were carried out to the road where a priest was to pass, in order that he might confess them. They had the custom of building little shelters of branches and leaves to protect the patient while he waited. This custom persisted still when Mendieta wrote.

What was it that drew these hosts of simple folk to seek confession? For, while Mendieta may have exaggerated somewhat the numbers who came, there must have been many. It does not seem to have been force, for they were in no sense obliged to do this, even if they had been forced to accept baptism. No economic benefit would result to them from it. Apparently they even wearied the priests themselves and sorely tried their patience by their insistence. Was it superstition, fear, or contagion which produced the phenomenon? Probably all of these entered. Or was it that there was a genuine spiritual stirring among a people ripe for the appearance of such a new faith? It may seem unscientific to say so but it does not seem impossible to this writer that such was the case. Here was a great opportunity for the spiritual conquest of a race. Some of the early priests were real spiritual leaders who sought to take advantage of the favorable movement toward Christianity. That the movement was stifled and mishandled, and a great opportunity lost through the cupidity and ruthlessness of the Spanish settlers and the lack of real spiritual interests on the part of many of the later clergy, does not at all disprove the genuineness of the acceptance of Christianity by many of the Indians in the earlier stages of the process.

THE EUCHARIST

The *Códice Franciscano* says that the sacrament of the eucharist was given to very few natives at first, and there were diverse opinions regarding it until a Bull came from Paul III, which, in view of the information he had concerning them, ordered that they be not denied it, but that it be administered to them the same as to other Christians.[22] Despite this Bull, the Indians were still not commonly admitted to the eucharist. In 1578 we find the king writing to the archbishop as follows:

We are told that in those provinces there are some Indians, good Christians, capable of receiving the sacrament of communion, to whom it is denied. After consideration in our Council of the Indies, it has appeared wise to us to order that they be not deprived of so great good and spiritual consolation.[23]

To this the *Códice Franciscano* answers,

Many Indians seek communion with great insistence and importunity, and to some of them it is denied, as already said,

[22] *Ibid.*   [23] *Ibid.*, p. 102.

because to some of the ministers it seems best. Other priests try to draw them to it since they find in them great sincerity and intelligence regarding the things of God. Some refuse it, saying that they are not yet prepared for so high a blessing from God, and postpone it for another year, declaring that they will try to prepare themselves for it.

However, even so, many do commune, especially during Lent, wherever there are *frailes*. In some villages as many as three thousand, or four thousand, or five thousand, in others fewer, according to the population, and also the care and diligence on the part of the priest. . . . If they are lax, the people soon fall away.[24]

According to this codex, definite preparation is made for the sacrament, the same as for the confession.[25] In brief summary, it is as follows: They must first satisfy their confessor that they are in conscience ready for it, that is they must have confessed and done penance. Second, they must know the articles of the Trinity of the Persons; the unity of the divine essence; the incarnation and passion of the Son of God and how he himself is in the Sacrament of the Altar, after the priest, using the words of the Redeemer himself has consecrated the bread and wine. In addition a talk is always given them about the divine Mystery. Third, the day before communion a talk is given on the cleanliness which is required of those who partake of the body of Christ, and on the necessity of their coming as clean as possible, for, although external cleanliness is not the principal thing with God, it is well that it be observed as a mark of high respect for the sacrament. At the same time it is a good example for those who may be present.[26] The same document tells of the good fruit which results from the sacrament. Those who confess and receive it regularly are in comparison with those who do not, "as man and beast." Wherefore, the

[24] *Ibid.*, pp. 103-5.
[25] *See ante*, p. 234.
[26] *Códice Franciscano*, pp. 102-5.

friars are urged to greater activity in getting the Indians to adopt so holy a practice.

EXTREME UNCTION

According to the *Códice Franciscano,* extreme unction was not much practiced among the Indians. "Since it is not 'necessitate salutis,' it is not given ordinarily among them, because they are so numerous and the ministers are so few and so occupied in teaching doctrine and administering the other more necessary sacraments. Nor are the homes of the Indians decent enough for it. To administer it there would be irreverent and would cheapen the sacrament. To bring them to the church when at the point of death would be to hasten the end, so, except in the case of some of the chiefs who ask for it, it is not given. For the chiefs it is administered according to the same form in use among the Spaniards."[27]

MARRIAGE

The first Christian marriage ceremony among the Indians took place in Tezcuco in 1526. The task of marrying the converts became one of the heaviest responsibilities of the priests. Motolinia writes that in 1540, by which time the early rush should have been over, one priest visited the town of Santa Ana and found twenty sick people to confess, two hundred couples to marry, many children and adults to baptize, and a burial, besides the preaching. In another nearby village there were baptized in a day fifteen hundred, using both oil and chrism, and fifteen persons were confessed. A week later in Santa Ana, four hundred more couples were married. In Zumpanzingo, people came from a league round about and four hundred and fifty couples were married. Motolinia records that on a journey of the priests in Tecoac, five hundred were baptized and one hundred pairs

[27] *Ibid.,* p. 109.

married. In one day, in another place, as many as six hundred pairs were joined. In Tlaxcala as many as one thousand pairs were wedded on a single day, and "in other places it was much the same, for there was at this time a fervor for marriage to only one woman among the Indians." This was in 1540. "What must it have been in the earlier years," says Mendieta, "when the eagerness for the sacraments first awoke!"[28]

But the question of marriage was a vexing one for the friars. In the case of young unmarried converts who wished to wed, it was simple, but what of the plural marriages that were so common, especially among the chiefs, for the poorer people generally had but one wife. Should they be allowed to continue in polygamy? Manifestly no. But which was the real wife, or indeed was any one of them really married? Did legitimate marriage exist before the coming of Christianity among the Indians? The question was debated frequently in assemblies of priests and in the first Apostolic Assembly, as Lorenzana calls it, in 1525. It was referred to Spain, three visits being made by priests for consultation on the matter.

A group of learned men, including Cayetano, gave it as their opinion that, when an Indian could not say which of his wives he had taken with real matrimonial intent, he should be allowed to choose the one desired. Previous to this it had been the opinion of a group in Mexico that he should take her who had been the first. Pope Paul III finally issued a Bull in which he declared that to anyone who should come into the faith should be given the first of his wives and in case he should not be able to say which was first, he should be given the one he wished. And even though it were true that another had been the first, in case of any doubt, his conscience should be at ease.[29]

[28] Mendieta, *op. cit.*, p. 300.   [29] *Ibid.*, p. 303.

After the receipt of the Bull of Paul III, an assembly was called in Mexico City, and, after much discussion, it was determined that without any doubt the natives of New Spain had practiced legitimate marriage. The chief difficulty in arriving at this conclusion lay in the frequent repudiation of women by men and vice versa, but "investigation proved that this ease in abandoning a consort had occurred only after they became subject to the Spaniards, for then began a relaxation of the watchfulness and the rigorousness of justice which had before been maintained. Having lost fear, they became bold, and frequently dared to do freely what had been permitted but infrequently before."

Among the Indians, according to Mendieta, separation had generally been sought judicially, and then only for serious reasons. Usually the judge inquired what sort of a union the pair had contracted. If it had been mere cohabitation by mutual consent, little constraint was placed upon them to keep them together, but if they had been joined by the ceremony current among them, every effort was made to reunite them, but they were never allowed to separate.[30]

Motolinia says that, in order to avoid mistakes, there were in each parish persons who knew all the inhabitants, and that in cases of plural marriages they aided in discovering just which had been the true wife. Those who wished to be married by the church came with relatives and friends, and each made allegations as to which was the real wife, and in what way the claims of the others should be satisfied, and they and their children be supported. "It was a sight to see them," said Fray Toribio, "for many of them brought a train of wives and children like a flock of sheep." When these were dismissed, other Indians well trained in the matter, and in the grades of consanguinity and affinity, talked over with the friars the various impediments which had been dis-

[30] *Ibid.*, p. 304.

covered. Any great difficulties were referred to the bishops and their councils to determine. These Indian helpers were called "licenciados."

Some argued that the Indians did not truly marry because they failed to make such fine distinctions as to consanguinity, as was common in Spain, for at times brothers and sisters lived together, sometimes a man lived with his step-mother, and in some cases even with his mother-in-law. However, Mendieta makes this interesting reply. "In this the object-ors are wrong, for they desire to impose upon these in their infidelity the divine law (the Mosaic and evangelical law of which they knew nothing), whereas, the infidels were obli-gated only to the natural law. . . . Wherefore, if they held it a legitimate custom for brothers to marry sisters, then was their marriage a true and legitimate marriage, and being con-verted to the faith they should not be separated, but allowed to go on as before."[31] As a matter of fact, such unions were very rare and utterly insufficient to serve to discredit the institution of marriage itself.

The *Códice Franciscano,* on the other hand, gives a de-tailed statement of how the Franciscans met the problem. We must however, repeat here an observation frequently made throughout the book, that this represents not actual practice, so much as the theory regarding it. That every friar conscientiously followed the prescribed plan, is too much to suppose, particularly when such large numbers of cases had to be handled. Cuevas says, in speaking of this, that until the contrary is proved, we are obliged to suppose that a majority of the priests did practice it. However, this particular statement would apply only to Franciscans, for it was notorious that the orders were not always a unit in their methods of work. So far no such detailed statement regard-ing the matter, coming from either Dominicans, Augus-

[31] Mendieta, *op. cit.,* p. 305.

tinians, or Jesuits, has come to our attention.   We summarize briefly the statement of the *Codice:*

One day of the week is designated on which all those who wish to be married present themselves, so that what would have to be told to each couple may be told them all at one time, thus saving the time of the priests.   Two or three Indians in each village are picked out to help the priests in the matter of doctrine and marriages.   These have the people ready at the time indicated and tell them beforehand that they must answer truthfully whatever they are asked by the priest without any fear, for the priest is their spiritual father, and seeks only their own good, and whatever he asks is only in order that their marriage may be legitimate.

When all is ready the priest appears and examines them, as to:

1. Whether they are baptized, for if they are not, this must be done before they can be married.

2. Whether they are confirmed.   If they are not, they must be the first time the bishop visits their village.

3. Whether the parties belong to that district or another, for if either the man or the woman is from another village where there is a priest, he must be informed of the intended union so that the banns may be published in their native town.

4. Their ages, for minors are not to be married.

5. Whether either is a slave, in order that the other may know it and know whether marital life is to be possible.   If not, they are not received.

6. Whether they are related within the grade of consanguinity to which marriage by the church is prohibited.

7. Whether either has been married before, so as to know whether there exists any impediment to the marriage.

8. Whether they come of their own free will, or whether either is forced into it, in which case the marriage would not be permitted.

After questioning each one individually, the minister advises the relatives present as to what constitutes an impediment to

marriage and urges them to declare it if they know of any
such, for in so doing they serve God and aid their relatives
in being married properly.

It was then required that the banns be published on three
successive Sundays in the church. If the parties to be
wedded had not known the necessary doctrine on first presenting themselves, they were required to learn it. They were
strictly enjoined against cohabitation before the final solem-
nization of the marriage. On the day set for the wedding,
care was to be taken to see that the proper preparation had
been made; a talk was given on the duties involved in
marriage, and the ceremony was performed.[32]

The Christianization of the marriage system was opposed
by two important factors, according to Motolinia. First of
all and perhaps most important were the "ancient carnal
customs" of the Indians which they found it so hard to
abandon. Second, the economic motive was in conflict with
the attempt to introduce monogamy. The possession of
wives was an economic asset, owing to their ability to work,
and the fact that the product of their labors could be sold for
profit. Thus Christian teaching and economic advantage
faced each other in this as in many other phases of the
conversion process.

That abuses should arise out of the confusion resulting
from the attempt to untangle former marriages and assure a
legitimate union, was most natural. One form of such abuse
appears in a letter from one Dr. Anguis, who, Cuevas warns,
was a priest and openly hostile to the friars against whom
he charges the abuses. However, after discounting his statement somewhat, he doubtless does give a not uncommon
picture of current practices. He writes:

I will tell of a case of abuse which I found in the diocese
of Michoacán, and I found so many cases of it that finally, I

[32] *Códice Franciscano*, pp. 105 ff.

gave up the idea of trying to discover a remedy. It happened that Pedro and María, Indians, were married by the church. Then Pedro became enamored of another woman and in order to rid himself of his wife and wed the other, had only to go to the friar and say that when he was married to María by the church, he was already married to the other. At once this was believed, and, without asking for further information the monk dissolved the union and married him to the other woman.

It happened afterward that Pedro became angry and dissatisfied with his latest wife, so he appeared again before the same friar and said that the story he had told on the former occasion was not true and that he had practiced deception in what he said. He asked then that his former wife be returned to him. Meantime, however, she had sought the protection of some other man and had married him. At once, not withstanding the admission of deception, with the same readiness as before, the priest accepted the second story, and there was thus created a matrimonial tangle which God alone could untangle, for there was a confusion of five or six marriages, all solemnized by the church.

This is very common and every day such marriages are performed and dissolved, as I have ascertained by repeated personal observation and investigation of many cases. . . . I sought by writing and by word to get the evils corrected, but accomplished nothing, for the friar simply said that the conscience of each one had to be relied upon. Even the protests of the prelates accomplished nothing more than to provoke a defense by the friars.[33]

THE STATE OF THE CHURCH AT VARIOUS STAGES

From the quotations thus far regarding the rapid progress of conversion, one is apt to get the impression that it was an uninterrupted triumph. But if this did seem to be true during the first few years, disillusionment soon followed, and we find all sorts of discouraging reports from different sections of the country as the century wore on. It is probably fair to assume that Motolinia, Mendieta and other enthusiastic, interested writers would report most fully

[33] Quoted by Cuevas, *op. cit.*, II, 219.

the successes and say less about the failures and difficulties. There is nothing odd in such a supposition. One has only to check his own reports on things in which he is interested to realize the force of such a tendency. Most interested accounts are open to the same criticism, and unfortunately, disinterested, critically historical accounts of the period are not to be had.

It is exceedingly difficult to judge accurately just what was the total situation at any given time. The best we can do, it seems, is to present a series of quotations from documents written at different periods, which reflect conditions at least in a particular section of the country at that time. Most of these are in the nature of reports. Here, one must remember that the whole truth does not always appear. An official desiring help at some particular point may paint a very dark picture of that especial section, while in the rest of his field of work he may be enjoying a real success.

Bishop Zárate of Oaxaca complains in a letter to Prince Philip in 1554 that his diocese is so large that three bishops would be insufficient for it, since it is rough and mountainous and people of many languages inhabit it. There are only two monasteries in the whole territory over three hundred miles long and but eight friars, who are unable, of course, to cover the whole field. "I have personally baptized and confirmed an infinity of Indians," he says, but he has to keep traveling so constantly that he cannot do what he ought to do. He complains of his poverty and the poor support he receives. Later, in 1571 he writes again that there are whole provinces in his area that do not know the true God.[34]

The document which describes in greatest detail the state of the church in all its various phases, is a letter of the archbishop of Mexico to the Royal Council of the Indies, in 1556. He paints a dark picture. It ought to be noted that

[34] *Documentos para la Historia de México,* VII, 543 ff.

he writes with the distinct purpose of securing the use of
the tithes, and it is therefore probable that he overstressed the
existing faults in order to move the members of the Council.
However, there must have been much of truth in what he
wrote.   Certainly no other authority might be supposed to
speak out of a better knowledge of the entire field than the
archbishop, under whose jurisdiction the whole country lay.
He writes:

The state of the church is this.   In some parts there are
monasteries of two or three friars, more frequently two, who
live in one center and visit the country within a radius of two
to thirty or more leagues around.   One priest remains in the
monastery while the other visits sometimes twenty or more
head towns to which still others are subordinate.   So the two
friars frequently have charge of over one hundred thousand
souls.   The towns are visited anywhere from once in two weeks
to once in six months and in some cases not more than two or
three times in five years; moreover, the visits are of necessity
hurried.   The priest arrives late, baptizes and marries those
who are waiting, says mass and passes on.   The people come in
at times to the center of the circuit for mass and the sacraments. . . .

The friars do not like to go out of the monastery to confess
the sick.   They say it is not the practice of their Order and
they only do it of their own free will and as an act of
charity. . . .

Here in Mexico City we would not think it a small matter
if as many as three or four thousand, out of the fifty or sixty
thousand who are accustomed to confess at all, should make
confession in a single year.   The rest of the Indians never confess. . . . There are some who have not confessed in four, ten,
or even twenty years, and others in their whole lives have not
done so; yet in the number of priests this is the best provided
for of all the provinces, and the best Christians are here.   If it
is thus here, what is the case in other places where only once
in a long time do they ever see a priest?

Herein is the great need for ministers. . . . Nearly all
the people die without confession or other sacrament than
baptism. . . .

There is great rivalry among the Orders. Even though there be but one monastery and two friars in an area where not even a dozen would suffice, one Order is unwilling that another come in to help. Each defends its territory as if the villages were its own property. There has been and is great feeling between the Orders, not about which can best care for the flock, but which can have the greatest number of places and provinces in its hands; and so they go, occupying the best centers, building monasteries close together (a league and a half apart) not wishing to live in the difficult and needy places. If we assign a priest to help them, they cause the Indians not to admit him. . . . So great is the fear which the Indians have of the friars because of the severe punishment they practice upon them that they do not dare to complain. And if this is true in the province of Mexico, what of the mountains?

Things being as I have described, and no priest will deny it, very little fruit, it may be suspected, has come of the gospel among the people. Taking out the children, how very few adults have been saved or will be saved? From what has been said and will be said you can easily conjecture. . . .

If the gospel consisted only of holy baptism, we might believe in the salvation of the majority of the people, but since it is true that it is necessary, besides being baptized, to believe and do and perform penance for sins, it would require some new theology to believe and say that some of these adults are saved.

With regard to belief, the fault which we find is that they do not believe those things which are commonly thought by theologians to be necessary, such as the articles of faith and the mysteries which the church celebrates. Many of the people know the articles of faith and the prayers of the church fairly well, though many do not know them, and, of those who do know them, many say them like parrots, without knowing what they mean.

With regard to works and penance, this people is much inclined to vices and carnal practices. Rare are the women who are chaste. They are inclined to drunkenness, stealing, lying, and taking usury. . . . There are few vices they will not commit, and so great is their lack of firmness in the faith that if any other great power, greater than the gospel should come along it would sweep them off their feet.[35]

Six years later, in 1562, Mendieta wrote a letter to the Commissary General of his Order regarding the state of the work at that time. It reads somewhat differently from his history, which we have quoted so much. He says in part:

From what we see and hear in our congregations, everywhere the superiors are resigning. In visiting the convents one hardly finds a single monk who is content and happy. Discontent is manifest everywhere; many are seeking leave to return to Spain. It is a miracle to find a friar who is seriously trying to learn the language, for those who know it use it with so little satisfaction and profit. . . . The old fervor and enthusiasm for the salvation of souls seems to have disappeared. The primitive spirit is dead. The newly converted Indians no longer throng the churches to hear the word, confess or receive the sacraments, etc.[36]

In 1567 Fr. Miguel Navarro writing to the viceroy recounted the necessity of closing eleven monasteries the previous year, owing to the lack of sufficient means, and particularly, the lack of men, due to the death of a number of the older priests, the return of several to Spain, and the failure to get reinforcements. He declared that for three years they had had no word from the crown relative to their repeated requests for additional priests.[37] A letter of Fr. Juan de San Ramón, in 1571, says:

There are many villages in this land where there exists a great need of doctrine, either because of the lack of a priest or because the priests do not handle the language. The bishops do not know the native tongue and have to speak through boys and *mestizos* in whom one cannot trust very much. As a result the state of Christian teaching is so low and so little esteemed by

---

[35] "Carta del arzobispo al Consejo Real," *Colección de Documentos Inéditos,* IV, pp. 494-99.
[36] García Icazbalceta, *Nueva Colección de Documentos,* I, 4.
[37] *Ibid.,* p. 58.

the natives as to make a Catholic weep. What happens is that
the Indians, enlightened by God, come to the viceroy and clamor
for doctrine and wholesome bread, but it is not given them.[38]

In a document bearing the date 1609, two or three villages
are described, indicating the condition of the church and its
support. Of Miguatlan it is said:

> There is one resident *doctrinero* who also visits two other
> villages. This *doctrina* is worth two hundred fifty *pesos* salary
> and with the perquisites, all told, about one thousand *pesos,*
> gold, half paid by the king and half by the *encomendero*. The
> natives pay nothing toward the salary, but the bishop levies a
> tax of five *reales* a year payable on certain feast days. They
> pay first-fruits of corn, *chile* and beans, and provide for the
> priest two Indians to bring wood and water, and two to make
> his bread.
> There are no friars. There were some formerly, but they
> left. No one knows to what Order they belonged. Each year
> the natives appoint a teacher who instructs the children in the
> doctrine and teaches them to read and write. For this he re-
> ceives no salary nor other reward than freedom from the pay-
> ment of tribute and from personal service.[39]

It is interesting to note that in 1644, a date a little beyond the period which our study is supposed to cover, a
petition was sent from Mexico City to Philip IV asking:
1. that no more convents be built, since of nuns, particularly,
there was already an excessive number and their servants
were far more than necessary; 2. that the lands of the convents be limited, otherwise they would be lords of everything
in a little while; 3. that no more monks be permitted to come
out from Spain; 4. that the number of feast-days be limited
because they tended to cause idleness. This may be taken as
an indication of the direction affairs were taking during the
latter part of the sixteenth century. As late as 1769 the

[38] *Ibid.,* p. 105.
[39] *Colección de Documentos Inéditos,* IX, 221-3.

archbishop writes that the governors ought still to see that the Indians attend mass. "It is indispensable until the Indians are more civilized and wish to know."[40]

THE DISAPPEARANCE OF PAGAN IDOLATRY

One of the most obvious results of the conversion efforts was the disappearance of the pagan idolatry. This we have already described, in part, in chapter five.[41] But the mere destruction of the idols and temples was not sufficient to destroy at once the faith of the Indians in their gods, and there was the greatest difficulty in keeping them from reverting to their idolatrous practices. Motolinia says:

Just when the friars were thinking that since they had taken away the idolatry of the temples of the demon, and the people had come to the doctrine and to baptism, all was accomplished, they found the most difficult thing of all, one which required a longer time to destroy, namely the natives gathered together at night and made feasts to the demon according to their various rites.

Later the friars were told how the Indians were hiding their idols and putting them at the foot of the crosses or in the steps below the stones so that while they appeared to adore the cross, they were really adoring the demon.[42]

It seems really remarkable that so swift a success were possible. That it could have been achieved by a form of religion which like modern Protestantism makes no use at all of images, is very doubtful. With the image of the Virgin, the cross, the Christ-child, the saints, and the elaborate ornaments of the church, which could easily become magical objects of veneration, it was possible for the Indian to embrace Christianity with less of a break with his past. He could, under Christian imagery, carry over many of his pagan ideas, and this he unquestionably did. In the last chapter an

---

[40] *Concilios Provinciales*, p. 7.
[41] *See ante*, pp. 163 ff.   [42] Motolinia, *op. cit.*, p. 31.

attempt is made to discover to what degree this was actually done.

Cuevas holds that the destruction of idolatry was almost complete. He writes:

> Idolatry was destroyed among the masses, though here and there cases of it were found. Human sacrifice was completely blotted out. . . . There are those who multiply gratuitously the cases of idolatry, deducing thereby that the Indians generally continued to practice it. The most insistent in sustaining this thesis have not been able to prove the historicity of even thirty cases. Even though they were able to prove three thousand cases, scattered over three centuries and the whole of the nation, it would mean nothing. In 1538 Motolinia wrote: "If there exist in any village an idol, it is either rotten or so forgotten or so secret that in a population of ten thousand souls, not five of them know anything about it and they hold it for what it is, that is, a stone, or as wood. Idolatry is as completely forgotten as if a hundred years had passed.[43]

Tylor quotes Clavigero regarding the charge that the Indians continue to practice idolatry:

> The few examples of idolatry which can be produced are partly excusable, since it is not to be wondered at that uncultured men should not be able to distinguish the idolatrous worship of a rough figure of wood or stone from that which is rightly paid to the holy image. But how often has prejudice against them declared things to be idols which were really images of saints, though shapeless ones. In 1754 I saw some images found in a cave, which were thought to be idols, but I had no doubt that they were figures representing the mystery of the holy nativity.[44]

MORAL RESULTS

What was the practical effect of conversion upon the moral character of the Indians? Any investigation would be incomplete which did not attempt at least to see whether

---

[43] Cuevas, op. cit., II, 20.
[44] E. B. Tylor, Anahuac, p. 206.

the coming of Christianity made people better in their ordinary living or not.   Did Christian morality replace pagan morality?

It would be unfair to judge the results obtained in the moral sphere by twentieth century standards, for the Christianity of the sixteenth century in Spain had little moral content.   The clergy were, many of them, corrupt and licentious.   It is not probable that the life of the people generally was any better, and more than likely it was worse. Reading through the history of the conquest, one is amazed at the deeds which the so-called Christians performed with never a question as to their rightness or wrongness.   Drunkenness, treachery, violation of women, plunder, are found all through the pages of the history of that period, the same history that recorded the pious exhortations of Cortés and the all-night prayer-vigils before battle.   It is difficult to strike a balance. Opinions of writers differ so widely.   One does not know, in the first place, just what the moral standards of the pre-conquest period were, and reports of moral conditions after the coming of Christianity are from sources which are open to suspicion of bias for or against Christianity.   Comparison of the best in Christianity with the worst in pagan faiths has too often been practiced.   On the other hand some of the critics of the church have compared the worst in Christianity with the best in the native practices, an equally unfair comparison.

Sahagún, who, better than any other earlier writer, seems to have represented Indian life and thought, gives accounts of moral instruction which, if correctly reported, would lift it well on to the plane of Christian morality.   It seems almost too ideal, when one reads the accounts of the cruelty of the Indians in their sacrifices and the frequent references in the writings of Bernal Díaz del Castillo, Gómara and others to the corrupt and vicious practices of the natives.   We will not, therefore, make the mistake of supposing that all parents used the forms of instructions we summarize here, nor that all those who were instructed thus obeyed every injunction received; but it is only fair to cite it as an example of what was actually found among them.

Zurita writes that parents were accustomed to give moral instruction and counsel to their children and that they had the instructions written down in the form of paintings such as they were accustomed to use. One of the friars had the substance of the teaching translated for him and wrote it down in Spanish. Then, without a single change, except to divide it up into paragraphs, and substitute for the name of the pagan gods that of the Christian God, he gave it to the Indians for instruction in Christian morality. Zurita does not name the priest, but in Father Olmos' grammar of the Mixteca language is found a code which parallels this so closely, that it was probably he who made the translation. In part it is as follows. We give it in a free translation and much abbreviated.

O my precious son, commend thyself to God that he may help thee, for he created thee and loves thee more than I. Think of him day and night, serve him with love and he will bless thee and free thee from danger. Reverence his images, pray devoutly before them and celebrate his festivals.

He who offends God shall die and great shall be his guilt.

Reverence and salute your elders, comfort the poor and afflicted with kind words and works of mercy.

Honor and love, serve and obey your parents, for the son who does not do so shall not succeed.

Love and honor all, and live in peace.

Have no company with those who, like animals, do not honor father nor mother, and who will not listen to counsel.

Never make sport of the old, the sick, the maimed, or of one who is caught in some sin, but humble yourself before God, lest a like thing befall you.

Do not give poison to any one, for in so doing you will offend God, yours will be the confusion and the harm, and you shall likewise die.

Be honest and well bred and do not bother nor annoy others. Go not where you are not called.

Injure no one. Do not commit adultery, nor be licentious for it is a great vice and destroys those who are given to it and offends God.

Do not be an evil example nor speak indiscreetly; do not interrupt while others are speaking. Unless it be your turn to speak, keep still. If you are asked anything, reply properly without deceit or flattery and without injury to others.

Do not give yourself to fables, tricks, or lies. Do not stir up discord where there is peace.

Seek not pleasure; do not loaf in the streets, the markets, or the baths.

Be not too queer in the matter of dress, for it is a sign of poor counsel.

Wherever you go keep your eyes quiet, not making eyes, certainly not with lascivious intent, for these are the works of the evil one.

Do not take another by the hand or the clothing. It is a sign of lightness.

Do not enter or leave before your elders, or cross in front of them. Always give them the advantage.

Commend yourself to God, for from his hand comes good and you know not when you are to die.

Do not marry without first telling your parents.

Do not be a gossip. If a secret is told you, keep it to yourself.

Do not murmur nor complain if you would live in peace.

Have nothing to do with a woman not your own, but live a clean life.

Offend no one.

If you live with another, be careful to serve and please him.

Be not proud of that which God gives you, nor depreciate others, for you will thus offend God who has given you the honor.[45]

[45] *Colección de Documentos Inéditos*, II, 59 ff.

In addition to these counsels, the text contains numerous directions as to matters of courtesy. Altogether it is an admirable code, in which will be found nearly all the ten commandments, in one form or another.

Sahagún gives also the instruction which mothers were accustomed to give to their daughters. Many of the items concern the care of the home, cleanliness, food, children, etc., but it also contains stern moral teaching, particularly regarding chastity. We quote parts of it, using the translation by Prescott:

". . . One thing remains to be said and I have done. If God shall give you life, see that you guard yourself that no stain come upon you. Should you forfeit your chastity, and afterwards be asked in marriage and should marry anyone, you will never be fortunate nor have true love. . . . See that not more than one man approaches you. . . . When you shall receive a husband . . . beware that you do not commit the treason against him called adultery. See that you give no favor to another, since this, my dear and much beloved daughter, is to fall into a pit without bottom from which there will be no escape. According to the custom of the world, if the crime be known, they will kill you; they will throw you into the street for an example to all people, where your head will be crushed and dragged upon the ground. . . . From this will come a stain and dishonor upon our ancestors, the nobles and senators from whom we are descended. And remember that though no man shall see you, nor your husband know what happens, God, who is in every place sees you and will be angry with you and will also excite the indignation of the people against you, and he will be avenged against you as he shall see fit. By his command you shall either be maimed or struck blind or your body will wither or you will come to extreme poverty for daring to injure your husband. . . . Our Lord is compassionate, but if you commit treason against your husband, God who is in every place shall take vengeance upon your sin and will permit you to have neither repose nor a peaceful life, etc.[46]

[46] Prescott, *History of the Conquest of Mexico,* III, 423-44.

We have elsewhere noted that the priests of the native religion were required to observe chastity and the testimony of all writers is that as a class they were faithful in this regard. While the same could possibly be said of the earliest missionaries, it could by no means be said of the later arrivals who brought over and gave free reign to the vicious customs so frequently practiced by priests in Spain.

Among the Spaniards generally there was little conscience on sex matters. They mingled with the greatest freedom with the native women, and while it is said that the native women gave themselves readily to the Europeans, the economic and political pressure upon them, joined with the near deification of the first white men, may have led them to greater freedom with the Spaniards than with their own people. On the whole, one gains the impression that in matters relating to sex, the contribution of Christianity was not in the direction of higher standards. This is certainly true if the whole century and the subsequent history of the country be taken into account.

Zurita says that the Indians severely condemned lying. Sometimes they even split the lip of a person given to falsehood, "Asked why they now lie so frequently, they say that they learned it from the Spaniards. 'There is no longer any punishment for it,' say the old men, and because of the fear they feel toward the Spaniards, they always try to say the thing that will please."[47]

An early writer says:

If you ask an Indian chief why now, under the law of God, there is more drunkenness and other vices than in the times of their infidelity, and greater shamelessness he will reply that in the time of infidelity, no one did his own will, but what he was ordered to do, and that now our greater liberty has done us harm, for we are obliged to fear or respect no one.

[47] *Colección de Documentos Inéditos,* II, 57.

Evidently the writer was himself convinced that conditions were worse under Christianity than before. The Indian evidently held the same view, though that would be but natural. Zurita writes further:

> On being asked why the Indians were so given to litigation and practiced so many vices, an Indian chief replied: "Because you neither understand us nor do we understand you nor know what you want. You have taken away our good order and manner of government and have replaced it with a system we do not understand, so that we are in confusion and without order or agreement. The Indians are given to law-suits because you have forced it upon them. . . . Where they live separately and have no dealings with you they live in peace, without litigation. If there were suits in the time of our infidelity, they were very few and were speedily concluded, for there was little difficulty in discovering where justice lay, nor did they know the tricks for delaying justice as now."[48]

From a memorial of the things for which the chiefs and natives of the city of Mexico seek some redress at the hands of King Philip, in 1574, we take the following:

> In the time of our infidelity we resorted but infrequently to litigation, and such cases as there were, were disposed of in a short time and without cost. Now, however, that we have turned Christians, we are in constant litigation, natives as well as Spanish, and in it we spend the little we have, at times our lives and our souls. And since it occurs that suits are started for a little matter of ten pesos and we spend one hundred pesos on them, extending over a year or two; seeing this, many of the natives allow their properties to be forfeited because of the excessive cost of securing justice from the Spanish.[49]

It would be utterly unfair to say that there were not many good results from the conversion of the Indians. Mendieta and others present many cases of fine faithfulness on the part

---

[48] *Ibid.*, p. 45.
[49] García Icazbalceta, *Neuva Colección de Documentos para la Historia de México,* IV, 185-186.

of the Indians to the very highest teachings of the gospel, and stories of restitution for sins committed before their conversion. Many of the Indians released their slaves and some who had sold them bought them back again and gave them their liberty. More than one writer has remarked on the ease with which they forgave injuries and insults and sought forgiveness when they themselves had done wrong. Many of them became so genuinely Christian as to forfeit their lives gladly that others might have the benefits of the gospel. It is true that the one great outstanding pagan evil, that of the sacrifice of human life, was completely abolished, yet the total result of the process leaves very much to be desired on the moral side. Observation of the moral situation at the time of the conquest and later has led many to agree with the judgment expressed by E. B. Tylor who says:

As it is, I cannot ascertain that Christianity has produced any improvement in the Mexican people. They no longer sacrifice and eat their enemies, it is true, but against this we must debit them with a great increase of dishonesty and general immorality which will pretty well square the account.[50]

[50] Tylor, *Anahuac*, pp. 289-90.

CHAPTER VIII

THE DEVELOPING NATIVE CHURCH

BRIEF REVIEW OF ORGANIZATION

Although we have made frequent reference to various phases of the organized life of the church, as one of the natural results of the conversion process, it will be of advantage to gather up in a brief chapter a sketch of the logical development of the church in Mexico down to the close of the sixteenth century. Particular attention will be directed to its means of support and to the rise of a native ministry.

It will be recalled that the first priests came with the conquering army of Cortés; that they were followed by three Flemish missionaries who came without any formal authorization from the ecclesiastical powers; and that it was not until nearly four years after the capture of Mexico that the first fully authorized group of Franciscan friars arrived in New Spain, under the leadership of Martín de Valencia, who became thus the first head of the church in Mexico, and who was confirmed in this by the unanimous vote of his colleagues. To him and to his companions were granted large powers, as befitting the situation into which they went, where they were the only representatives of the church and where communication with the church authorities was so difficult as to make it impossible for close supervision to be exercised upon them.

Valencia's first act was to summon the whole company of missionaries into conference where many days were spent in discussing the best plan of procedure in their work. This resulted in the division of the total group into four smaller groups of four each, three of which went to establish themselves in centers outside the capital, while four monks besides Valencia the leader, undertook to open work in Mexico city. This was early in 1524.

In the closing days of the same year and the beginning of 1525, Valencia summoned the entire force into a conference called the *Junta Apostolica,* where, on the basis of the experiences of the year they had already had, they discussed again the problems relating to their task. No formal actions of that body are preserved, but Bishop Lorenzana, in his volume, *Concilios Provinciales,* includes a summary of their action, gathered from Mendieta, Torquemada, and other sources. The group was still small and the organization still very simple. Cortés and a few other laymen had met with this assembly.

But the next year saw a new group of Franciscans arrive, and scarcely a year passed thereafter that new companies of padres did not appear in Mexico. In 1526 the Dominicans came. So long as the majority of the priests were Franciscans, Valencia, though reluctantly, continued as head of the church, but as other orders came and secular priests also, need arose for the appointment of a bishop. Accordingly, in 1528, Don Juan Zumárraga, provincial of the Franciscan Order in Concepcion, Spain, was named by Charles V, bishop and protector of the Indians of New Spain and in the same year arrived in Mexico as bishop-elect, though he was not consecrated until he revisited Spain in 1532. He exercised the episcopal functions from the first, however.

The expansion during those early years was rapid. By 1539, when, at the request of the king, a council was held, we find three bishops signing the report. They were the bishops of Antequera, Guatemala, and Mexico City. In 1533 Zumárraga had been raised to the dignity of archbishop. Later were added the bishoprics of Puebla, Chiapas, Michoacán, and Yucatan. Even with all these, Cuevas laments that there were not more and cannot explain to himself why there was no protest on the part of the priests at the inadequate number of bishops. He finds it embarrassing that, in the midst of this silence on the part of the priests, the voice of the Indians should be heard pleading for bishops. They wrote Charles V as follows:

> There is great need that your majesty order an increase of the number of bishoprics for Spaniards and Indians, for each diocese is now so great that it is impossible for the bishop to cover it. There are neither friars nor parish priests in many of the remote principal villages, nor does any one take account of this fact, as would happen if there were a prelate who would look upon them as his own.[1]

With the coming of larger numbers of secular priests, a controversy arose over the transfer of parishes to their care, a controversy so bitter that we referred to it as one of the factors hindering the work of conversion of the Indians. By authority of the pope, in commissioning the Franciscan friars to go to Mexico, they were given very full powers. As a result of the controversy, apparently, the rights of the friars to administer the Holy Sacraments was withdrawn. Mendieta, in a letter, deeply resents this withdrawal, declaring that it has occasioned irreparable damage to the work of conversion. The right was restored in 1567, according to the *Recopilación de Leyes*.

In 1555 occurred what is called the First Provincial Council of Mexico, the former assemblies not having been considered as true Councils. The Second Council was held ten years later in 1565, and a third which established the norms that were to stand until into the eighteenth century was held in 1585, under the presidency of archbishop Pedro Moya y Contreras.

From the first, the crown was careful to keep the direct control of the church in the New World in its own hands, just as it had always done in Spain. Two chief methods were employed, one through the control of the tithes which

[1] Cuevas, *op. cit.*, I, 354-5.

had been granted the king by the pope as a part compensation for the expense of the conquest, conversion, and government of the new lands. How this worked out may be seen as we discuss the whole matter of the support of the churches.[2]

THE SUPPORT OF THE CHURCH

Obviously, complete self-support of the work among the Indians could not be expected at first. Reliance for buildings was upon two sources, aside from the Indians, the king's tithe and the contribution of the Spanish *encomenderos* who, with the help of the Indians, were supposed to provide suitable buildings for instruction and worship. This is clearly set forth in a memorandum of Don Antonio Mendoza, the viceroy, to his successor.[3] The part of the Indians seems to have been principally labor, which they gave freely, in many cases not receiving even their meals while so employed, though sometimes this was furnished them. Since in the villages, particularly, the cost of materials was very slight, the heavy part of the expense would have been the labor, so that the Indians did contribute heavily. They did also contribute to the support of the mendicant friars who at first lived in great poverty and simplicity, relying for their maintenance upon what was provided by the community. An order of the king in 1534 reads as follows:

We order that the Indians of each village or neighborhood build houses adequate for the clergy to live in, in comfort. They should be alongside the churches and be used by the clergy who are occupied in the instruction and conversion of the Indians of the parish, and they must not be applied to other uses.[4]

Whether this means the provision of materials or only the labor is not clear, though if there were no other indications elsewhere, one would naturally take it to include both.

[2] See the section on the government and conversion, *ante,* pp. 181 ff.
[3] *Colección de Documentos Inéditos,* VI, 497.
[4] *Recopilación de Leyes,* I, 19.

One of the concessions made to the Indians was that they were not to pay the tithe as did the Spaniards and lords. There was a great controversy over the matter. Generally, the Orders were opposed to exacting it from them. Excerpts from a letter of the archbishop to the Royal Council of the Indies show the situation that existed. He writes:

All the prelates of the church in New Spain in the Council which we celebrated, voted to request your majesty in our name and that of the churches, that the natives pay tithes as well as Spanish Christians, according to the royal orders hitherto sent, but with which the religious orders have interfered.[5]

The letter continues, alleging the reasons why this should be done and setting forth the attitude of the Orders:

The friars say that the Indians are in no way obligated to pay tithes, but rather that your majesty has the obligation to support all the ministers necessary for the preaching of the doctrine and the administration of the sacraments, and that failure to do so must put a burden on your majesty's conscience. They say that this is your only title to the land and the tribute you receive from it, nor was there any other reason for its conquest; and, further, that the going of ships laden with gold and silver for your majesty's use, without having first provided for the necessity of ministers for the indoctrination of the Indians, is an evidence of bad faith.

They say that tithes were instituted for the sustenance of the ministers of the church, and since they have been and are the ministers, nothing is owed them, and that if they do not make a demand for it, no one else has a right to do so. Where there are secular priests, let their salary and food be sent them, for they are not at present necessary (to the Indians, we take it), for they do not know the Indian tongue.[6]

The archbishop replies, saying that while the friars may say that tithes ought not to be collected, "it is notorious and frequently commented upon that, in many places, they them-

[5] *Colección de Documentos Inéditos,* IV, 504.
[6] *Ibid.,* pp. 507-8.

selves collect two or three tithes." He charges that they do not receive his visits, and that it is unjust of them not to expect to support their prelate who has the care of so many souls. The more reason do they owe the prelates who, solely as a matter of charity and without obligation, do what is done for the Indians.

He states that the friars support their opposition to the tithes by reference to St. Thomas, who declared that tithes were not to be paid in a new country where there was no custom of doing so, since among a weak and new people such a requirement would be an offense. He replies to this by recalling the offerings of the people in the time of their infidelity, even to their blood. The fraires say that perhaps after a hundred years or so, the natives may be asked to pay them, which thinks the bishop is as if they should say that in a hundred or two hundred years they will be saved, but in the meanwhile be condemned.

The archbishop complains of the great expense of personal service, the sumptuous and superfluous buildings which the monks cause to be built in the villages, and all at the expense of the Indians. Monasteries are elegant in their appointments and extensive, even though there be but two or three friars. As many as three have been built one over against the other in the same village, the last the best of all, and all by enforced labor of the Indians by turns, receiving not even their food, while they were compelled to bring in materials also.[7]

THE IMPERIAL DOMINATION OF THE CHURCH

Apart from the indirect method of controlling the clergy through the tithes, the king did so directly by means of the famous *patronato* of the Indies. The kings of Spain exercised greater authority in ecclesiastical matters than even the

[7] *Ibid.*, pp. 491-519.

pope himself. The following royal decree shows just what prerogatives they claimed:

Since the right of the royal patronage in the Indies belongs to us . . . we order and command that this right be reserved to us and the royal crown. No person, secular or ecclesiastical, shall mix in any thing pertaining to the royal patronate; neither providing a church nor benefice, nor ecclesiastical office, nor receiving such without our representation or that of the persons to whom we by law or other provision may commit it. Whosoever does so, if a laymen, shall incur the loss of any favors which we have shown him in all the Indies and shall render himself incapable of obtaining others, and he shall be banished perpetually from our dominions; if an ecclesiastic, he shall be held as a stranger and shall be ineligible to hold any benefice or ecclesiastical office in our kingdom; and both shall incur such other penalties as established by our laws.[8]

Cuevas, a modern Jesuit, severely criticises the system. Every religious order, all the rites and ceremonies, the publication of books—everything came under it. But the worst, he thinks, was the attempt to isolate the church from Rome, for all Bulls and communications addressed to it had to pass through royal hands.

But do not think that these were all the prescriptions upon the church and its institutions. All of the twenty-four titles of the first book with a total of six hundred ninety laws, with numberless offspring of royal orders, viceregal notes, orders of *Audiencias,* and other interpretations of governing powers, which had every one, from the patriarch of the Indies to the last poor sacristan, from provincial councils to the Indians' hospitals, completely tied in such form that, if the king or his under officers had wished to abuse their power, they could have had the church, and indeed they did so have it, in many cases in the very greatest humiliation and most difficult situations.[9]

In 1524 Charles V sought and obtained from Pope Alexander VI, a Patriarchate of the Indies, that is Latin America

---

[8] *Recopilación de Leyes,* VI, titulo vi, ley 1, fol. 2.
[9] Cuevas, *op. cit.,* II, 52-3.

as it is now called. The first to hold the dignity was Don Antonio de Rojas who had been bishop of Mallorca. He was succeeded in 1532 by Cardinal Guiena who lived in Rome. In 1572 he sought to have the patriarch reside in Spain as a sort of second pope. But in 1591 at the request of the same monarch, the patriarchate was withdrawn. It seems never to have exercised any considerable power. Cuevas declares that he has been unable to discover any trace of evidence of its work. It was, apparently, no more than an honorary title and in no way affected practically the conduct of the ecclesiastical organization in the New World.[10]

THE INQUISITION

In the study of the conversion of the Indians in Mexico we need say but little about the Inquisition except as it directly touches our subject. It will not, however, be out of place to sketch briefly its introduction into New Spain. In 1517 Cardinal Cisneros, Inquisitor General, had given the power of Inquisitor to all the bishops of the Indies. Perhaps by delegation of the bishop of Santo Domingo, the priests who accompanied Cortés tried an Indian of Alcohuacan, named Marcos, for adultery, as early as 1522. Fray Martín de Valencia founder of the Franciscan order in Mexico, on passing through Santo Domingo was delegated as Inquisitor for all New Spain in 1524, but he seems to have made little or no use of his powers. However, on the arrival of the Dominicans who were especially privileged as Inquisitors, Fray Tomás Ortíz became Inquisitor and a year later Betanzos was named, and he became more active. Seventeen persons were tried and convicted of blasphemy during his regime which lasted till 1528.

In 1535 Bishop Zumárraga became Inquisitor, and he was much more active than his predecessors. Formal establishment of the office was made in 1536. In the seven years

[10] *Ibid.*, I, 303-04.

which he held the position one hundred and forty-one trials are reported, one hundred and eighteen against Spaniards, and thirteen against Indians. One of the most important cases was that of Don Carlos Chichimectecotl, an Indian chief of Tezcuco. He was accused of having begun by murmuring against the priests, speaking disrespectfully of them, and warning others to abandon Christian practices as being vain and useless, so that all who heard were scandalized. Another charged that he had persuaded him not to teach the Christian doctrine nor to disturb the Indians in their ancient customs, but let them live like their forefathers.

His home was searched and a book of Indian paintings was discovered, also certain idols. No witness could be found who had ever seen him worship before them. They were apparently kept merely as objects of curiosity. However, a son was made to testify that his father had forbidden him to go to the church and that he knew no doctrine, not even being able to repeat the Lord's Prayer. The most serious statement put into the mouth of Don Carlos was, "Brother, listen to me, and let no one set his heart on this law of God . . . all that they have taught you regarding this God is false. . . . Have not these Christians many wives? Do they not get drunk? Their priests can do nothing with them. Then what is it that they would compel us to do? It is not our place or our law to hinder anyone from doing whatever he wishes. Let us let these things alone and put behind us what they say." He would not confess any idolatry or heresy or sacrifice, though he did confess living illicitly with a niece. His trial began in June. On Nov. 30, 1539, he was delivered into the hands of the government to be burned.

This case brought a rebuke from the Inquisitor General, probably because the victim was an Indian. However,

Cuevas, a Jesuit, writing in 1921, almost four hundred years afterward says:

Despite this fact (that of being an Indian) we judge that it was well to have punished some guilty ones. Unless it can be shown otherwise, we believe that these punishments were very salutary for New Spain.[11]

It has been urged by some that Don Carlos was the last Indian punished by the Inquisition, but Cuevas cites several, two in 1544 for idolatry; again in 1546, in 1547 and as late as 1560, Indians were tried for blasphemy. The order exempting the Indians from the Holy Office, Cuevas says, was in 1575. He gives a summary of the activity of the Inquisition in Mexico, prior to 1600.

A total of nine hundred and two accusations were recorded, of which six hundred were sentenced. Seven hundred and forty-four cases involved were minor ones, such as evil words, witchcraft, bigamy, etc. For formal heresy sixty-eight, for propagating Judaism fifty, against priests soliciting in the confessional forty. Only seventeen were condemned to death.[12]

THE RISE OF THE NATIVE MINISTRY

One of the usual results of the Christianizing process in any land is the rise of a native ministry to carry on the work. We have made an effort to trace this rise in Mexico, without finding within the limits which we have set for this study, the sixteenth century, any indication that the Indians themselves were admitted to full clerical orders. This was by no means due to the lack of interest and desire on the part of the natives, for many of them earnestly sought to be admitted; but by deliberate action of the authorities of the church they were excluded. How much later it was before this privilege was extended to them we have not been able to discover, though finally they did come to share fully in the

[11] Cuevas, *op. cit.*, I, 378.   [12] *Ibid.*, p. 273.

priesthood. Is not this an unusual case? Are there other great fields where the natives were held so long unfit for the higher offices within the church?

We have seen that from the very first, use was made of the young Indian students, first as interpreters, then as teachers or *doctrineros,* and as preachers, but they were not allowed either to enter the orders or to be ordained. Mendieta tells us that the Franciscans had the custom of receiving a few Indians as *donados,* who lived in the company, not marrying, but serving somewhat as lay brothers, a practice he had not observed in other orders. They were *donados* in name only, however, for they took no vow, nor were they bound by any rule. They simply wore a brown tunic tied with a cord. If they proved satisfactory they remained in the monastery, if not, they were returned to the world. He continues:

I have favored as far as possible those who have come in this way, although others opposed it. It has seemed to me terrible inhumanity and a thing for which God will require an accounting, to wish to deprive a whole nation of innumerable people of all the help and recourse for living religiously and spiritually. . . .

If these miserable Indians are not allowed to take the vows in any Order (for in none of them are they admitted even as lay brothers), shall they be deprived of even the slight privilege of wearing the tunic like the stewards of the order and the privilege of serving the monks? . . . Especially since if they do what they ought not, they can without difficulty be dismissed without prejudicing the cause.

Not to permit them the long tunic like the habits of the monks nor mantles nor the hat by which they would come to appear like friars, seems to me to be wise, as also not to allow them to walk alone outside of the monastery; but for the rest, I can see no reason for opposition. . . .

Some of them thus received, have given an excellent example. The first fathers who came to this land, began to receive a few Indians in this form of *donados* and it resulted very well.[13]

He then continues to mention particular cases that have shown remarkable devotion.

He relates an interesting story of one Indian chief who was converted, and reading the life of St. Francis which had been translated into the Indian tongue, was so impressed by it that he vowed with many tears to live the life and wear the dress of St. Francis. So he left the clothing of his class, as a chief, for a poor roughly woven robe. He set his slaves free, telling them of the law of God and of His holy way. He renounced his chieftainship, gave away his jewels and possessions to the poor, and sought entrance into the monastery of Michoacán. Refused entrance there, he went to Mexico City and begged admittance to the monastery. Refused again, he demanded of the archbishop that the doors be opened for him. The archbishop, seeing the great devotion and perseverance of the man, desired to do something for him, but he knew that the monks would not agree to his admission. After a long time and much insistence he was finally permitted to live among the monks with the habit he wore and was promised that if he proved worthy he would be allowed the probationer's habit. The excellence of his life and his perseverance were notable, but after much discussion, the monks agreed to dissimulate with him and delay the fulfillment of their promise, in order not to open the door to others. Finally the Indian died, still in the habit of a *donado*.

Mendieta enters into a discussion as to why the Indians were denied this privilege.

What then is the reason why the Indians are denied the habit not only of priests but of lay brothers, since in the primitive church gentiles and Jews, newly converted to the faith, were elected as priests and even bishops? Rather it would

---

[13] Mendieta, *Historia Eclesiástica*, p. 444.

seem of great benefit in the conversion of the natives, for these know the languages better and could preach and minister more acceptably in them; furthermore the people would receive the gospel at the lips of their own brothers more freely than from strangers.

To this question, it will be enough to reply confessing that in the primitive church it was thus, and that it was fitting then, for God worked by miracles on the new converts and they became saints and even martyrs to the name of Jesus. But in these times, the church, illumined by the Holy Spirit, and taught by the experience which it has had of the many backslidings among the new Christians, has ordained that by determination of the High Priests, the Vicars of Christ, that there shall not be admitted to the profession of priesthood or the orders, the descendants of any infidel in the fourth degree, and this is especially provided in the constitution of the Franciscan order. But I would add further that even providing that they would not return to the vomit of their rites and ceremonies (which is the reason why the church deprives them of this privilege) there exists among them a greater cause than in other descendants of infidels why they should not be admitted even as lay brothers, namely, that the majority of them are not fitted to command or rule, but to be commanded and ruled. . . . I mean to say that they are not fitted for masters but pupils, not for prelates but for subjects, and as such the best in the world. So good are they in this regard that poor and weak as I am, with only the backing of the king and his favor, I could with little aid from my companions have a province of fifty thousand Indians so well ordered and Christian that it would seem to be a monastery.[14]

Mendieta says that he himself on one occasion brought some of the Indians into his own monastery, but after a year's probation it became evident that they would not prove out, and so they were dismissed.[15]

In the council of 1539 action was taken granting to the Indians the right of receiving ordination to the four minor orders, which are porter, reader, exorcist, and acolyte, but

[14] Mendieta, *op. cit.*, pp. 448-9.   [15] *Ibid.*, pp. 445-9.

these are not regarded as sacramental, the ceremony by which they are conferred differing very markedly from that of the sacramental ordination. Those so ordained were not bound to celibacy and might lawfully marry, though by marriage they forfeited any benefice they might be holding. The action of the council was as follows:

For the service of such parishes and the aid of such priests, let some of the most capable Indians and *mestizos* be ordained to the lower orders of the church. They should know how to read and write and, if possible, should know Latin, and should know the native languages and reside in the said parishes in order to serve them and to care for the baptism and other matters as may be necessary. These four orders were established by the church for its service in a time when there was a lack of priests, such as now exists, to assist the priests and ministers of the sacraments, and to handle reverently the sacred and blessed things of the altar. . . . They may retire from the service and marry if they so desire.[16]

The attitude of the Dominicans toward their ordination is set forth in a letter which they wrote to the emperor in 1544. They treated not alone of ordination but also their general fitness for study.

It seems well to write regarding the study of the Indians, their preaching and their ordination. We say that these Indians ought not to study because no good result can be expected from it, first, because they will not be fit to preach for a long time to come, since in order to preach, it is necessary that the preacher have some authority among the people, and the natives do not have this; for truly those who study are vicious beyond the common people and are not persons of any seriousness, nor are they different from the ordinary people either in dress or conversation. . . . Second, because they are an unstable people to whom the preaching of the gospel ought not to be entrusted, for they are new in the faith and are not as yet well grounded in it. The result would be many errors, as we al-

[16] Cuevas, *op. cit.*, I, 430-1.

ready know by experience, having tried it. Third, because they
are not skillful in the correct understanding of the things of
the faith nor the reasons therefore, nor is their language such
that they can explain it without improprieties which might
induce great mistakes.

It follows from this that they ought not to be ordained, for
they would be held in but light esteem even if they were.[17]

The first regularly constituted Provincial Council, that
of 1555, evidently discussed the matter thoroughly. Probably this action may be regarded as evidence that there were
those who favored the ordination of the Indians. But their
declaration was categorical:

If the candidate is or has been known to be connected with
any infamous or vulgar act, or if he be descended from parents
or grandparents, burned or *reconciliados,* or of the lineage of
Moors, or if he be *mestizo,* Indian or mulatto, he shall not be
admitted to orders. And if it be known that at present or recently he has not lived a clean life and abstained from carnal
sins, or if he has been a player of illicit games, or if he has not
habitually confessed nor taken communion as required by canon
law, etc. . . . he shall not be admitted to ordination.[18]

In 1556 the archbishop, in his long letter regarding the
state of the church, from which we have already quoted in
various connections, discussed the matter of admitting the
Indians to the priesthood. He said:

So unstable are these confused people, that it is certain that
if any greater power should appear, there would be no resistance on their part to its acceptance. Because of this instability,
we dare not ordain them nor entrust them with the administration of the Holy Gospel, leaving them as the apostles did, over-
seers and ministers among the newly converted people.

In the villages where there are no priests, certain Indians
brought up in the church are appointed to teach the doctrine,

[17] *Colección de Documentos Inéditos,* VII, 541-2.
[18] *Concilios Provinciales,* p. 106.

but among these, many great evils have been found, such as robbing the church and violating women and girls, and even boys.[19]

An undated document in the *Nueva Colección de Documentos para la Historia de México,* expresses belief in the possibility of future fitness for the high office of priest, but it is very clear that the writer regards them as quite unfitted for immediate ordination.   It reads as follows:

Nor will they be fit to receive orders in these our times, for although there may be intelligent Indians who would be capable in ecclesiastical affairs, nevertheless, their ability is of such a quality that in no way would it be fitting to entrust to them the offices of the church until Our Lord, with the change of times, and according to his good pleasure, should be pleased to change their being and capacity in such manner that those who understand will, in future times, adjudge them fit and perceive that their time has arrived.[20]

All this hesitation on the part of the church to confide priestly powers to the natives on the score of inability is somewhat strange in comparison with the government policy of permitting them to hold public office of honor and responsibility.   It is interesting to note that as early as 1530, the empress wrote to the *Audiencia* of New Spain permitting them to name Indians as *regidores* and *alguaciles.*

Apparently the *mestizos* were more highly esteemed by the church than the Indians, for they were admitted to orders long before the same privilege was given the Indians.   How soon the order was actually put into practice we do not know, but we find a royal order given in 1588 charging that *mestizos* be ordained to the priesthood.   The order reads:

We charge the archbishop and bishops of our Indies that they ordain the *mestizos* of their dioceses to the priesthood,

[19] *Documentos para la Historia de México,* IV, p. 499.
[20] *Nueva Colección de Documentos,* II, 110.

provided they possess the necessary qualifications for the office, but only after thorough investigation by the prelates as to their lives and habits, and on finding that they are well educated, capable, fit and born legitimately in wedlock. And if any *mestizos* desire to be nuns and to take the habit and veil, they are to be admitted to the convents and to the professions, notwithstanding any constitution that may exist to the contrary, provided, of course, the same careful investigation as to their life and habits has been made.[21]

That the order was obeyed is clear from another order given in 1636 in which the king charges that they refrain from ordaining so many, especially *mestizos* and illegitimates.

We charge the archbishop and bishops that they refrain from ordaining so many clergy as they are doing, especially *mestizos,* illegitimates and others who are defective; and that they do not allow in their dioceses those who have been expelled from Orders, or other scandalous persons.[22]

Besides the Indians and *mestizos* there was a not inconsiderable number of negroes and mulattos, but these labored under even stricter limitations than the Indians. Never did they rise in the social scale, and they were never admitted to any ecclesiastical orders.[23]

The chief dependence of the church was upon foreign priests and the creoles or people of pure Spanish blood, born in Mexico. These had the advantage over foreigners in that they spoke the native language naturally and, of course, knew and understood the natives better. The first of these to enter the priesthood was the child, Alonso de Molina, who became the first interpreter of the priests, later entered the Franciscan order and became a conspicuous leader in the early church. It was he who prepared the catechism from which we noted the content of instruction given the natives. The founding of the University of Mexico was partly in obedience to the

[21] *Recopilación de Leyes,* Lib. I, titulo vii, ley 8.
[22] *Ibid.*   [23] Cuevas, *op. cit.,* I, 397.

demand for the preparation of creoles for the priesthood. Before this, however, between 1535 and 1542 a school had been founded in Michoacán for this purpose by Don Vasco de Quiroga. Writing in 1565, he says:

> Many years ago, I founded in Michoacán the College of San Nicolás, because of the great lack of ministers of the sacraments and divine worship in Michoacán, in order to provide ordained clergy; for truly, if from here the need of priests who know the language cannot be supplied, they never will be forthcoming.
>
> In the college of San Nicolás students of pure Spanish blood are prepared for language priests, as many as can be accomodated and who have the qualities necessary, as well as the required purity of blood.[24]

Though a discussion of the whole matter would carry us far beyond the limits of this study, it may be remarked that it seems to have been the deliberate policy of the crown to keep the control of the church throughout all the dependencies, and particularly in Mexico, in the hands of foreign priests. The present attitude of the Mexican government toward foreign priests, doubtless has its roots in this fact. Mexico now seems to be determined that at last the loyal, native, Mexico-loving priests shall lead the people, and that an end must be made to the influence of a foreign clergy. Did the reluctance to ordain native Indians to the priesthood depend in part on the unwillingness to permit native leadership through fear of possible loss of direction by the mother country? A more detailed investigation at this point might yield some very interesting and valuable results.

[24] *Ibid.*

THE PERMANENT INFLUENCES OF THE NATIVE RELIGIONS OF MEXICO UPON ROMAN CATHOLIC CHRISTIANITY

We have, in the course of this study, seen something of the character of the two religions when they met. We have watched as first the conquerors, then the missionaries came, each, in his own way, affecting the religious situation. We have seen the methods whereby the representatives of the new faith sought to establish it among the Indians; the factors favoring and hindering them; the results of the conversion as registered in the documents of the sixteenth century; and have watched the unfolding life of the national church. One step remains to be taken before our study is ended. We have yet to inquire, skipping over the intervening centuries to the present, what are the permanent influences, if any, of the native cults upon present day Catholicism in Mexico.

MODERN CULTURAL TENDENCIES IN MEXICO

If, after four hundred years, surviving elements of the pagan religion are still found in Catholicism, it will be clearly evident that there must have been a marked interpenetration of religious cultures in that first century of contact, since the tendency throughout the succeeding centuries has been toward a more complete Europeanization of Mexican life. The constant influx of foreign blood; the multiplied contacts, political and social, with the European countries and the United States; the spread of popular education, which has followed foreign patterns; the extension of the use of the Spanish language—all these would tend naturally to the disappearance of the ancient cultural elements.

The Cathedral in Mexico City, Erected Upon the Site of the Great Aztec Temple, and in Part from Materials Employed by the Pagan Builders.

SURVIVALS OF ANCIENT CUSTOMS

Naturally, they disappear first in the great centers of the land. One would not expect to find marked pagan survivals in the cathedrals in the principal cities, just as he would expect to find in such centers but few other ancient cultural survivals. Some of these have become, particularly Mexico City, great cosmopolitan centers, very similar to the great cities of other lands. Nor would one expect to find among the educated well-to-do, pure-blooded classes the same vestiges of the older culture that he would find in the pure Indian or even the mixed-blood groups, most of whom have had but meager opportunities of education. C. Sartorius, an interesting and authoritative writer upon the life of Mexico, is perfectly right when he says:

In Mexico the religious festivals have assumed a peculiar character. Indian customs have been in part retained and are most singularly interwoven with the ceremonies as practiced in Europe. These peculiarities, however, must not be sought for in the cities, for on the whole surface of the earth, civilization there levels ancient customs, and fashion scorns that which in distant country towns and villages is still regarded as sacred.[1]

That there are numerous vestiges of the pagan cult in existence in Catholicism, practically every writer who has given any attention to the religion of the country asserts. One could quote opinion to this effect indefinitely, and on the whole, probably well-founded opinion, but the writers who trouble to give any reasoned basis for their opinions are very few. In conversation with many natives and others who have lived in Mexico, one finds the same impression current, but few of them have been able to adduce any practical examples of such permanent remains of paganism. We shall quote a few of such opinions, but we shall go farther and give concrete illustrations of such existing vestiges. We

[1] C. Sartorius, *Mexico and the Mexicans*, pp. 154-5.

have examined scores of books of travel and description, popular and scientific, mission-books and encyclopedias, folk-stories and songs, and have sought by interviewing Mexicans, both erudite and ignorant, to find what they are. We do not attempt to present all that each has contributed, but only significant examples of the various elements which seem to have survived. We quote at length the cases cited, instead of merely summarizing them. This chapter is therefore rather more of the source-book type. We do not pretend to have exhausted the list of surviving elements. Many exist, undoubtedly, which are so subtle and intangible as to escape detection, survivals which result from the peculiar psychological make-up of the natives, that register themselves in attitudes of mind and heart, rather than in formal visible fashion.

Given the peculiar organization of the Roman Catholic church, with its common creed, common requirements upon believers everywhere, and its common hierarchical organization all over the world, we need not expect to find any considerable changes in these, unless it be that the recent struggles of the state with the church have as its result the complete emancipation of the Mexican church from foreign influences and the formation of a new organization that will be indigenous and, therefore possibly, quite different from what it has hitherto been by reason of the pressure of outside authority.

We believe there is conclusive evidence of the survival of the following elements:

1. The native pagan dances on certain religious occasions.

2. The perpetuation of certain pagan feasts as Christian festivals.

3. The pagan custom of making offerings before the images, sometimes of flowers, copal, and even animals.

4. The taking over of pagan shrines or divinities under Christian names, or in other words the exchange of deities. Under these main divisions will appear minor elements which vary from place to place. It does not so much concern us here to know how widely these practices are distributed throughout the country, though the impression that one gets from reading of the different sections of Mexico is that these practices, or their counterparts, are very widely scattered among the Indians and the *mestizo* group.

We begin by citing characteristic opinions of travelers to that land at different periods during the last century. First, we present the statement of a man whom we cannot but recognize as having a strong anti-Catholic bias. Yet, recognizing this, his opinion may well be given here, for, underneath his prejudices, there are certain bases in fact.

And this is Christianity? And the worship of the true God —to introduce which, in the place of existing superstitions, the blood of millions of the blind heathen of this vast region was shed by the Spanish conquerors. The plea for the cruelties exercised upon the Aborigines was their idolatry and their inhuman sacrifices. The most exaggerated statements, suited to exercise the horror and extinguish the compassion of the bigoted Catholic of Europe, were found necessary and were made to palliate in some measure the undeniable enormities perpetrated upon the Indians.

The detestable character of the ignorant idolatry in exercise among the ancient race, needs no demonstration; yet at the present day, with the exception of the single item of human sacrifice as a part of the religious system, it may well be asked, by what has it been supplanted—fewer and more dignified divinities? less disgusting ignorance? purer rites? a less degrading superstition? a better system of morality?—who will dare to assert it?

As to the charge of the inhuman rites and the bloody festivals of the later generations of the Aztecs, the magnitude of which, as asserted by the Roman Catholic historians, is almost incredible, no one offers to palliate them.

You are shown with obsequious eagerness, the huge round stone of sacrifice; you are told to mark the hollow for the head of the victim and the groove which carried off his blood; your ears tingle when they are filled with the number of those who are supposed to have been immolated upon this carved surface. You turn and see the huge and detestable figure of the goddess Teoyamiqui, before whom as Spanish historians relate, the hearts of the victims were torn out. Yes, but no officious cicerone leads you to the court of the Dominican convent and points out the broad perforated stone where the hundreds of thousands of poor benighted, ignorant Indians expired at the stake amidst smoke and flame.[2] No one reminds you that about the time the idolatrous worship of the Aztecs was extirpated in Mexico, the same Inquisition then in the first flush of power, burnt eighteen thousand victims at the stake in the old world and consigned two hundred and eight thousand to infamy and punishment scarcely better than death itself. The simple fact is that at the present day, dark as we consider it, the Roman Catholicism of Europe is light when compared to that established in Mexico and practiced by its inhabitants.

A change of names—a change of form and garb for the idols—new symbols—altered ceremonials—another race of priests—so much and no more has been effected for the Indians.

The change was easily made. The ancient superstition abounded with fasts, feasts and penances; so did the new. The whole system of the aboriginal hierarchy bears a striking resemblance to that which took place under the domination of Spain. Even the monk found that his vocation excited no surprise; the existence of regular orders of celibates of both sexes whose lives were devoted to the service of certain amongst their gods, seems indisputable.

With the Indians, Teotl, the unknown God, "He by whom we live," as he was termed, he whom they never represented in idol form, is still the supreme being under the name of God. They continue to adore the god Quetzalcoatl, the feathered serpent, under the name of St. Thomas. It is indifferent to them whether the evil spirit is called the devil or Tlacatecolotl. They retain their superstitions, their talismans, their charms, and as

---

[2] In this statement the author clearly indicates that he is not familiar with the facts. On the Inquisition in Mexico, *see ante,* pp. 267 ff.

they were priest-led under the old system, so they are kept in adherence to the church of Rome by the continual bustle of festivals and ceremonials and processions of the church. But, as to change of heart and purpose, a knowledge of the true God as a spirit who is worshiped in spirit and in truth; a sense of their degraded and fallen state as men and an acquaintance with the truths of the true gospel; its application to their individual state and its influence upon their lives and characters, they are as blind and as ignorant as their forefathers.[3]

Now, having had a vigorous Protestant opinion, let a Catholic priest who traveled extensively in Mexico about the middle of the last century speak. He was a keen observer, and has done a very valuable piece of work in the study of the religion of the Indians of North America.

The Mexican is not a Catholic. He is a Christian simply because he has been baptized. I speak here of the masses and not of the numerous exceptions which are to be found in all classes of society. I affirm that Mexico is not a Catholic country, because the majority of the Mexican Indians are semi-idolaters; because the majority carry ignorance of religion to the point of having no worship but that of form. Their worship is materialistic beyond any doubt. It does not know what it is to adore God in Spirit. The idolatrous character of Mexican Catholicism is a fact recognized by all travelers and above all by our officers of the French army who have traversed Mexico in every part. The worship of saints and madonnas absorbs the devotion of the people to such an extent that they have very little time left to think of God. It is vain to look for good fruits from this hybrid tree, which makes of the Mexican religion a singular collection of lifeless devotions, of haughty ignorance, of unhealthy superstitions and of horrible vices. It would take volumes to recount the idolatrous superstitions of the Indians which are still left in existence. On account of the lack of painstaking instruction, there appear in the Catholicism of the Indians numerous vestiges of the Aztec paganism.

[3] C. J. Latrobe, *The Rambler in Mexico,* pp. 164-7.

Sacrifices of turtles and other animals are still practiced by thousands of Indians. In the state of Puebla they used to sacrifice, not many years ago on St. Michael's day, a small orphan child, or else an old man who had nothing better to do than to go to the other world.[4]

An interesting comparison of Mexican Catholicism with that of Europe, by an English writer who visited in Mexico and wrote very informingly of many phases of its life, is that of Brantz Mayer:

Although there is much that is singular to Protestants who are accustomed to a simple ritual in the splendor of the Roman church in Italy and France, yet there is always a picturesque fitness of the ceremony to the season and there is an evident meaning in its dramatic effect, illustrating the incidents of the time. In those countries, we can never free ourselves from the associations of the place and the ceremony upon which no corrupt grafts of heathenism appear. The rites at the altar are gorgeous, but chaste and beautiful; the music is select and suitable to the moment; the temple in which you kneel is hallowed by historical memorials; the dead of hundreds of years—illustrious through all time—rest in the carved tombs about you; and the masterpieces of the greatest artists realize once more, on their eloquent canvas, the triumphs of saints and martyrs. But not so here. The ritual is Indian, rather than civilized or intellectual. The show is tasteless, barbaric. The altars display a jumble of jewelry, sacred vessels and utensils of the precious metals mixed up with glass through which is reflected the tints of colored water, and the whole is overlaid with fruits and flowers.[5]

In another place, speaking of certain religious practices, he says:

Those painful exhibitions, which cannot fail to strike a stranger as disadvantageous, both to the true and the pure and

---

[4] J. H. McCarthy, *Two Thousand Miles Through the Heart of Mexico*, p. 229.
[5] *Mexico as it Was and Is*, pp. 151-2.

spiritual adoration of God; the mixture of antique barbaric show and Indian rites, may have served to attract the native population at the first settlement of the country, but their continuance is in keeping neither with the spirit of the age nor the necessities of a public.[6]

We have also the opinion of two men, both noted for their contributions to the world's knowledge, largely through personal observations. It is true that Baron Humboldt's claim to fame is as a geographer, rather than as a student of religion, and it is not always safe to follow such authorities into fields other than their own. However, E. B. Tylor is known as a student and interpreter of the customs and practices of mankind, particularly primitive man. If, as seems probable, his studies of the history of the early Mexican peoples gave him a knowledge of their religion, then his judgment here ought to carry considerable weight. Humboldt, who traveled and studied in Mexico about the beginning of the nineteenth century, wrote:

The introduction of the Romish religion had no other effect upon the Mexicans than to substitute new ceremonies and symbols for the rites of a sanguinary worship. Dogma has not succeeded dogma, but only ceremony to ceremony. I have seen them, naked and adorned with tinkling bells, perform savage dances around the altar, while a monk of St. Francis elevated the host.[7]

Tylor writes as follows:

Practically, there is not much difference between the old heathenism and the new Christianity. We may put dogmas out of the question. They hear them and believe them devoutly and do not understand them in the least. They had just received the Immaculate conception, as they had received many mysteries before it; and were not a little delighted to have a new occasion for decorating themselves and their churches with flowers,

[6] *Ibid.* Preface, p. v.
[7] Quoted by Winton, *Mexico Today,* p. 84.

marching in processions, dancing, beating drums and letting off rockets as their custom is. The real essence of both religions is the same to them. They had gods, to whom they built temples and in whose honor they gave offerings, maintained priests, danced, walked in processions—much as they do now, that their divinities might be favorable to them and give them good crops and success in their enterprises. This is pretty much what their present Christianity consists of. As a moral influence, working upon the character of the people, it seems scarcely to have had the slightest effect, except, as I said, in causing them to leave off human sacrifices which were probably not an original feature of their worship, but were introduced comparatively at a late time, and had already been abolished by one king.[8]

THE RELIGIOUS DANCE A SURVIVAL

The religious dance is not wholly a pagan custom. Indeed it has appeared frequently within Christianity. It was practiced in Spain in the middle of the eighteenth century according to Stockdale, who traveled through Spain in that period. He says that in the religious procession in Holy Week "the people ran about masked, they danced, they sang, they tore themselves with scourges, then with faces covered, but naked to the waist, they tore their shoulders until the blood gushed out, with the rod of discipline."[9] Tylor, in describing a church-dance, in Mexico adds a footnote declaring that an eye-witness had told him of having seen a dance in the cathedral at Seville which consisted of minuets or some stately, old-fashioned dances, performed in front of the high altar by boys in white surplices, with the greatest gravity and decorum.[10] However, the religious dances that exist in Mexico today are not imported dances, coming from Spain, but are native dances which were permitted by the priests to be carried over into Christianity. Auguste Genin, writing

[8] E. B. Tylor, *Anahuac, Mexico and the Mexicans, Ancient and Modern,* pp. 289-90.
[9] J. J. Stockdale, *History of the Inquisition,* p. 351.
[10] Tylor, *op. cit.,* p. 212.

on the *Dances, Music and Songs of the Ancient and Modern Mexicans,* quotes Torquemada as saying:

One of the dances, called Tocotin, was so beautiful and fitting, and so solemn, that it was admitted into Christian temples.[11]

We have already described the deliberate adoption of the dances by Pedro de Gante and others.[12]

With this general statement, it will be sufficient to give descriptions of present day religious dances as recorded by travelers and observers. With but one exception, the dances described are native as are also the costumes, and generally, also the music. The one exception we have found is recorded by Tylor and, even there, the costumes were of the ancient sort. Did this description not come from one so well known as an observer, one would be tempted to doubt its accuracy. Probably some local explanation of it could have been found, had Mr. Tylor attempted to seek for it. It occurred in a mountain village. He writes:

We took our places in the great church with the monks who had mustered in full force to be present at the dancing. Presently the music arrived, an old man with a harp and a woman with a violin, and then came the dancers, eight Indian boys with short tunics and head-dresses of feathers and as many girls with white dresses and garlands of flowers on their heads. The costumes were evidently intended to represent the Indian dress of the days of Montezuma, but they were rather modernized by the necessity of wearing various articles of dress which would have been superfluous in the olden times. They stationed themselves in the church opposite the high altar, and to our unspeakable astonishment began to dance the polka. Then came a waltz, then a schottische, then another waltz, and finally a quadrille, set to unmitigated English tunes. They danced ex-

[11] *Annual Report Smithsonian Institute,* 1920, p .662. (Translated by permission for the Smithsonian Report from the Revue d'Ethnographie et de sociologie, Paris, 1913.)

[12] See *ante,* p. 155.

ceedingly well, and behaved as though they had been used to European ball-rooms all their lives. The spectators looked on as though it were a matter of course for these brown-skinned boys and girls to have acquired so singular an accomplishment in this out-of-the-way village among the mountains. As for us, we looked on in open-mouthed astonishment and, when in the middle of the quadrille, the harp and violin struck up no less a tune than "The King of the Cannibal Islands," we could hardly help bursting out into fits of laughter. We restrained ourselves, however, and kept as grave a countenance as the rest of the lookers on, who had not the faintest idea that anything odd was happening. The quadrille finished, in perfect order, each dancer took his partner by the hand and led her forward and, so forming a line in front of the high altar, they all knelt down and the rest of the congregation followed their example; there was dead silence in the church for about the space of an Ave Maria, then every one arose and the ceremony was over.[13]

In describing a certain dance witnessed in Dinamita, Mexico, Auguste Genin writes:

In the morning the dancers, led by the queen, move to the altar, dancing in two ranks, flanked by the fool, the devil and the master, who to some extent plays the clown. These are the only persons whom one sees laughing at times. The others display only religious gravity and ritualistic or hieratic poses and signs. After a series of dances and prayers before a rustic altar, other ensemble figures are danced outside, but always, at determined intervals, they return toward the altar.[14]

In proof of the essentially religious character of the feasts, the author tells how in passing one of these dances with a priest, on his way to bless a graveyard, the whole dancing company fell in behind and followed them, dancing and gesticulating to the accompaniment of their weird music. The priest accepted their company as a fitting and pious act.

---

[13] E. B. Tylor, *op. cit.,* pp. 211-12.
[14] Auguste Genin, "Notes on the Dances, Music and Songs of the Ancient and Modern Mexicans," *Annual Report of the Smithsonian Institute,* 1920, p. 673.

At the cemetery, they made him sit on one of their two thrones, rustic armchairs garlanded with flowers ribbons and colored papers, and

bent devout knees during the benediction of the tombs and of the ground destined for future burials. They accompanied, mutely, the litanies and the rosary, then returned with us without stopping their dancing and without their presence causing the least scandal.

This seems to me to demonstrate that these dances had a distinctly religious side. Traditionally, some of their freshness and of their early simplicity has undoubtedly been lost at obstacles on the journey traveled during four centuries. But they have, nevertheless, preserved a pagan element borrowed from the ancient myths of Mexico, together with the skillful grafting on done by the Catholic missionaries. It is a mixture of the cross of the Savior of the world, the basis, bond and symbol of the Christian religion, with the cross of Quetzalcoatl, which represents the four winds or the four cosmogonic suns of the Aztecs. But it is also, alas, the reflection of a considerable part of the population of Mexico, Indian or half-breed, semi-pagan, semi-Catholic, ignorant and fanatical, among whom the thin veneer of civilization, the very superficial civil instruction, and the religious education, consisting almost entirely of affectations and outward practices of a cult, scarcely conceal the ferocity of the redskin.[15]

Usually the dances are performed outside of the churches but not always. Professor Starr writing of the celebration on December 12, at Guadalupe, says:

Groups fantastically garbed dance through the crowded streets in the virgin's honor, and in their songs and dances, modern though they be, can be found suggestions of the olden time. Now and then one may witness what I saw in December, 1895, a group of Indians, pilgrims from a distant town, singing and dancing to the virgin within the great church itself.[16]

[15] Genin, *op. cit.*, p. 673.
[16] Frederick Starr, *In Indian Mexico*, p. 395.

Perhaps the typical attitude of the church toward these old survivals is expressed in the remark of a priest to Father Domenech, about the middle of the nineteenth century.

One day I was present at an Indian dance celebrated in honor of the patron saint of the village. Twenty-four boys and girls were dancing in the church in the presence of the priest. An Indian with his face concealed under a mask of imaginary deity resembling the devil, with horns and claws, was directing the figures of the dance which reminded me of that of the Redskins. I remarked to the priest, who, for all that, was an excellent priest, that it was incongruous to permit such a frolic in a church.

"The old customs," he replied, "are respectable; it is well to preserve them, only taking care that they do not degenerate into orgies."[17]

While we have noted the statement of Tylor that he heard the Indians use modern music in their dances, and while Professor Starr's statement regarding the celebration at Guadalupe mentions modern songs, much of the music formerly used was certainly the music of the ancients, and it is still widely used in the out-of-the-way villages. A writer on the popular arts of Mexico, says:

There exists also a type of music which may be called religious, which some of the peoples execute before the images of the saints and especially before the Christs and the Virgins, such as Señor de Chalma, the virgin of Guadalupe and of Zapopan. This music is played on an ancient instrument called *teponaxtli*, and is composed with "unas cuantas notas." It is undoubtedly the same rhythm which the temples heard before the coming of Cortez. Nor has the instrument varied. Some of these *teponaxtli* are heirlooms of the villages and have been passed down from fathers to sons for centuries.

Until a little while ago, the custom of dancing to the sound of the *teponaxtli*, dressed in fantastic Indian costumes and executing the dance before a Catholic image, was common in

[17] Quoted by Winton, *Mexico Today*, p. 86.

all the villages of Mexico. Now, only on the anniversaries of Guadalupe and on certain feasts of the sanctuaries of Michoacán or in the state of Mexico or Jalisco, does the custom persist.[18]

The tendency here noted toward the disappearance of these ancient survivals will be much more rapid than hitherto, with the penetration of the modern moving-pictures, the phonograph and, perhaps, most important of all, the radio, into all parts of the country.

PAGAN ELEMENTS IN RELIGIOUS FESTIVALS

Most of the dances occur at special feast-times which are themselves survivals of the pagan cult, or at least are conducted much after the fashion of those in honor of the ancient gods. It is in connection with these feasts that most of the sacrifices which we have noted as also pagan vestiges, occur. We will, therefore, make no attempt to present the two items separately.

Some pagan festivals have survived, which are not now particularly religious feasts, but which had at one time a religious significance. One writer believes, for example, that the Fiesta de las Flores (The feast of the flowers) celebrated in April, on the Viga canal, was originally a day devoted to the Aztec god, Quetzalcoatl. The festival has lost all its religious significance, he says, but it is celebrated much the same as in Aztec days. During the entire feast day boats large and small rowed by sturdy Indians fill the canals. Crowds of girls and women garlanded with poppy wreaths move along singing and dancing as they go, while on shore the wealthy ride in flower-decorated carriages.[19]

SACRIFICE STILL PRACTICED

One of the most interesting writers as well as one of the most accurate observers of the native customs in all classes in

[18] Atl, *Las Artes Populares de Mexico,* II, 201-2.
[19] Nevin O. Winter, *Mexico and Her People Today,* p. 235.

Mexico, is C. Sartorius, who wrote in the latter half of the nineteenth century. We let him describe the feast of Corpus Christi as celebrated in a village in the heart of the mountains. Here is a fine example of the persistence of the custom of sacrifice as practiced in the ancient cult.

On the four sides of the square in front of the church the Indians construct a green avenue of trees and branches and trees, an arbor, closely interwoven at the top and at the sides, and lavishly decorated with flowers and wreaths. In the four corners of the square, flower altars are constructed, where the responses are sung; the ground is profusely covered with flowers and earthenware basins are seen on all sides, in which copal and storax burn. That which is most singular and a relic of ancient times, which the Christian priests have permitted to be continued as a harmless amusement, is the sacrifice of sylvan beasts which the Indians offer to the divinity as their ancestors offered to Quetzalcoatl and to Tlalloc. Every living wild beast that can be procured is bound and suspended in the green alley. The jackal and the fox, the armadillo and the opossum, the raccoon and the nasua are seen struggling in their bonds; birds of prey, ravens, wild ducks and turkeys; quails and turtledoves flutter in the snares in which they were caught, and a quantity of small singing birds flutter and twitter in cages of bamboo from all sides of the green foliage. Even in the church, before the festively decorated high altar, the melodies of the mocking bird are heard and the metallic notes of the brown silvia.

This innocent gratification may well be conceded to the child of nature. The Indian generally, and more particularly, the inhabitants of ancient Anahuac, exhibit in their lives many traces of the primeval nature worship of the Toltecs, to whom subsequent generations owed this civilization and religion. Mountains and springs, he still conceives as tenanted by tutelary genii; the goddess of the clouds still draws her nets over the sky to fertilize the earth. . . . His love for flowers too, his selection of them to adorn his churches and altars, his skill in decorating religious performances was not taught by Spaniards, nor is it accidental; but since many centuries interwoven with his life, and derived from another race than that of the Aztecs with their bloody rites. The offering of living animals may also belong to an earlier form of worship.[20]

The festival of All Saints and All Souls as practiced also includes the element of sacrifice. The same writer describes their manner of celebrating it.

Another festival which is kept by the whole people, but which is of peculiar significance for the Indians, is that of All Saints and All Souls. ... With the Mexicans the festival of All Saints received a national coloring, dating from the aborigines, but gradually adopted by the *mestizos* and even by the creoles. It is not the feast of the Roman church, for this is here only a secondary consideration. It is an ancient Indian festival which the prudence of the Christian priests who found it too deeply rooted amongst the neophytes, added to the Christian holidays. . . .

The Ancient Aztecs held an annual festival in honor of the dead and offered the departed dead, sacrifices. The Christian priests suffered these rites to be combined with those of All Souls and thus the heathen, probably Toltec custom has maintained itself until the present day. . . .

In the Indian villages the proceedings are as follows. On the evening of the last day of October the house is put in order and when it is dark, a new, parti-colored woven mat is placed on the floor of the dwelling. The whole family is assembled in the kitchen waiting for the meal being prepared, which consists of chocolate, sweet maize, porridge, stewed chicken and little tortillas. A portion of each is put, if possible, into new vessels and conveyed by the members of the family into the house where it is placed on the mat; to this is added a kind of maize bread, called *elotlascale* and death-bread, a kind of wheaten bread without fat, sugar and salt, which is baked for this day only, shaped like a rabbit, a bird etc. and prettily ornamented. On clay candlesticks, corresponding with the number of dishes, thin wax tapers are lighted, not much thicker than a quill; roses, marigolds and the blossoms of the "datura grandiflora" are laid between the plates; and now the head of the family invites the dead children, that is to say, his own imme-

[20] C. Sartorius, *op. cit.,* pp. 160-1.

diate house (his own children, grandchildren, brothers and sisters) to come and regale themselves with the offering. The whole family now returns to the kitchen to consume the remainder of the meal which has been prepared abundantly enough to regale also the living. This is the offering of the children and every child, according to the age it had attained, has its dish and taper. Saucers with incense are placed around the mat and fill the chamber with a dense cloud.

The following day, offerings are prepared for adults in a similar manner. . . . With the adults, less care is exhibited in adorning the room with flowers, but with the things which belonged to the deceased—sandals, hat or hatchet. The whole house is filled with incense which is placed before the picture of the patron saints who were undoubtedly introduced three centuries ago in place of the house idols.[21]

The author believes that the Indians still think as did the ancients, that the souls of the departed hover about places they loved in life, sometimes fluttering about as humming birds or floating as clouds above it, though he admits that he has never been able to gain confirmation of it from the mouth of an Indian. The food of the offering was usually sent to a friend or a relative after the ceremony.

A festival dedicated to the Virgin de los Remedios, next to Guadalupe, the most popular of the many Mexican Virgins, is described by Brantz Mayer. It includes the dance as well as offerings, the native music and other pagan survivals. It is celebrated not more than ten miles outside the Mexican capital. The writer considers it an Indian corn-dance with a Catholic setting.

We sallied forth from the chapel as the mass commenced. Gradually the church began to fill with the half-naked Indian crowd. Deputations of natives from the different villages next arrived, bearing their offerings of flowers and wax candles to the Virgin, headed by a band of Indian musicians with their tom-tom drums and flageolets, making a low monotonous music.

---

[21] *Ibid.*, pp. 161-4.

The offerings were taken to the altar, under banners of flowers, and, after a wild dance of the Indians to their music, before the image, they were deposited in the sacristy. A constant succession of these oblations poured in until near two o'clock, when the morning services being finished, the image was taken from the tabernacle and put under a canopy, while a priest bore the consecrated wafer, and the procession began its march. All heads were at once covered, and I went to the upper story of the church to have a better view of the ceremony. At the door of the church stood a ragged Indian with a large firework on his head, made in the shape of a horse, surrounded with squibs and rockets; behind him were five men and a woman from one of the villages, neatly dressed, their heads being covered with red silk or cotton handkerchiefs. The men bore thin staves in their hands and small hoops made of cane were strapped on their backs. The woman held a covered basket before her, and one of the men thrummed a guitar, giving forth the same monotonous tune of the flageolets and drum. As soon as the procession reached the portal, the whole crowd knelt and a number of small rockets and cannons were fired by the Indians.

The huge flowers which I have before described as ascending and descending on ropes from the church tower to the gate, were pulled open by a secret spring and a shower of rose leaves fell from them over the passing priests and images. Juan Diego's knees were bent by some equally secret machinery and he continued on his slack rope pilgrimage through the air. The flageolets and the drum were once more put into requisition and the Indian with the horse firework, accompanied by six others began retreating in a trotting dance as the holy image approached, whirling and hopping to the barbarous music, ever careful to keep their faces to the Virgin. Suddenly an Indian stole behind the one who bore aloft the firework and touched its match. At this moment the bells began to chime, and thus amid their clang and the detonation of the squibs, cannons and rockets and the loud cracking of the exploding horse, the procession sallied from the courtyard to the village, to make a tour of the plaza among the gamblers, *pulque* shops and fruit sellers, all of whom suspended their operations for the moment and knelt to the sacred figure.

After the return of the Virgin to the church there was another grand explosion of the fireworks on a wheel and more cannons were discharged. The multitude then gathered together and made their frugal meal of fruits, dulce, tortillas and the never-failing frijoles and chile. By four o'clock, the majority of the Indians had trotted off once more to their villages, some of which were at a distance of not less than twenty or thirty miles.

The whole ceremony of the day seemed to me nothing more than an Indian corn-dance, and it is, no doubt, among the simple-minded Indians, a festival of thankfulness to God for the crops with which the bountiful seasons have blessed them; in other words a substitute for the sacrifices which they once made of fruits, flowers and birds to their goddess Centeotl.

The fault is in the permission of these idolatrous rites, before the mock image of another image, although it may be urged, perhaps, that as the Catholic is the blending of the rituals of many nations, there is no harm in these innocent Indians being allowed to mix up the relics of the worship of their fathers, so long as the whole service is offered in honor of the ever-living God.[22]

EXCHANGE OF DEITIES

The other way in which paganism influenced Christianity was by the carrying over into Christianity some of the ancient gods in the guise of saints or the virgin, or by the appropriation of shrines and places sacred to their old gods for some form of Christian worship. A number of present day survivals of this sort are recorded by the travelers and students of Mexican life. Mr. N. O. Winter, writing of religion in Mexico today asserts that at the time of the conversion not a few of the ancient Aztec Gods blossomed out as saints of Christianity, thanks to the ingenuity of the priests, who found this an effective method of getting the new religion accepted. Along with them, according to Mr. Winter, they brought the same powers and characteristics which they

[22] Brantz Mayer, *op. cit.,* pp. 145-7.

had enjoyed before; thus, for example, a goddess of rain much worshipped in a particular region of light rainfall may be recognized in Our Lady of the Mists, or Our Lady of the Rains, of the present day church in Mexico. In not a few cases, he adds, proof is not lacking that an ancient altar to the pagan goddess stood on the very spot where today the virgin is invoked.[23]

The "Virgen de los Remedios," rival of Our Lady of Guadalupe in popularity among the Mexican people, is the particular figure to which appeal is made in case of drought. Many times has her image been carried in procession through the streets of the capital and even of distant places in order to secure rain. She is lent, or more strictly speaking rented out for such purposes, according to some writers. Guadalupe on the other hand, is the protector against floods. On more than one occasion she is said to have stayed the rising floods threatening the city of Mexico, when appealed to do so.

G. B. Winton, one of the most careful of the observers of the life and customs of the people, and one who has studied the early history of the land, declares:

The Indians had indeed merely exchanged their indigenous superstitions for new and foreign ones. The Virgin Mary was promptly identified with Mother Earth (Nana Curaperi) who had long been a favorite deity among an agricultural people. The periodic feasts of the church were celebrated with garlands and the processions and dances just as the Mexicans had been accustomed to observe the festivals of their own religion. The traveler who chances to be in Mexico City now on December 12, the day sacred to the origin of Guadalupe, will see in the village of Guadalupe, a suburb of the city, Indian pilgrims from neighboring mountains, dancing their quaint rounds and chanting their native songs as in the days before the Spanish priests and monks came.[24]

[23] Winter, *op. cit.,* pp. 310-11.   [24] Winton, *op. cit.,* p. 87.

Another writer, Carleton Beals, who lived for some time in Mexico and has written discriminatingly of other features of Mexican life, writes:

Yet the spirit that burned in those ancient hearts and caused them to spend so much of their energy upon massive religious edifices and majestic ceremonies, still burns in the breasts of the modern sons and indeed, in few countries may be encountered such intrenched religious zeal! In few places have native barbaric pomp and impressiveness dovetailed so well into the elaborate Roman ritual.

But push through a crowded church festival such as that of Santa Anita or the "Fiesta de los Naturales" above Guadalupe and catch the sunny laughter of paganism behind it all. You will see in the uplifted figures of saints, the images of the ancient gods; and in the flowers garlanded about the heads of men and women, that unabashed pantheistic love for nature and beauty which throbbed in the pre-Spanish art. The modern tribes still fall down in worship before the majesty of the snow capped mount Orizaba, clipping a triangle from the dawn—that mountain of the star Citlaltepetl—for on that lofty summit was not Quetzalcoatl, the greatest of earth, consumed in divine fire?

This old pagan civilization may be clearly traced beneath the surface. Even today, in the shadows of far-off *barrancas* and beside the tropic seas, the natives secretly prostrate themselves before their stone gods and in remote districts, the crude carved idol may often be encountered behind the Christian saint or the bleeding Christ. The name has changed; both are still the grotesque, fear-filling shapes of unseen powers of earth, air and water. Thus the Indians of Tixtla cut from bamboo or the pith of the "calchual" a body resembling that of the Christ, which they coat with terra cotta, then paint with a brilliant scarlet, fairly bathing it in blood. After a priestly blessing, it is installed on the altar of the domestic "teocalli," among the household gods of similar fabrication. Yet, did not the early Christians, as is told in Marius the Epicurean, set out food for the old gods? Only here the process is reversed.[25]

[25] Carleton Beals, *Mexico—an Interpretation,* pp. 13-14.

Quinn, writing in *Beautiful Mexico,* says of the Tarascan Indians:

Today, the Tarascan Indians are the most fervent Catholics; but their worship of the Virgin and the saints is delight-
fully mingled with their pagan worship of Our Father The
Sun, and Our Mother the Moon, and with the many superstitions that still exist among them. They live in deadly fear of
the evil eye. The only protection against this terrible witch-
craft is something red, for red blurs the sorcerer's sight. Thus
always a red feather from the wood-pecker is worn in the hair,
or a red string is tied about the wrist or the ankle; a bit of red
flutters over the door of the hut, and a piece is tied to a maize-
stalk in the corn-patch. As a further protection for their crops
a talisman that will bring abundance of maize, an idol of one
of their gods is buried in each field.[26]

The same writer finds another vestige of the old cult in
the near deification of Fray Martín de Valencia, the leader
of the first group of twelve Franciscans to Mexico. He
writes:

So greatly was Fray Martín de Valencia loved by the Indians that when he died . . . he soon was revered as a saint and
then almost as a god. And as the years passed and the centuries, the place where he had been accustomed to spend much time
in prayer and meditation became so sacred that today, hundreds
of thousands of Indians make pilgrimages every year to this
shrine, to pray to the saint and to a remarkable image of the
Christ. This image, while life size, weighs only three pounds.
. . . It is probably made of the pith of maize stalk and it is
colored in a way that makes it more showy than beautiful, but
whatever its origin, it is regarded with fanatic veneration by
the Indians.
The sacred hill is about four hundred feet high and the cave
of the good friar is protected by a chapel. Stone stairs cut into
the hillside lead steeply to the top, and many of the worshipers
ascend those steps on their knees, murmuring as they go rhyth-
mic, semi-audible prayers. Other Indians stand for hours in

[26] Quinn, *Beautiful Mexico,* p. 383.

an ecstatic trance communing with the spirit of the good Fray Martín, dead now these four hundred years.

Unwashed garments, articles of clothing torn from the body, human hair pulled out of the head in exalted frenzy, lie spread out on the trees and bushes where the spirit of the saint in passing will pause to give them blessing.[27]

Frederick Starr, than whom few keener observers have studied Mexican life, writes interestingly of his contacts with the Indians of widely separated sections of Mexico on his various scientific expeditions. He has given a number of pictures of Indian religious customs which illustrate this point. One of the most interesting is as follows:

The young man who had been most interested in our proper understanding of the *costumbre* was anxious that we should see the village idols. These are kept concealed, apparently in a cave, though it is possible that they are buried in the ground. At all events, they exist, and in considerable number. A lively discussion ensued as to whether it would be proper to show them to us, and it was decided that nothing should be done until the old woman who is at the head of the pagan practices of the village should be present. It seems that in the *costumbre* already described, there are four priests or leaders. One of these is the old woman just mentioned, and the other three are men. She was sent for and while we waited, we were told that if we desired to see the lanterns of the last *costumbre,* they were still preserved in the *santocalli.* This is a mongrel word from the Spanish *santo* and the Aztec *calli,* house. It was a little structure of adobe and canes, close to the school house, and fronting with it upon the plaza of the village. It had a two-pitched thatched roof and a single door in front. After some demur, it was opened and we entered. It consisted of a single plain room with two benches of beams along the wall. At the back was a terrible Christ and Virgin, and to the right and behind, another Virgin. These Virgin figures were both small and unattractive and wore *quichequemils*. In front of the Christ and the larger Virgin was a simple altar built against the wall. In the floor, directly in front of it, were four small hollows. To the right of the altar, stood a table upon which were censers and candlesticks. Underneath the table, the space between the four legs was occupied by a heap of ashes; in front of this and behind were ill-defined basin hollows. To beams in front of these were hung the almost globular paper lanterns already mentioned.

When we had seen the lanterns and were about to leave, the old *bruja* appeared, with her female acolyte. She was furious over the desecration of strangers entering the *santocalli,* without her presence. She was a striking figure; very small, with wrinkled, shrewd and serious but not unkind face; her white hair was almost concealed by her *rebozo,* which was folded square and laid upon her head with a portion of it flowing behind. The most striking thing was her great devotion and complete unconcern regarding all around her.

Entering, she hastened to the altar, knelt, touched her forehead to the edge and in a clear, but not loud voice crooned an impassioned cry to Christ and San José and to the Virgin. Imperiously turning to her acolyte, she seized the censer, filled with copal and having lighted it, incensed the figures. Turning to the *presidente,* she asked whether he were going to placate the saint for the invasion by giving spirits and candles, both of which appeared as if by magic, when she was given money. Pouring the spirits from the bottle into a glass, she poured into the four basins in the ground before the altar, before the virgin; before and behind the heaps of ashes under the table, and then placed it to the lips of the virgin and the Christ, lovingly requesting them to partake. She then compelled each of the three men priests to make the same libation. Taking the unlighted candles, she made passes with them over and across the figures, first to one side and then to another, brushing the wicks against them.[28]

Two interesting cases of the taking over of Christian elements into the still persistent pagan religion serve to indicate something of the interpenetration that went on. Professor Starr is authority for the following story:

These Indians of Chamula have a love of liberty and a desire for independence. The most serious outbreak of recent

[28] Starr, *op. cit.,* pp. 353-5.

times was theirs of 1868, when, under the influence of the young woman Checheb, they attempted to restore the native government, the Indian life and the old time religion. Temples were erected to the ancient gods whose inspired priestess the young woman claimed to be; but three hundred years of Christianity had accustomed them to the idea of a Christ crucified; an Indian Christ was necessary, not one from the hated invading race; accordingly, a little Indian lad, the nephew of the priestess was crucified to become the savior of the race.[29]

Quinn, in *Beautiful Mexico,* contributes the other example.

In the wildest mountains of Durango and Sinaloa are the Huichol Indians. Having little use for the white man or his methods, this tribe lives in the deepest barrancas, on the most precipitous hillsides and in the most inaccessible fastnesses. In the days of the Franciscan friars, five churches somehow were established among the Huichols; but today they are used for pagan worship, those saints of whom the Catholics left visible images being accepted as heathen gods and worshiped alongside the Huichol idols. Especially is the rain dance performed inside these old churches so that the saints may participate and be so pleased that they will intercede with the sky gods for rain.[30]

Perhaps the best example of all, of the taking over of a pagan shrine and the transference of the attributes of the ancient divinities to the Catholic figures is the conspicuous case of the appearance of the Virgin, Our Lady of Guadalupe, upon the very place sacred to the goddess, who among all the figures in the Mexican pantheon most closely resembled her. Today she is the patron saint of all Mexico, and all over the world, among Catholic peoples, she is highly venerated. Hardly a house in Mexico, and no church in the country is without some image or reminder of the blessed Virgin. At the foot of the hill where she appeared is one of the most costly churches in Mexico, reputed to have cost

[29] *Ibid.,* pp. 366-7.   [30] Quinn, *op. cit.,* pp. 374-5.

over two million dollars, and to the shrine, countless thousands of Indians and other Mexican folk flow yearly to gaze upon the figure of Our Lady, which is supposed to have appeared, miraculously painted, upon the poor *tilma* or cloak of the Indian to whom she showed herself. We take the description of the shrine and its origin from an American source, the Catholic Encyclopedia, and thus avoid the wild extravagance of some of the native descriptions.

The picture really constitutes the shrine. It occasions the devotion. It is taken as representing the Immaculate Conception, being the lone figure of the woman with the sun, moon and star accompaniments of the apocalyptic sign, and in addition a supporting angel under the crescent.

To a neophyte fifty-five years old named Juan Diego, who was hurrying down Tepeyac hill to hear mass in Mexico City on Saturday, December 9, 1531, the blessed virgin appeared and sent him to bishop Zumárraga to have a temple built where she stood. She was at the same place that evening and Sunday evening to get the bishop's answer. He had not immediately believed the messenger, having questioned him and had him watched, he finally bade him ask for a sign of the lady who said she was the mother of the true God. The neophyte agreed so readily to ask any sign desired, that the bishop was impressed and left the sign to the apparition. Juan was occupied all Monday with an uncle who seemed dying of a fever. Indian specifics failed, so at daybreak on Tuesday, December 12, the nephew was running to the St. James convent for a priest. To avoid the apparition and untimely message to the bishop, he slipped around where the well-chapel now stands. But the blessed virgin crossed to meet him and said, What road is this thou takest, son? A tender dialogue ensued. Reassuring Juan about his uncle, whom at that instant she cured, appearing to him also, and calling herself Holy Mary of Guadalupe, she bade him go again to the bishop. Without hesitation, he joyfully asked for a sign. She told him to go up to the rock and gather roses. He knew it was neither the time nor the place for roses, but he went and found them. Gathering many into the lap of his cloak, he came back, the Holy Mother rearranging the roses, bade him keep them untouched and unseen until he reached the bishop. Having got to the presence of Zumárraga, Juan offered the sign. As he opened his cloak, the roses fell out and he was startled to see the bishop and his attendants kneeling before him; the life size figure of the virgin Mary just as he had described her was glowing on the poor *tilma* or cloak. . . . The picture was venerated, guarded in the bishop's chapel, and soon after carried processionally to the preliminary shrine.

The picture has been conserved carefully, mounted in a heavy silver frame, and it has been the object of veneration of untold millions of Mexicans during the almost four hundred years since it was first seen. Elaborate apologies for the genuineness of the miracle have been written. In the Vatican library there are innumerable testimonies of supposed witnesses of its original appearance and of the miracles which it has wrought throughout the years. The present pope is the nineteenth, according to the Catholic Encyclopedia, to favor the shrine. This is no place to enter into the question of exactly how this remarkable appearance was arranged. It is very much like other supposed appearances of the Virgin in other places. It certainly created no problem in the minds of the credulous Indians, and it did much to win them to Christianity, for it served to transfer to the Virgin the veneration which the Indians had for the goddess who inhabited that hill.

The relation between the Virgin and the original goddess Teotenantzin who was worshiped in this place appears in many Mexican writings where the contrast between the Virgin and the goddess is a matter of special emphasis, but which clearly supports the contention we hold, of a transference of deities. Padre Florencia, one of the most noted writers regarding Guadalupe, writes of it as follows:

In the time of their infidelity the Mexicans had a shrine upon this hill in which they worshiped an idol which in their tongue, they called Teotenantzin, which means mother of the gods. . . . Here it pleased the most holy Virgin to perform the miracle of her blessed image and that a temple be founded to dispossess this false mother of the false gods . . . vainly worshiped by the Indians, and to show them with many blessings, that she only was the true mother of the true God, and true mother of mankind. In this mountain where evil abounded, it pleased her to appear that grace might much more abound; that the site of the once infamous altar to a stupid idol should be the sacred throne of the most pure virgin; that in the place where such sacrilegious rites and such inhuman sacrifices were practiced, and in the place where such false responses and deceitful oracles were given, a temple should be erected in honor of God and his mother, such as that which now stands there, in which the sacraments are administered to the Indians and the bloodless sacrifice for our redemption is made in the many masses which are daily said, and where the true law is preached. There the doctrine is taught, and the mysteries of the rosary of the Most Holy Virgin are recited in chorus.[32]

Apparently, not content with this statement, he returns again to the theme a little farther on in his book, where he says:

The devil got himself worshiped in the idol Teotenantzin, which I said in the beginning, was in the same place where Our Lady appeared, under the name of mother of the gods, usurping thus the glorious renown of the Mother of God, with this name of pretended mother, and with the reality of a stepmother of the miserable Indians of this extended empire, possessed their souls for centuries, tyrannizing over their bodies, cutting them up in bloody sacrifices, etc.

The Holy Virgin dispossessed her of her stolen title putting in the place of the idol, her own miraculous image of Guadalupe; took away from her the souls of the Indians which he held, freed their bodies, etc.[33]

The same author notes that the Virgin appeared in the garb of a woman of the country, a woman of rank. This

[32] Padre Francisco de Florencia, *La Estrella del Norte,* p. 85.
[33] Florencia, *op. cit.,* p. 498.

which, to the modern scholar, is but another evidence of a deliberate purpose to render the Virgin as attractive as possible to the people, and doubtless to make her resemble as closely as possible the appearance of the goddess Teotenant-zin, is explained by the pious father as a gracious act on the part of the Virgin. To prove that Indians were not mere animals, without souls, as the Spaniards were already declaring, in order to justify their exploitation of them, but that they were humans with souls like the white men, she appeared in the garb of an Indian. In the face of this could any deny to them a complete humanity? It was a custom, in earlier times, according to the author, to celebrate her festival with great pomp and ceremony, with enormous spectacles and dances representing in them the war of the Mexicans with the Chichimecas and of the Spaniards and the Mexicans. But these were gradually abandoned, perhaps, because of the decreasing number of the Indians and their poverty.

Another writer of the seventeenth century carries the analogy, or rather the contrast between the pagan and Christian objects of worship a little farther than Father Florencia. He says:

In the times of their Gentility, the Indians adored an idol called Teotenantzin which means the mother of the gods. The Virgin desired that in this same mountain the miracle should be performed and a temple built to punish the devil for the idolatry and to teach that there was but one true Mother of God, making of the altar of the sacrilegious idol, the throne of a most pure image, so that where the pretended mother of the false gods was worshiped, the mother of the true God might be adored. In the temple the holy sacraments are now administered to the Indians who once received there deceitful oracles.[34]

To the points of similarity disclosed in the foregoing quotations, may be added that, according to some authorities,

[34] "Relación sacada de la Historia de al aparición de Nuestra Señora de Guadalupe," by Miguel Sanchez. 1662. In the *Colección de Obras y Opusculos pertenecientes a la Aparición . . . de Guadalupe,* 1785.

Teotenantzin, in becoming the mother of the gods, like Mary, had conserved her virginity, and that a son was called Tehuiznahuac, or the Lord of the Crown of thorns. One writer, Dr. Mier,[35] a priest who had the temerity to question the traditional story of the appearance, thought to see in it the reappearance of a Christian virgin, known to the Mexicans as Teotenantzin, who had been brought originally by Quetzalcoatl, or, as he thinks, St. Thomas. He cites Torquemada as authority for believing that the figure under which the Virgin was venerated was that of an Aztec girl, dressed in a shining white tunic and a sea-blue cape, sprinkled with stars, which, he says, is just the figure of the Virgin of Guadalupe.

Mier says that the natives celebrated several feasts in her honor, the principal being the second of February, which coincides with the purification, and the presentation of Jesus in the temple. The other was the twenty-second of December, which, according to Becerra Tanco, was the day of the appearance of the Virgin to Juan Diego. While Dr. Mier's statement may have been the result of some bias, it would, if true, be but interesting, added proof of the prudent adoption of Teotenantzin and her shrine under the figure of the Virgin Mary, in order thus to win to her standard the vast numbers of Indians who were said to resort to the pagan shrine at special feast times every year.

CONCLUSION

It thus appears that while Catholicism, backed by the power of a superior civilization, nominally won the struggle with the native religion of Mexico and so become the dominant faith, she still bears the distinct imprint of many features of the ancient cult. The fundamental principle of interaction is seen to have operated in the realm of religion

[35] Dr. Sewandro Teresa Mier, *Cartas al Cronista de Indias, sobre la Tradición de Nuestra Señora de Guadelupe.*

no less certainly than in the other phases of the two cultures which met. It is true that as European culture, through education, through economic and political pressure, and through a variety of social forces, increasingly pervades the life of the people, these pagan vestiges will gradually fade out. Thus far, however, due to the mutual interpenetration of the two types of religion which met in the conquest, the resultant religion is to a degree different from either of the original cults.

ESSAY ON THE SOURCES

The casual reader will have been satisfied to accept uncritically the source materials presented in the body of this book, however much he may have dissented from the writer's conclusions drawn from them. Students of history particularly will want, however, to know something about the sources employed, by whom written, under what circumstances and to what degree it is probable that they report the facts correctly. For such readers a brief critical evaluation of the chief sources is here attempted.

One group of sources is the considerable number of books or codices which have been preserved. The Mexicans possessed the art of picture-writing and of book-making. There were many codices in existence at the time of the conquest and a few of them have been preserved. Some of those that remain were produced about the time of the coming of the white man, others shortly after. Some of them are clearly the work of Christians, and the interpretation of all of them has been the work of Christians, though employing in that task the aid of the older Indians, who still were able to read them.

Alfredo Chavero, to whom we are indebted for much of the information regarding the sources, has written at length regarding them in the introduction to the first volume of *México á través de los Siglos*. There is just one thing to be noted about Chavero which may have affected his judgment in regard to questions of religion. He has displayed in his writings an anti-Catholic bias, at times almost violent. Yet it has seemed to the writer that, in his weighing of the sources, he has kept this feeling under control and that his estimates of the value of the religious material is essentially sound.

Regarding these codices and their interpretation, made for the most part shortly after the conquest, "some by aged Indians who translated them into the common tongue," he says:

It would seem at first sight that such interpretations ought to be given entire credence, but they must be taken cautiously in all that refers to religion, for from the beginning the Spanish writers and, naturally, the Indian neophytes who followed them, showed the tendency to correlate aboriginal traditions with Biblical narratives and since then have sought in their paintings to discover the accounts of the flood, the tower of Babel, the confusion of tongues, etc. They sought also from time to time to hide all that might encourage the conservation of the dethroned idolatry, which resulted in their leaving the explanations incomplete.[1]

Speaking particularly regarding the interpreter of the Codex Vaticanus, Padre Rios, he says,

He shares the defect already indicated of wanting to explain all their antiquities by biblical ideas.[2]

Of the interpreter of the Codex Borgiano, Padre Luis Fabrega, he says,

He likewise falls into the common error of subjecting the beliefs of the Mexicans to the traditions and ideas of the Christians.[3]

One of the most valuable of the Codices is the Codex Ramírez. It was written by an Indian about the time of the conquest. He was doubtless a Christian. He refers with severity to the ecclesiastics, calling them indolent in the matter of Christian instruction, saying that they did not baptize Montezuma because the priests who came with the Spaniards were more concerned with seeking riches than in catechising

---

[1] *México á través los Siglos,* I, p. xxii.
[2] *Ibid.*   [3] *Ibid.*

the poor Indians. The Codex purports to have received the facts narrated from eye-witnesses. Its early date is evidenced by the fact that the author speaks of the ruins of the great temple as it still existed at the time he wrote. Chavero considers this the purest of the historical sources and the most important for the genuine tradition of the Mexican people. It contains a long story regarding the patron god of the Mexicans quoted in part on pages 43-44. This codex has been published recently in English by Paul Radin,[4] who also rates it very highly.

There exist also a few other ancient poems and writings which throw some light on the native religion. Brinton has collected these and published them with an introduction telling their origin.[5] Some of them very clearly antedate the period of the conquest. Care must be taken in the use of these writings to consider them as the expression of a very limited number of people out of the mass of Indians. They do not in any sense reflect the thought of the people as a whole.

The most complete description of the religion of the Indians is to be found in the works of the early Spanish writers, most of them ecclesiastics, though not all. Great care must, of course, be exercised in taking the description of a religion from its opponents. Even though some of the writers were laymen and soldiers, they were without exception so thoroughly Catholic that they could but look with horror upon the religious practices of the natives. The chief authorities of this sort are as follows:

Bernardino de Sahagún was born early in the sixteenth century in the town of Sahagún, in Spain; was educated in the University of Salamanca, and arrived in New Spain in 1529 together with nineteen other priests to help in the conversion of the Indians. He became a close student of the

---

[4] *Sources and Authenticity of the History of the Ancient Mexicans.*
[5] Brinton, *Rig Veda Americana, Sacred Songs of Ancient Mexicans.*

Indian languages and history. He wrote a considerable number of books in the native tongue and about 1566 finished his great history of New Spain in twelve books. This was written in the native language and later translated into Spanish. The manuscript was sent to Spain but was not published for more than two hundred years. It was finally discovered in the Franciscan convent at Tolouse, in Navarre, and published almost simultaneously by Kingsborough in London and by Bustamante in Mexico, about 1829.

It will be worth our while to examine the method which the author employed in securing the material which the books contain. Fortunately a detailed description of his procedure is given in his introduction. He says:

All writers seek to authenticate their writings as fully as possible, some by trustworthy witnesses, others by reference to previous writers who have secured sure testimony as to the facts, still others by reference to the Holy Scriptures. But these means are wholly lacking in my case for the twelve books I have written, and I see no other way of authenticating what I have written than by stating here the extreme care which I exercised in securing the data. As stated elsewhere, I was ordered by my superiors to write, in the Mexican tongue, whatever I thought would be useful for the doctrine, the culture and the maintenance of the Christianity of the natives of New Spain and would help those who are seeking to indoctrinate them. As soon as I received the command, I made, in Spanish, a list of all the subjects that ought to be treated. I then went to the town of Tepeopulco and began to seek material. I went about it in this way. I had the head man of the village, D. Diego de Mendoza, an old man of great ability, well practiced in things priestly, military, political and even idolatrous, call together the chief men of the place. When they were met, I proposed what I wished to accomplish and asked that they furnish me with skilful and experienced persons with whom I could talk, who would be able to explain to me the things I might ask. They replied that they would confer together about it and would let me know next day. . . . Next day they came together again and with much solemnity assigned ten or twelve of the chief older men, saying that I might communicate with them and that they would explain all that I might ask. . . . With these I conversed over a period of two years (following the list that I had made). Everything about which we conferred they gave me in paintings, which was their method of writing. The grammarians (four of these had been pupils of his in an earlier period) translated them into the common language writing the explanations at the bottom of the pictures. I still have these originals. . . . Later I went to live at Santiago de Tlaltelolco, where I gathered together another group with whom I might explain what was already written. The governor assigned eight or ten of the chief men who were well trained in their own language and well acquainted with the ancient traditions. With these and with four or five students, all of whom spoke three languages, we spent more than a year amending and adding to what I had brought already written from Tepeopulco.

He then relates in detail how he submitted the work to different individuals and groups and secured their approval of it. What shall we say as to his writings? Certainly no more careful piece of work was done in that early day. But may we trust it as a true description of the religion, remembering that he was a priest, and that most of the men whom he questioned were Christians, at least nominally? In his introduction to the book dealing with the religion of the people he states as his reason for writing it that the physician who would cure an ill must know what the ill is. He says:

It is not enough to say that among these people there exist no longer sins of drunkenness, dishonesty and carnality. There are other sins and much more serious which are in great need of a remedy, the sins of idolatry, idolatrous rites, idolatrous superstitions and auguries and idolatrous ceremonies. These are by no means all ended.

To preach against these things and indeed to be able to know whether they exist or not, it is necessary to know how they were used in the time of idolatry.[6]

[6] Sahagún, *Relación de las Cosas de la Nueva España,* I, xiii.

It seems to the writer that, notwithstanding his bias, he has come nearer giving the facts than any other writer of his time save possibly one other, Bernal Díaz del Castillo, of whom we shall speak later. As simple description of what was done, Sahagún can probably be safely considered as trustworthy, though where interpretation enters in, caution should be used in following him.

Fray Toribio de Motolinia was another of the very early writers whose works are still preserved. He was a Franciscan monk who came to New Spain as a missionary in 1524. His principal work appeared in 1541 under the title *Historia de Los Indios de la Nueva España*. Prescott, author of the *History of the Conquest of America,* says of him,

Never losing sight of his mission for a moment, the author interrupts the sequence of the subject which immediately occupies him to relate an anecdote or tell of some event which illustrates his ecclesiastic interests. He recounts the most marvelous happenings with grave credulity. . . . He repeats as true a host of miracles more than sufficient to provide for the rising religious communities of New Spain. Nevertheless in the midst of all this, the investigator of Mexican antiquities will find much important and curious material. The long and intimate association of the author with the Indians gave him opportunity to acquire a vast knowledge of their theologies and science. The deduction in which the superstitions of the age and the peculiar character of the author are reflected cannot be taken with entire confidence; but since his integrity and his means of gaining his knowledge are indisputable, he is a first authority in the study of the antiquities of Mexico.[7]

Alfredo Chavero says of him:

We consider Motolinia as the first and principal source of our written history and whatever eulogy we might write regarding his work would be of little account in comparison with his merit.[8]

[7] Prescott, *History of the Conquest of Mexico,* II, p. 98.
[8] *México á través de los Siglos,* I, xlv.

It will be noted that he is rated very highly by both these men as an authority in purely historical matters, but not so highly in matters religious.

Other early authorities are Gonzalo Fernando de Oviedo y Valdés who published, in 1535, an extensive general and natural history of the Indies, *Historia General y Natural de las Indias.* What he did not actually see himself he took from eye-witnesses. He is not so valuable a source for religious investigation as for historical and geographic study.

Among the most valuable ought to be the writings of Ixtlilxochitl, himself a descendant of the emperors of Mexico. His mother was the daughter of the next to the last Mexican emperor. He served in his later years as interpreter in the Indian court. However, he is not to be relied upon as exact in all his statements. In the first place he was a Christian and writes from that standpoint. What seems to be one of the most important stories pointing toward an advanced idea of the One God, we owe to him. It is recounted twice in his different books. We cannot be sure, however, that he has not read back into the experience more than was really there. Chavero says of him:

He wished to represent his forbears always as conquerors and twists the history of Mexico to that end. He invented for them an impossible culture, given the epoch and the social milieu in which the people lived.[9]

Spence in his book *Myths of Mexico and Peru,* says:

He was cursed with or blessed by a strong leaning toward the marvelous and has colored his narratives so highly that he would have us regard the Toltec or ancient Nahuan civilization, as by far the most splendid that ever existed. His description of Tezcuco, if picturesque in the extreme is manifestly the outpouring of a romantic and idealistic mind, which in its patriotic enthusiasm desired to vindicate the country of his birth from

[9] *México á través de los Siglos,* I, xlviii.

the stigma of savagery and to prove its equality with the great nations of antiquity.[10]

If one approaches his writings with this fact in mind and is careful in using his materials, there is a great deal of value to be found in his work.

Bernal Díaz del Castillo was one of the companions of Cortés throughout the whole conquest and seems to have been quite close to his commander. He was not a learned man in any sense, nor praticed in the art of writing. His history is just the story of what he saw and heard during the years of fighting that won Mexico to the crown of Spain. He makes no pretense of any literary skill, indeed he constantly laments his inability as a writer. Nevertheless, or it may be chiefly just because of this, his narrative is generally accredited to-day as true. Chavero says of him:

This soldier-historian, companion of Cortés, was eye-witness of the events which he describes. He has written only that which he saw with his eyes and heard from the Indians. He is an honest and trustworthy witness. His genuineness is revealed on every page and his account may be taken as the very truth.[11]

Although one must recognize the extremely Catholic bias of Díaz, the very naiveté of his descriptions strikes the writer as being the best evidence of the accuracy of what he writes. Ramírez says of him:

With his genius for investigation he inquired into everything and with his natural frankness told everything, leaving us, thus, in his rude writings the most precious gem of Mexican history.[12]

Invaluable in any study of the period of the conquest are the letters of the man whose genius made it possible, the

[10] P. 46.

[11] *México á través de los Siglos*, I, 1.

[12] José F. Ramírez, "Bautismo de Moteuhzoma Novena Rey de México," *Boletín de la Sociedad Mexicana de Geografía y Estadística, la epoca* (1863), X, 366.

Conquistador himself, Hernando Cortés. He wrote five long letters to the emperor, Charles V, relating the story of his adventures, at some points in very great detail. They were written very soon after the events they narrate, so that it may be supposed that the reports are faithful accounts of what happened, unless we are to suspect that, in some cases in which Cortés' own character or his own fortunes are involved, he may have colored his narrative. He has been charged with this by his enemies. The dates of the letters are, July 10, 1519; Oct. 30, 1520; May 15, 1522; Oct. 15, 1524; and Sept. 3, 1526. Fortunately these have been made available to English readers by Francis A. MacNutt who has edited them and added valuable notes and comments, in two large volumes, published by Putnam's, N. Y., in 1908.

Aside from these longer letters, scores of letters and government orders of all sorts from the hand of Cortés are to be found in the great collection, *Colección de Documentos Inéditos*,[13] which are quite as valuable, or possibly even more so, as those to the emperor, since many of these were doubtless written without thought of their reaching the imperial eye, and may therefore be more trustworthy.

Two others of Cortés' companions have left brief records of the conquest which are highly regarded by historical students. The author of one is unknown, being known simply as El Conquistador Anónimo. It was edited and published by Joaquín García Icazbalceta, in volume two of his *Colección de Documentos para la Historia de México*. Chavero thinks it may have been written by Francisco Terrazas, father of the early Mexican poet Terrazas. It has but little to say regarding religion, aside from one chapter which describes the native temples, rites, and ceremonies. The other was by Andrés de Tápia, one of the officers of the conquering army, under the title *Relación sobre la Conquista de*

[13] *See post,* p. 323.

México, and is published by Icazbalceta in the same volume with the former. In the introduction he says of it:

> This document, until now entirely unknown, is of the greatest importance. Its author was one of the most notable captains in Cortés' army. He was in all the wars and expeditions, figured prominently in the discord between the governors of Mexico, went with Cortés to Spain, and returning, lived neighbor to him until his death.[14]

Perhaps the best known of all the early writers on Spain in the New World is Bartolomé de las Casas, fiery champion of the Indians against their exploitation at the hands of the Spaniards. His writings have enjoyed probably a wider circulation than those of any other writer of the period, having been translated into English, Dutch, French, and German at least, particularly his one work *Brevísima Relación de la Destrucción de las Indias,* which he first published in Seville in 1552. In it he recounted the fearful cruelties and injustices practiced upon the Indians by their conquerors. It doubtless made very interesting reading and effective propaganda against Spain in the enemy-countries, though many of them were no less guilty than she of grossly mistreating the conquered peoples under their sway in the New World.

While, doubtless, there was much of truth in what Las Casas wrote, he is too much under suspicion as a propagandist for his writings to rank high as sober history. He wrote with such passion, and in some cases so evidently overstated his case that his statements require rigorous checking before they can be used. Oddly enough, one of his most powerful opponents and critics was the gentle self-effacing Franciscan friar, Toribio Benevente, better known by his Indian *sobre-nombre* Motolinia, concerning whose

[14] García Icazbalceta, *Colección de Documentos para la Historia de México,* Intro. p. lxi.

work we have already written,[15] himself also a staunch friend of the Indians. Several of his letters condemning Las Casas are extant.

Only slight use of Las Casas is made, in one section of the paper. The fact that he is not used more extensively, given the character of his writings and the popular esteem in which he is held, requires this explanation. What is said here is no reflection at all on the great service which the fearless and tireless friend of the Indians rendered them, and no man in the whole history of this stirring drama of conquest proved himself a more genuine or more powerful friend of the oppressed natives. The judgment here is wholly as to the merit of his literary work as source-material for our present purpose.

Francis A. MacNutt, the translator of Cortés' letters, has written a monograph on Las Casas, including the translation of the *Brevísima Relación,* in which he vigorously defends the "protector" and assigns greater worth to his historical writings than that conceded by most Spanish writers.

Other first-hand writers consulted have been so little used that they need not be discussed here. They are Suarez de Peralta who wrote in 1589 his *Noticias Historicas de la Nueva España;* Dorantes de Carranza, *Sumaria Relación de las Cosas de la Nueva España;* Saavedra Guzmán, who wrote a lengthy poem, *Peregrino Indiano,* which, while lacking great poetic merit, does furnish valuable material, particularly for the secular historian.

Among the most valuable sources, especially regarding the work of conversion by the priests and the development of the church in Mexico, are the following:

Concilios Provinciales, primero y segundo, celebrados en la Ciudad de México en 1555 y 1565, published by Arch-

[15] *Ante,* p. 314. See *Documentos para la Historia de México,* VII, 261-3, 266, 283.

bishop Francisco Antonio Lorenzana of Mexico City. It bears the date of 1769, but was taken from the original proceedings of these councils, the manuscripts of which were preserved in the Metropolitan church in the capital. The third council, held in 1585, is said by Lorenzana to have furnished the norm for ecclesiastical procedure in his own time. Unfortunately a copy of its decrees has not been found in any of the libraries to which we have access. It was published by Don Juan Perez de la Serna in 1622. However, the volume of the Archbishop is of very great value, for it gives not only the proceedings of the two formal councils, but of the very first *Junta Apostólica,* which took place during the closing days of 1524 and the early days of 1525. The original minutes of the gathering have been lost but the summary taken from Torquemada and Mendieta is given and probably represents fairly well what was done at that time. It was not dignified with the name of Council, because at that time there was no bishop or archbishop in Mexico. By means of a comparison of the three documents it is possible to see something of the progress that was being made and of the problems that were emerging. These are official pronouncements, and while they probably by no means always represent what was actually practiced, they do show what the church was attempting to do and the ideals for which she stood.

There exists also an interesting appendix to these council reports, though it is not always bound with the volume by Lorenzana. The copy found in the Ayer Collection at the Newberry Library (Chicago) was bound separately. It is called *Apéndice a los Concilios, Primero y Segundo Mexicanos,* and contains a *Carta Original de los Obispos de México, Guatemala y Oaxaca,* asking for instructions regarding the matter of attending the general Council of Trent; inquiring concerning different points, such as tithes; and seeking directions for the sound planting of the faith in the new world. This letter, written in 1537, was the result of a meeting held at the request of the king through the viceroy, that they might discuss matters relating to the good of the Indians and their conversion and instruction in the Holy Faith. It is signed by the three bishops; Zumárraga of Mexico City, Zárate of Antequera, and Marroquín of Guatemala.

In reply to this letter the emperor expressed the desire that they should assemble the bishops and other ecclesiastical leaders to draw up rules for governing the church and the spreading of Christianity. Such an assembly met in 1539. The bishops had drawn up for their consideration a tentative set of rules which were discussed and the response of the clergy to each section was inserted in the margin. Why this was not technically called a council, does not appear. The document is found also in the *Apéndice a los Concilios*, thus furnishing a complete file of the group pronouncements of the early church of Mexico.

Another source of very great value is the *Recopilación de Leyes de los Reinos de las Indias,* printed and published by order of King Charles II. The royal order for its printing is dated 1681. The edition from which quotations are taken is the second edition, Madrid, 1756. It consists of four large volumes of some six hundred pages each, double column. The first book, containing two hundred forty-six pages is wholly devoted to religious and ecclesiastical matters. Some of the titles of chapters are: Concerning the Holy Catholic Church; Concerning Archbishops, Bishops and Visitors; The Clergy; Religious Teachers. Some of the chapters or titles, as they are called, have as many as fifty laws or more. Besides this first book, laws relating to like matters are scattered throughout the whole compilation, which may be easily found by a system of cross-references.

Here are brought together the royal orders and those of the royal council of the Indies which were promulgated from time to time from the very beginning of the new era of discovery. In each case the date of the order and its author are given. The place to which it is particularly meant to apply usually appears also, though most of them are general prescriptions for use throughout the whole domain. It is, of course, the source-book for all official pronouncements regarding the conversion of the Indians and their treatment. Just the reading of the headings of the various chapters and laws provides an excellent running commentary on the world of that day.

No other single individual has contributed more to the study of the history of Mexico, particularly the phase of it that engages us here, than has Don Joaquín García Icazbalceta, who has edited and published so many valuable original source-documents and provided sound critical introductions to them. It was he who edited and published Motolinia's great work in Volume I of his *Colección de Documentos para la Historia de México*. It was he who, in the second volume, gave us the *Relación de Andrés de Tapia, El Conquistador Anónimo* and various other documents of great worth. It was Icazbalceta who edited Mendieta's *Historia Eclesiástica Indiana,* one of the very best sources, discussed in more detail on pages 325-326; and it was he who edited a remarkably valuable collection of documents in five volumes under the title, *Nueva Colección de Documentos para la Historia de México*.

Volume one of this collection entitled *Cartas de Religiosos de Nueva España, 1539-1594,* contains a wealth of material which reflects the religious conditions at various periods during the sixteenth century. If it offered no more than the eight letters of Mendieta which appear there, it would be of immense worth, but it has a great many other letters as well; for example, one expressing the opinion of the Franciscans regarding the *repartimiento* of the Indians in 1594.

Volume two, *Códice Franciscano,* is one of the most important sources for this study. It gives more explicitly than any other document just what the Indians were to be taught. The doctrine which they used is here presented both in Spanish and the Indian dialect. In addition there are many letters, mostly of ecclesiastics, all Franciscans, covering the years 1533-69. Volume three contains two *Relaciones,* one that of Pomar, a half breed of Tezcuco who wrote of his own people in 1582, and that of Zurita who wrote under the title *Breve y Sumaria Relación de los Señores y Maneras y Diferencias que había en la Nueva España y en Otras Provincias.* Neither is of great value for our purpose save as they here and there open up a window through which one catches momentary glimpses of the religious changes that were taking place. Volumes four and five form what he calls the *Códice Mendieta.* Not all the letters and documents are by Mendieta, but Icazbalceta thinks that many of those not specifically attributed to him were really his.

Another collection of original documents is the large work, *Colección de Documentos Inéditos Relativos al Descubrimiento, Conquista, y Colonización de las Posesiones Españoles,* the second series of which is still being published. These include hundreds of letters and government orders, many of them having direct reference to the religious phase of the conquest. The orders given by Cortés "for the good government of the people," orders from the king to the viceroy, reports from the viceroys to their kings, reports of law suits, criminal trials, and commercial contracts—all throw some light on our problem. The particular sources within the collection are cited when quotations are used from them. Just the titles of those read in the search for pertinent material would fill many pages.

Other less extensive and less valuable collections exist, and they have been consulted, but so little material has proved to be germane to this particular field of investigation, that they need not be discussed here. They are merely named in the bibliography.

Thus far the sources discussed have, in the main, been original first-hand writings by people who lived during the period covered by their writings. Passing to the group of writers at second-hand, probably Gomara ought to be mentioned first, for he wrote much earlier than many of those who were actual participants in the events which they so graphically describe. His great work *Historia de las Conquistas de Hernando Cortés,* was finished in about 1553. The sources of his information were various. He is said to have had personal contact with many of the conquerors who returned from Mexico. Ramírez declares that Gomara's work may be thought of almost as the testimony of an eyewitness, and to have the authority of Cortés' own writings, since it was likely written under his inspiration and perhaps even his dictation. In a footnote,[16] Ramírez quotes Garcilaso de la Vega, the Peruvian writer (*Comentarios Reales del Peru,* Libro II, capítulo viii) as saying that Cortés himself wrote it. He affirms that he knows "trustworthy gentlemen" who told him so, and he laments that Cortés did not publish it under his own name. Ramírez adds that where Cortés' own personal character is involved, the book should be read with caution, for Gomara was an apologist for Cortés whom he served as chaplain while the latter was in Spain. Bernal Díaz del Castillo criticizes his narrative at many points, indeed one motive which the "true historian" alleges for writing his own confessedly imperfect narrative is that he may correct the mistakes of Gomara.

[16] Ramírez, *loc. cit.*

Mendieta, of whose letters we have already spoken, is for this study one of the chief sources, for he wrote particularly of the subject which engages our attention, the conversion of the Indians, under the title *Historia Eclesiástica Indiana* (Ecclesiastical History of the Indies). Chavero says of him:

If he is not one of the first hand writers, he must not be confused with those who wrote at second hand, although he himself says that he made use of the writings of Olmos and Motolinia. Although less original than Motolinia, he writes more extensively and observes better order and more precise method. At every step he reveals his vehemence of character which is still more clearly shown in his letters.[17]

García Icazbalceta who, as stated above, has edited much of his work, says that his *Historia Eclesiástica* was finished in 1596, but that it was sent to Spain for publication and he never saw it again. No writer after Torquemada made use of it though he used the manuscript extensively. It was not until 1861 that the manuscript again came to light and it was published by Icazbalceta in 1870. He says of the writer:

Mendieta, a man of strong character, possessed of the spirit of his Order (Franciscan), jealous for the honor of God, lover of justice and truth, living more nearly in the times of the conquest, witness of the great miracles of the Indians and their hardy defender, although not blind to their defects, looses his pen and without fear or favor points out and even exaggerates the vices, disorders, abuses, tyrannies and evils of the conquerors, not excepting the governors, nor even the king himself. If Mendieta is not in the strict sense of the word an eye-witness, he is original in his acts as well as judgments and merits a distinguished place among our historians.[18]

Of course, for the purposes of this study, while he is not an eye-witness of the earliest attempts, he is a prominent actor

[17] *México á través de los Siglos*, pp. li-lii.
[18] *Nueva Colección de Documentos para la Historia de México*, I, xxxix.

in the later efforts at conversion and deserves high rank as indicating the progress which Christianity had made.

Fray Diego Durán based his work chiefly on the *Codex Ramirez,* but greatly enlarged it, taking much of his material from contemporaries. Says Chavero:

> We do not hesitate to say that his *Historia de las Indias de la Nueva España y las Islas de Tierra Firme* is the best and most complete account we have of the ancient history of the Mexicans.[19]

He was a Dominican monk, born in Mexico shortly after the conquest. He finished his work in 1581, but it was not published until 1867 and 1880. The elements used by him that were not found in the *Códice Ramirez* were taken from ancient Mexican paintings, and from Indians and Spaniards contemporary with the conquest.

La Historia Natural y Moral de las Indias, by the Jesuit Fray José de Acosta appeared in 1590 in Seville. The work has been extensively circulated, for it was translated into English, German, Flemish, Latin, and French. It was very highly regarded by earlier historians, but Chavero denounces it as simply a plagiarism of the work of an Indian writer who gave us the *Códice Ramirez.* This, however, while it discredits José de Acosta, does not take away from the value of the work itself which has very great merit.

Next to Mendieta, perhaps Juan Torquemada, among secondary authorities, is of most importance for this study, for of his great work, *Monarquía Indiana,* written during the first decade of the seventeenth century, he devotes the greater part to the religion of the natives and the efforts at their conversion. He relied largely on what had already been written, but he himself lived early enough and was keen enough observer to record much invaluable material for

[19] *México á través de los Siglos,* I, lii.

tracing the progress of the gospel among the Indians. Chavero says of him:

He took word for word whatever he found in Motolinia, Olmos, Sahagún and Mendieta, paying no attention to the contradictions which arose from such different opinions. Yet his work is very important for he gathered up what had already been said. He lacked the critical faculty, but the materials for criticism are there.[20]

Ramírez calls him the "most illustrious and *recomendable* of our historians."

We have thus far discussed the original sources and the writings of those who were but little removed in point of time from the events which they recounted. There were many later writers who have left very valuable material, but they depended largely on those already mentioned, adding very little that was not at least implied in the earlier works. Herrera, Solís, Betancourt, Boturini, Clavigero, Baron Humboldt, Orozco y Berra, Palacios, Alfredo Chavero, our own Prescott and Bancroft, and others have made rich contributions to the field, but all on the basis of the originals. Most of these have been examined from time to time for the benefit of their critical judgment, but we have from the outset attempted to work from the original sources as far as possible. In not a few cases we were unable to accept the conclusions of some of the later writers, arrived at on the basis of their study of the originals.

In the matter of native myth and tradition we acknowledge indebtedness particularly to Daniel G. Brinton, the American writer who has gone most thoroughly into the study of Mexican religions. He rendered a very useful service to all students of the subject by editing and publishing many original Indian writings. We cannot always agree with Brinton in his interpretation of the myths, for he seems to be entirely obsessed with the notion that all myth-

[20] *Ibid.,* p. liii.

ology centers about light and darkness, but if this be kept in mind as he is read, his books are filled with excellent material.

Lewis Spence writes much more popularly than Brinton and is not so profound a student as the latter, but does make a contribution to the field. Albert Reville, the French historian of religion, in his *Native Religions of Mexico and Peru,* has given perhaps as satisfactory a discussion as any that has appeared.

Listed in the bibliography will be found a large number of books of travel and description of Mexico written at intervals throughout the history of Mexico. In these we have constantly sought to find mirrored the religious life of the period with the view of comparing the situations and trying to determine what has been the religious trend since the beginning of the conversion. Unfortunately few writers of books of that character are skilled observers, and most of them had no particular interest in the matter we are studying. Hence a great deal of reading has netted but meager results. One of the most valuable works of the sort was E. B. Tylor's *Anahuac; Mexico and the Mexicans, Ancient and Modern.*

In the attempt to follow down one conspicuous instance in which an ancient Mexican shrine was taken over and devoted to the Virgin, a number of books recounting the story of the Virgin of Guadalupe have been consulted, all of them save one bearing the *imprimatur* of the ecclesiastical authorities. What a queer mixture of fact and legend! No historical accuracy is demanded of these sources, for their interest lies not so much in the exactness of their statements, as in the fact that such statements and claims could be made and believed. They do, nevertheless, establish clearly enough that the Virgin did displace the ancient pagan goddess Teotenantzin.

BIBLIOGRAPHY

I. EARLY WRITERS

Acosta, Fray José de: *Historia Natural y Moral de las Indias.* 2 tomos. Madrid, 1590. Present edition Madrid, 1894. Translated under the title *Natural and Moral History of the Indies* by Edward Grimston, 1604, edited by Clements R. Markham, London, 1904.

Advertencias para Confesores de Indios. Mexico, 1601.

Codex Telleriano-Remensis, in Kingsborough: *Mexican Antiquities,* Volumes II and VI.

Concilios Provinciales, Primero y Segundo, 1555 y 1565, Editado por F. A. Lorenzana, Mexico, 1769. The appendix of this work contains two other important documents which are sometimes bound separately: *Carta Original de los Obispos de México, Guatemala y Oaxaca,* and *Copia de un Original muy Precioso de la Junta de los Obispos Zumárraga y Otros en 1539.*

Cortés, Hernando: *Cartas y Relaciones al Emperador Carlos V.* Escritas 1519-26. Translated and edited with valuable notes and comments by Francis A. MacNutt, 2 vols., under the title *Letters of Hernando Cortés to Charles V.* New York, 1908.

Díaz del Castillo, Bernal: *Verdadera Historia de la Conquista de México, 1568.* Translated by John Ingram Lockhart under the title *The Memoirs of the Conquistador, Bernal Díaz del Castillo.* 2 vols. London, 1844. All references to this author are to this edition.

Dorantes de Carranza, Baltazar: *Sumaria Relación de las Cosas de la Nueva España.* Written before 1604. Mexico, 1902.

Durán, Diego: *Historia de las Indias de Nueva España y Islas de Tierra Firme.* 1579-81. Edited by José F. Ramírez. Mexico, 1867-80.

El Conquistador Anónimo. Written before 1556. Editado y publicado por Joaquín García Icazbalceta, en *Documentos para la Historia de México.* Vol. II.

Fernandez, Alonzo: *Historia Eclesiástica de Nuestros Tiempos.* Toledo, 1611.

Gomara, Francisco Lopez: *Historia de las Conquistas de Cortés.* Written before 1560. Ed. Carlos María de Bustamante, Mexico, 1826.

Gonzales Dávila, Gil: *Teatro Eclesiástico de la Primitiva Iglesia de Indias.* 2 tomos. Madrid, 1649.

Herrera y Tordesillas, Antonio de: *Historia General de los Hechos de los Castellanos en las Islas y Tierra Firme del Mar Océano.* 9 vols. About 1599. Published in Madrid, 1726-28.

Ixtlilxochitl, Fernando de Alva, 1568-1648: *Obras Históricas de.* Anotadas y publicadas por Alfredo Chavero, Mexico, 1891-92.

Landa, Diego de: *Relación de las Cosas de Yucatan.* Text in French and Spanish with notes by L'abbe Brasseur de Bourbourg. Vol. III in *Collection des Documents dans les Langues Indigenes.* Paris, 1864.

Las Casas, Bartolomé de: *Historia de las Indias.* Ed., El Marqués de la Fuensanta del Valle. 5 tomos. Madrid, 1876. *Historia Apologética de las Indias.* Ed. Madrid, 1909.

Mendieta, Gerónimo de: *Historia Eclesiástica Indiana,* escrita a fines del siglo XVI. Ed. Joaquín García Icazbalceta, Mexico, 1876.

—— *Códice Mendieta,* Vols. IV and V in *Nuevos Documentos para la Historia de México.* Mexico, 1892.

Montenegro, Dr. Alonzo de la Pena: *Itinerario para Párrocos de Indios.* Nueva Edición, Madrid, 1771. Written originally about the middle of the seventeenth century.

Montúfar, Arzobispo de México, "Al Real Consejo de Indias Sobre Recaudación de Tributos y Otras Asuntos Referentes a las Órdenes Religiosos." 1556. Published in *Colección de Documentos Inéditos.* IV, 491-530.

Motolinia, Fr. Toribio de: *Historia de los Indios de la Nueva España.* 1541. Publicado por Joaquín García Icazbalceta: *Documentos para la Historia de México,* I, pp. 1-250. Mexico, 1868.

Muñoz Camargo, Diego: *Historia de Tlaxcala.* Written before 1600. Ed. Alfred Chavero. Mexico, 1868.

Notícias Secretas de América. Escritas fielmente según las instrucciones del Excelentísimo Señor Marqués de la Ensenada, Primer Secretario del Estado, y presentados en informe secreto a Fernando VI, por Don Jorge Juan y Don Antonio de Ulloa, sacadas a luz por David Barry. London, 1826.

Olmos, A. de: *Grammaire de la Langue Nahuatl u Mexicaine,* composée, 1547. Paris, 1875.

Oviedo y Valdés, Gonzalo Fernandez (1478-1557): *Historia General y Natural de las Indias, Islas y Tierra Firme del Mar Océano.* 1535-37. Ed. Don José Amador de los Rios. Madrid, 1851-55.

Palafox, Rev. Don Juan (Obispo de la Puebla de los Angeles): *Carta Pastoral a los Súbditos de su Obispado sobre la Debida y Necessaria paga de los Diezmos y Primicias.* Aug. 26, 1647.

Pomar: *Relaciones Antiquas.* Siglo XVI. Publicadas en *Nueva Colección de Documentos* por Joaquín García Icazbalceta.

—— *Recopilación de Leyes de los Reinos de las Indias,* mandadas imprimir y publicar par la Majestad Catolica del Rey Don Carlos II. Ordered published 1681. 2nd ed. 4 vols. Madrid, 1756.

Román, Fr. Gerónimo: *Chronica de la Orden de los Ermitanos del Glorioso Padre Sancto Augustin* etc. Salamanca, 1569.

Sæavedra Guzmán, Antonio de D. (1599): *El Peregrino Indiano, Poema de la Conquista.* Published 1599. Mexico, 1880.

Sahægún, Bernardino de: *Historia General de las Cosas de la Nueva España.* 1566. Ed. Carlos María de Bustamante. 2 tomos. Mexico, 1829-30.

—— *Historia de la Conquista de México.* The twelfth book of the *Historia General de las Cosas de la Nueva España.* 1566. Ed. Carlos María de Bustamante, Mexico, 1829.

Tápia, Andrés de: *Relación hecha sobre la Conquista de México.* Written probably before 1550. Published by Joaquín García Icazbalceta in *Documentos para la Historia de México,* Vol. II.

Tezozomoc, Fernando de Alvarado: *Crónica Mexicana*. Written before 1651. Published in Kingsborough, *Mexican Antiquities,* Vol. IX.

Torquemada, Fr. Juan de: *Monarquía Indiana*. Written near the end of the sixteenth century. Edited and published by A. Gonzales de Barcía Carbillido y Zúñiga. 3 vols. Madrid, 1723.

Velades, Didaco: *Rhetorica Christiana*. Perugia, 1579.

Zumárraga, Fr., Juan (Arzobispo de México): *Carta de, a su Majestad*. Published in part in MacNutt: *Letters of Cortés to Charles V*. Vol. 2, appendix.

———— *Lettres de,* in Ternaux-Compans, *Pieces sur le Mexique*. Paris, 1840.

Zurita, Alonzo de: *Breve y Sumaria Relación* etc. About 1574. Vol. II, *Colección de Documentos Inéditos,* pp. 1-127.

Suarez de Peralta, Juan: *Notícias Históricas de la Nueva España*. 1536. Ed. Justo Zaragosa. Madrid, 1878.

II. Collections of Early Documents

Colección de Documentos Inéditos Relativos al Decubrimiento Conquista y Colonización de las Posesiones Espanoles. . . . Sacadas en su Mayor Parte del Real Archivo de Indias. I Series, 42 volumes. Madrid, 1864-84. Second series in course of publication, 1885-. This has been referred to in footnotes as, *Colección de Documentos Inéditos*.

Cuevas, P. Mariano de: *Documentos Inéditos del Siglo XVI*. 2 tomos. México, 1908.

García, Genaro: *Nuevos Documentos o muy Raros para la Historia de México*. 36 tomos. México, 1905-11.

García Icazbalceta, Joaquín: *Colección de Documentos para la Historia de México*. 2 tomos. México, 1858-66.

———— *Nueva Colección de Documentos para la Historia de México*. 5 tomos. México, 1886-1892.

Kingsborough, Lord: *Antiquities of Mexico*. 9 vols., containing numerous codices with their translation and explanations, and a number of ancient Spanish documents. London, 1830-48.

Radin, Paul: *Sources and Authenticity of the History of the Ancient Mexicans.* University of California Press, 1920. Contains translations of parts of important codices, particularly the Codex Ramírez.

Ternaux-Compans: *Pieces Sur le Mexique.* Paris, 1840.

III. MODERN WRITERS

General Historical

Alegre, P. Francisco Javier: *Historia de la Compañía de Jesús en la Nueva España.* 3 tomos. Ed. Carlos María de Bustamante, Mexico, 1841.

Bancroft, H. H.: *History of Mexico.* Volumes IX-XIV of Bancroft's Works. San Francisco, 1883-86.

Biart, Lucien: *The Aztecs.* Translated into English by J. L. Garner. Chicago, 1892.

Callegari, G. V.: *L'Antico Messico.* Roverto, 1907.

Cavo, Andrés: *Los Tres Siglos de México.* Ed. Carlos María Bustamante. 3 tomos. Mexico, 1836.

Chavero, Alfredo: *Historia Antigua y de la Conquista.* Vol. I of *México á través de los Siglos.* Barcelona, 1888.

Clavigero, Francisco Xavier: *Ancient History of Mexico.* 3 vols., translated from the Italian by Charles Cullen Richmond, 1806.

Cuevas, P. Mariano de: *Historia de la Iglesia en Mexico.* 5 vols. Revista Católica, El Paso, Texas. 1928. All citations are to the first edition. Imprenta del Asilo Patricio Sáenz, Tlalpam, Mexico, D. F., 1921-.

Espinosa Isidro, Feliz de: *Chrónica Apostólica y Seráfica de todos los Colegios de Propaganda Fide de esta Nueva España, de Misioneros Francisanos.* 1746.

García, Genaro: *El Clero de México.* Vol. XV, *Documentos para la Historia de México.*

Helps, Arthur: *The Spanish Conquest in America.* 5 vols. New York, 1867.

—— *Hernando Cortez.* New York, 1872.

Mayer, Brantz: *Mexico; Aztec, Spanish, and Republican.* 2 vols. Hartford, 1848.

Orozco y Berra, Manuel: *Historia Antigua y de la Conquista de Mexico.* 4 tomos. Mexico, 1880.

Prescott, W. H.: *The History of the Conquest of Mexico.* 3 vols. Lippincott, Philadelphia, 1874.

Plancarte y Navarrete, Francisco: *Prehistoria de México.* Mexico, Tlalpam, 1923.

Riva Palacio, Vicente: *México á través de los Siglos.* 4 tomos. Barcelona, 1888.

Solís y Rivadeneyra, Antonio de: *Historia de la Conquista de México.* First published Madrid, 1684. Edition Paris, 1838.

Spence, Lewis: *Civilization of Ancient Mexico.* New York, 1912.

Spinden, Herbert Joseph: "Ancient Civilization of Mexico and Central America." *American Museum of History Handbook,* Series III, 1917.

Winsor, Justin: *Narrative and Critical History of America.* Vol. II. Boston and New York, 1884.

Studies in Religion and Mythology

Brinton, Daniel G.: *American Hero Myths, A Study of the Native Religions of the Western Continent.* Philadelphia, 1882.

—— *Ancient Nahuatl Poetry.* Philadelphia, 1886.

—— *The Prophetic Books of Chilan Balam. The Prophetic and Historic Records of the Mayas of Yucatan.* Philadelphia, 1882.

—— *The Maya Chronicles.* Philadelphia, 1882.

—— *Rig-Veda Americana. Sacred Songs of the Ancient Mexicans.* Philadelphia, 1890.

—— *The Myths of the New World.* New York, 1868.

Encyclopedia of Religion and Ethics. 12 vols. Chas. Scribner's Sons. New York, 1908-1925.

Catholic Encyclopedia. The Encyclopedia Press. New York, 1913.

Nuttal, Zelia: "A Penitential Rite of the Ancient Mexicans," *Archeological and Ethnological Papers of the Peabody Museum.* Harvard, Cambridge, 1904.

Reville, Albert: *Native Religions of Mexico and Peru.* Translated by P. H. Wickstead, 2nd ed. London, 1905.

Spence, Lewis: *Myths of Mexico and Peru.* London, 1917.

On Religion in Spain

Altamira y Crevea, Rafael: *Historia de España y de la Civilización Española.* Barcelona, 1900.

Chapman, Charles E.: *A History of Spain.* MacMillan, New York, 1918.

La Fuente, Don Modesto: *Historia General de España desde los Tiempos Primitivos hasta la Muerta de Ferdinando VII* etc. Tomos VII y VIII, Barcelona, 1888.

Lea, Henry C.: *A History of the Inquisition in the Middle Ages.* New York, 1888.

—————— *A History of the Inquisition in Spain.* 4 vols. New York, 1906-7.

—————— *Chapters of the Religious History of Spain Connected with the Inquisition.* Philadelphia, 1890.

—————— *The Moriscos of Spain—Their Conversion and Expulsion.* Philadelphia, 1901.

McCrie, Thomas A.: *A History of the Progress and Suppression of the Reformation in Spain in the Sixteenth Century.* Edinburgh, 1829.

Merriam, Robert Bigelow: *The Rise of the Spanish Empire in the Old World and the New.* Vol. III. MacMillan, New York, 1925.

Meyrick, Frederick: *The Church in Spain.* London, 1892.

MacNutt, Francis A.: *Bartholomew de las Casas, His Life, His Apostolate and His Writings.* New York, 1909.

Plunket, Ierne L.: *Isabel of Castile and the Making of the Spanish Nation.* 1451-1504. Putnam's, New York, 1915.

Prescott, W. H.: *History of the Reign of Ferdinand and Isabella the Catholic.* 3 vols. Philadelphia, 1872.

Stockdale, J. J.: *The History of the Inquisition, including the Secret Transactions of those Horrific Tribunals.* London, 1810.

Wilkens, C. A.: *Spanish Protestants in the Sixteenth Century.* London, 1897.

*Travel, Scientific, and Mission Books
on Modern Mexico*

Atl. Dr.: *Las Artes Populares en Mexico.* 2nd ed. Mexico, 1923.

Ballou, Maturin Murray: *Aztec Land.* Boston, 1890.

Beals, Carleton: *Mexico, An Interpretation.* Huebsch, New York, 1923.

Bourne, E. G.: *Spain in America.* Harpers, New York, 1904.

Brasseur de Bourbourg, Charles Etienne: *Quattre Lettres sur le Mexique etc.* Paris, 1868.

Brocklehurst, Thomas U.: *Mexico Today.* London, 1833.

Browning, W. E.: *New Days in Latin America.* New York, 1925.

—— *Roman Christianity in Latin America.* New York, 1924.

Bullock, Wm.: *Six Months Residence and Travel in Mexico.* London, 1824.

Calderón, F. García: *Latin America, Its Rise and Progress.* London, 1913.

Calderón de la Barca, Madam: *Life in America.* Boston, 1843.

Domenech, L'abbe, Henri: *Missionary Adventures in Texas and Mexico.* London, 1858.

Enock, C.: *Mexico, Its Ancient and Modern Civilization,* New York, 1909.

Ferry, Gabriel: *Vagabond Life in Mexico.* New York, 1856.

Franck, Harry A.: *Tramping through Mexico.* New York, 1921.

Fyffe, H.: *The Real Mexico.* London, 1914.

García Cubas, Antonio: *The Republic of Mexico in 1876.* Mexico, 1876.

Genin, Auguste: "Notes on the Dances, Music and Songs of the Ancient and Modern Mexicans," *Annual Report of the Smithsonian Institute, 1920.* Washington, D. C.

Gooch, Mrs. Fanny Chambers: *Face to Face with the Mexicans.* New York, 1887.

Gilliam, Albert M.: *Travels in Mexico during 1843-4.* Aberdeen, 1847.

Gringo, A.: *Through the Land of the Aztecs.* London, 1892.

Hague, Eleanor: *Spanish American Folk Songs.* New York, 1917.

Hale, Susan: *Mexico.* Putnams', New York, 1889.

Humboldt, Baron A.: *Ensayo Politico sobre Nueva España.* Translated from the French by Gonzalez Arnao. Paris, 1836.

———— *Vues des Cordilleres etc.* Paris, 1810.

Latrobe, Charles Joseph: *The Rambler in Mexico.* London, 1836.

Lyon, G. F.: *Journal of a Residence and Tour of the Republic of Mexico in 1826.* London, 1828.

Lumholtz, Karl S.: *Unknown Mexico.* New York, 1902.

McCarty, J. H.: *Two Thousand Miles through the Heart of Mexico.* New York, 1886.

Mayer, Brantz: *Mexico as it Was and Is.* New York, 1844.

Martin, Percy F.: *Mexico of the Twentieth Century.* London, 1907.

Mexico, Dirección de Antropología: *La Población del Valle de Teotihuacán.* 2 vols.

Morris, Charles: *The Story of Mexico.* Philadelphia, 1914.

Moses, Jasper T.: *Today in the Land of Tomorrow.* Indianapolis, 1907.

Ramos y Duarte, Feliz: *Diccionario de Curiosidades Históricas.* Mexico, 1899.

Quinn, Vernon: *Beautiful Mexico.* New York, 1924.

Ross, E. A.: *The Social Revolution in Mexico.* New York, 1923.

Starr, Frederick: *In Indian Mexico.* Chicago, 1908.

Sartorius, C.: *Mexico and the Mexicans.* London, 1859.

Thompson, Wallace: *The Mexican Mind.* Boston, 1922.

———— *The People of Mexico.* New York, 1921.

Tweedie, Mrs. Alec: *Mexico as I Saw It.* 2nd ed. New York, 1902.

Trowbridge, E. D.: *Mexico, Today and Tomorrow.* New York, 1919.

Tylor, E. B.: *Anahuac, Mexico and the Mexicans, Ancient and Modern.* London, 1861.

Wilson, Robert A.: *Mexico, Its Peasants and Priests.* New York, 1856.

Winton, G. B.: *Mexico Today.* New York, 1913.

Winter, Nevin O.: *Mexico and Her People Today.* Boston, 1907.

Bibliographical and Critical

León, Nicolás: *Apuntes para una Bibliografía Antropológica de México.* Mexico, 1901.

García Icazbalceta, Joaquín: *Bibliografía Mexicana del Siglo XVI.* Mexico, 1886.

Chavero, Alfredo: Introduction of Vol. 1, *México á través de los Siglos.* Madrid, 1888.

Radin, Paul: *Sources and Authenticity of the History of the Ancient Mexicans.* University of California Press, 1920.

Ramírez, Don José: "Bautismo de Moteuhzoma, Noveno Rey de Mexico," in *Boletín de la Sociedad Mexicana de Geografía y Estadística.* Primera época, tomo X, 1863.

García Icazbalceta, Joaquín: Various introductions to the documents included in the collections he has edited, listed elsewhere in this bibliography.

Concerning Our Lady of Guadalupe

Cabrera, Miguel: *Maraviglia Americana . . . della Madonna de Guadalupe.* Ferrare, 1780.

Colección de Obras y Opusculos Pertenecientes a la Milagrosa Aparición de la Bellísima Imagen de Nuestra Señora de Guadalupe. Madrid, 1785.

Exquisitio Historico. . . . Sobre la Aparición de Nuestra Señora de Guadalupe. Jalpa, 1893.

Florencia, Padre Franciso de: *La Estrella del Norte de México.* Madrid, 1785.

Mier, Dr. Servandro Teresa: *Cartas al Cronista de Indias, sobre la Tradición de Nuestra Señora de Guadalupe,* 1797.

Rosa, Padre Agustín de la: *Dissertatio Historico-Theologico, de Apparitione . . . Guadalupe.* Guadalajara, 1887.

INDEX